Latin Literature

This highly accessible, user-friendly work provides a fresh and illuminating introduction to the most important aspects of Latin prose and poetry.

Readers are constantly encouraged to think for themselves about how and why we study the texts in question. They are stimulated and inspired to do their own further reading through engagement with both a wide selection of translated extracts and a useful exploration of the different ways in which they can be approached. Central throughout is the theme of the fundamental connections between Latin literature and issues of elite Roman culture.

The versatile structure of the book makes it suitable for both individual and class use.

Susanna Morton Braund is Professor of Classics at Yale University and previously taught at the Universities of Exeter, Bristol and London. She has written numerous books and articles on Roman satire and epic, and has also translated Lucan's *Civil War* into English verse.

Classical Foundations

The books in this series introduce students to the broad areas of study within classical studies and ancient history. They will be particularly helpful to students coming to the subject for the first time, or to those already familiar with an academic discipline who need orientation in a new field. The authors work to a common brief but not to a rigid structure: they set out to demonstrate the importance of the chosen subject and the lines of recent and continuing research and interpretation. Each book will provide a brief survey of the range of the subject, accompanied by some case studies demonstrating how one may go deeper into it. Each will also include guidance of a practical kind on sources, resources and reference material, and how to pursue the subject further. When complete, the series will comprise a critical map of the whole field of ancient studies.

The series is planned to include:

Early Christianity
Greek History
Greek Literature
Greek Philosophy
Late Antiquity
Latin Literature
Roman Social History
The Roman Empire

Books currently available in the series:

Latin Literature
Susanna Morton Braund

Roman Social History
Susan Treggiari

Latin
Literature

Susanna Morton Braund

London and New York

**For Josiah, Giles and Tim –
best of students**

First published 2002
by Routledge
11 New Fetter Lane, London EC4P 4EE

Simultaneously published in the USA and Canada
by Routledge
29 West 35th Street, New York, NY 10001

Routledge is an imprint of the Taylor & Francis Group

Typeset in Times by
Florence Production Ltd, Stoodleigh, Devon

Printed and bound in Great Britain by
TJ International, Padstow, Cornwall

British Library Cataloguing in Publication Data
A catalogue record for this book is available from the British
Library

Library of Congress Cataloging in Publication Data
Braund, Susanna Morton.
    Latin literature/Susanna Morton Braund.
        p. cm. – (Classical foundations)
    Includes bibliographical references and index.
    1. Latin literature – History and criticism.   2. Rome –
    In literature.   I. Title.   II. Series.
    PA6003.B73 2001
    870.9 – dc21   2001031920

ISBN 0–415–19517–9 (hbk)
ISBN 0–415–19518–7 (pbk)

Contents

CONTENTS

Illustrations

About this book

This book belongs to the year 2000. I started writing it on 1 January 2000 and I finished by writing this introductory note on 24 December 2000. Just as the year 2000 has been claimed by the past and the future – as the final year of the second millennium and as the first year of the third – so my year 2000 has two allegiances. In this year I have moved from England to New England. I have left Royal Holloway (University of London) in leafy Surrey to move to Yale University in leafy Connecticut. And I find that my new home of New Haven really is a new haven from the lunacy of the audit and assessment processes that currently dominate British academic life.

This book has been shaped by many individuals. There have been conversations with friends and with colleagues, too numerous to name here, though I thank you all for your ideas, advice, enthusiasm and encouragement. There were discussions with Richard Stoneman of Routledge and with the other Routledge authors involved in this exciting new series. There were discussions with my co-panelists and with the audience at the panel on the future of literary history at the Classical Association AGM (Bristol, April 2000), when I presented an outline of this project. Thanks to all of you, too. But more than anything, this book has been shaped by my teaching and by my students. At Royal Holloway I taught an introductory course on Latin literature in English translation, which generated many ideas and strategies for this book. I have been influenced by my graduate students at Royal Holloway, Giles Gilbert and Tim Hill, who co-taught on the introductory course and whose research interests – the representations of battle in Roman epic poetry and Roman attitudes to suicide – have inspired some of my emphases in this volume. And at Yale I have benefited enormously from the intelligence and acumen of another graduate student, Josiah Osgood. Josiah took my typescript, removed embarrassing errors, filled in missing data, made copious suggestions for further reading and came up with some stunning ideas for further study. That this book has been completed before 2000 is out is thanks to him.

This book is not intended to be comprehensive. There are some glaring gaps both in the primary texts culled and, inevitably, in the secondary literature referred to. For example, there's nothing here from one of my favourite prose authors, Sallust, and my coverage of later Latin authors is scanty and random, to say the least. I make no apology for these gaps because the book is intended as an introduction. That is why the chapters are relatively short. It is an introduction to Latin literature and also an introduction to some of the fine translations currently available. Where I have adapted an existing translation I have indicated this. Otherwise, the translations are my own. I have provided a list of all the authors and texts, Latin and Greek, referred to, along with all the translations which I have adapted, at the end of the book. What's more, I have also tried to avoid using abbreviations or Latin titles that will deter those meeting this material for the first time. This book is intended to be very user-friendly.

I imagine that use of this book will vary. I hope that teachers who choose to use it will have students read just one chapter or a part of one chapter before a class and then use the material as a launch-pad. I have numbered the paragraphs to make this easier and I have inserted ample cross-references so that anyone interested in how topics interconnect can pursue such questions on their own. It is not essential to read the chapters in the sequence presented. Nor is it essential to read the whole book (for example, Chapters 11–13 on literary texture could easily be omitted from an elementary course). I chose to organize my material into fifteen short chapters to fit with likely patterns of teaching. In a fifteen-week semester, a class could study one chapter per week. In a shorter term or quarter, the teacher can select the eight, ten or twelve most germane chapters as a basis for study.

This book is not intended to replace the big conventional literary histories and works of reference but to complement them. I am anxious about the fact that, in the words of the literary critic Roland Barthes, 'the work escapes' when it is the subject of literary history. You see, I fear that reading literary history is often a substitution for reading the texts themselves. I would like to think that literary history can rise to this challenge and offer its own challenge to readers to engage directly instead of indirectly with the texts. That is why I decided that my introduction to Latin literature need not follow the conventional diachronic path centred upon the sequence of significant individuals and events, but could instead move between texts, with ample quotations from those texts. I can imagine a host of objections to this approach, including an objection that my book is not a work of literary history. Perhaps not. But perhaps it is time to reconsider what literary history is, or might be. Without dispensing with vital works of reference, let us also have books that unashamedly present a particular point of view on Latin literature, books that focus upon the central characteristics of Roman literary culture and that give such a strong sense of the works of Latin literature that the reader new to Latin literature is inspired, invited and enticed to set aside introductions like this and go directly to the texts themselves.

In the remainder of this introductory note, I shall explain the philosophy and organization of the book and give an overview of its content, particularly for the benefit of teachers in schools, high schools, colleges and universities who are considering using it as a course book or as a complement to their lectures.

I decided that it was essential to plunge into study of ancient texts right away (*in medias res*, as we like to say when we dispense with preliminaries) and that's why I devote the first two chapters to case studies of what I regard as central texts. I chose to write about Virgil and Livy, with extensive quotations (in translation, of course) from the texts. This choice is designed to be representative of some of the quintessential features of Latin literature and mutually complementary: one text is in verse and the other in prose; the approaches applied here are broadly speaking synchronic for one and diachronic for the other.

Chapter 1 I call 'Virgil and the meaning of the *Aeneid*'. I first acknowledge that readers and critics in different places and eras have emphasized different themes in the epic, producing readings structured as oppositions, such as male versus female, order versus disorder and reason versus emotion, or readings that see tensions between the spheres of action, variously defined as heaven and hell, East and West, future and past, epic and tragedy, collective and individual, or readings that resist these polar antitheses and instead emphasize the ambivalences built into the text. But my own emphasis is upon the *Aeneid* as a foundation poem, strongly teleological in its anticipation of the construction of the city of Rome and the Roman nation which lies in the narrative future. After a brief discussion of Virgil's relationship with his predecessors in the genre of epic, Homer and Ennius, I attempt a socio-political contextualization of the poem in terms of Virgil's relationship with Augustus, looking at what we can crudely label as the pro-Augustan and anti-Augustan readings of the *Aeneid* and readings which emphasize the text's blend of positive and negative elements, held in a complex, ambivalent tension. Since most of these readings hinge upon the interpretation of the close of the poem, I then examine the spectrum of views of the end of Book 12, paying close attention to the text itself. The result is, I hope, an appreciation of how suggestive and elusive this text is: its richness for interpretation is visible in the sheer range of its reception and interpretation by different critics and readers throughout the centuries and in the continuing intensity of the debate now and, presumably, in the future. Finally, I acknowledge my own historical situatedness at the turn of the twentieth into the twenty-first century in seeing the issues raised by the close of the *Aeneid* as essentially concerning the nature of power. In short, my opening chapter provides a case study which deals briefly with the literary context of the *Aeneid* in terms of earlier epic but focuses primarily upon the socio-political context of the work.

In Chapter 2 my chosen author is Livy and my chosen text the story of the rape of Lucretia from the end of Book 1. I first use this text to demonstrate the essentially Roman habit of mind which we can label exemplarity – the deployment of historical figures as positive and negative role models. This is an idea which Livy presents vividly in the preface to his history, which he represents as a highly visible monument replete with images (the Latin word is *exempla*). Livy's articulation of the story of the rape of Lucretia represents a paradigm of the functioning of exemplarity in narrative. I then show how this text is highly political in its engagement with contemporary political issues and with political philosophy about the nature of the good and bad ruler. I then take a quick look at ways in which theories of narrative can enhance analysis of the story and I argue that Livy's narrative is remarkable for its focalization via the female perspective. Finally, I glance at dominant features in the later reception of Livy's story in literature and art, including some of the issues connected with gender that are raised by the story in the versions by the Greek historian Dionysius of Halicarnassus, by the Roman poet Ovid, by Shakespeare, and in paintings by Titian, Tiepolo and Artemisia Gentileschi.

I selected these two texts for my opening case studies because I felt they would represent some of the issues most crucial to an understanding of Roman literature and culture and because they illustrate a wide range of the kinds of approaches that readers and critics of different kinds can bring to bear on such texts. After this plunge directly into the texts, I use Chapters 3 and 4 to pause and draw breath. In Chapter 3 I interrogate the terms 'Latin' and 'literature' and in Chapter 4 I discuss what the study of Latin literature can or might involve in terms of the debate between 'traditionalists' and 'theorists'. And then, I devote the rest of the book to discussions of Latin literature organized around a set of 'collecting points' which I chose to try to dispense with the conventional approach based upon period or genre or author.

One basic element of organization I have adopted is a division between texts that seem to relate to public life and those that relate to private life. Within the sphere of public life – and we have to remember that the life of the Roman male elite was largely lived in public – I have distributed my material into the following three chapters. First (Chapter 5), the creation of Roman identity, *Romanitas*. This cannot be separated from the question of the creation of Rome itself and hence involves issues of nationalism and multiculturalism, militarism and masculinity. I start with the representation of war in Latin literature and then look at the domination of Augustan literature by imagery of the ceremony of the military triumph, for example in *Aeneid* 8 and Horace *Odes* 1.37. I then discuss the formation of *virtus* – the quality of being a man – in Roman literature and thought, especially in terms of the paradox that the virtues are represented as female personifications in literature and in the iconography of statuary and coinage. Finally I argue that the father–son relationship is central to the inculcation of *virtus* because of the force of tradition (*mos maiorum*) in Roman society, using as my examples Horace's *Satires* and the dream of Scipio at the end of Cicero's *Republic*.

The second chapter devoted to texts relating to public life (Chapter 6) takes as its theme the role of performance, display and spectacle in Roman literature and culture. This chapter looks first at the performance of masculinity in the context of the speeches made in public by orators such as Cicero. Then I consider the phenomenon of performing on stage and in the gladiatorial arena and explain that this kind of performance was viewed as a threat to the performer's masculinity and therefore outlawed for members of the elite. The spectacle of two gladiators fighting to the death in the arena takes us to the topic of death as performance. Gladiatorial combat is a central underlying theme of Lucan's epic on the civil war between Caesar and Pompey: I examine Lucan's narrative of the death of Pompey to demonstrate the importance of 'face' and then consider the phenomenon of the Stoic suicide, epitomized in the stories about Cato. Finally I take an episode from Tacitus' *Annals* which makes a funeral procession into a highly spectacular performance in which all the 'players' are acutely aware of the impression they are making.

The third of these chapters (Chapter 7) discusses the effect of political power and patronage upon creativity and freedom of speech. Here I examine the phenomenon of panegyric and I relate it to the circumstances of the production of literature in terms of the structures of patronage that pervaded Roman elite society. As an example of the workings of *amicitia* (literally 'friendship') I examine the so-called Scipionic circle of writers and intellectuals in the second century BCE, a pattern that I see as largely replicated later in the case of patrons like Pollio, Messalla and Maecenas and, of course, in the imperial court from then on. I then consider the way in which powerful men use and abuse their power, with discussions of Petronius' Trimalchio and Juvenal's Domitian in *Satire* 4 and the exploitative host in *Satire* 5. Finally I look at how authors of panegyric and satire manage to combine praise and blame of the most powerful people in society.

The next three chapters are devoted to an examination of what I term aspects of 'private life' that emerge from Latin literature. First (Chapter 8) I deal with two forms of annihilation experienced by men of the Roman elite. Life in exile, as portrayed by Cicero, Ovid, Seneca and Boethius, amounted to a kind of invisibility or living death because of the loss of status and removal from Rome. Another form of invisibility occurred when a Roman male assimilated himself to servile status by becoming the slave to his emotions and to a mistress. This picture of private life is revealed by Roman love poetry, with its inversion of the norms and ideals of public life articulated in the *militia amoris* ('campaign of love'). The chapter concludes with two further discussions of non-entity, from the philosophical writings of Lucretius and from a poem by Catullus about terrifying religious devotion. The next chapter (Chapter 9) tackles the question of representing 'real' lives in literature. My starting point is the fabrication of women in the pages of love poetry. After this I move on to the representation of the lives of individual men and women in epitaphs, biography, autobiography and letters, including Suetonius' *Caesars*, Augustine's *Confessions* and Cicero's *Letters*. I close with a glance at the evidence offered by magic spells and curses. The final chapter in this group (Chapter 10) examines questions of the representation of introspection and the contestation of identity and 'the self' in just two examples from Latin poetry, Ovid's treatment of Narcissus in his epic poem *Metamorphoses* and Seneca's portrayal of Medea in his tragedy. A brief example of the confusion of identity that is provided by the satirist Persius closes the chapter – a very long way from the performative aspect of Roman life that was the subject of Chapters 5–7.

After these six chapters which have had as their emphasis the themes and contexts which dominate Latin literature, it is now time to focus upon the qualities of the literature in its own right and to study three textual phenomena which seem to pervade Latin literature: intertextuality, metapoetics and allegory. So, in the next trio of chapters, I discuss different aspects of the surface of Latin texts and the self-consciousness with which Latin texts were written. Chapter 11 deals with some of the ways in which literary texture is created, not least through intertextuality, that is, through the relationships between texts. I draw examples of textuality from the 'poetry' of Apuleius' prose and of intertextuality from Horace and Persius and from Statius' relationship with his epic predecessors, concluding with a discussion of the difficulties of translating Latin literature. Chapter 12 considers what happens when the surface of the text is disrupted by self-referentiality, which happens in both narrative and dramatic genres when the text draws attention to its own functioning in a process we often call metapoetics. Examples here come from Plautus' comedy, Ovid's character Pygmalion, Seneca's tragedies and the prologue to Apuleius' *Metamorphoses*. Chapter 13 discusses allegory in Latin literature, a phenomenon which involves multiple 'messages' operating on different levels simultaneously, without necessarily disrupting the surface of the text but invariably adding layers of interpretation. Lucretius, Virgil, Statius and Prudentius furnish examples of philosophical, political and moral allegories in Latin texts.

The book is completed by two final chapters which tackle the enormous debt of Latin literature to Greek literature and the creation of a truly 'Roman' literature. Chapter 14 discusses the Romans' inferiority complex about Greek literature and explores the ways in which Greek literature was adapted by Latin authors, using Greek tragedy and specifically Medea as a case study. After discussing the influence of the Greek poets of Hellenistic Alexandria on Latin poetry, especially Catullus and Virgil, I end the chapter with a brief exploration of the generic hierarchy inherited from Greek literature and of the implications of using 'genre' as a tool of literary criticism. The book concludes with my assertion that the Romans finally overcame their inferiority complex to Greek culture under the emperor Augustus and that the creation of Roman literature, as opposed to literature in Latin, is connected with the physical fabric of the city of Rome itself. This is borne out, I argue, by the monumental imagery found in Virgil's *Georgics* and in Horace's *Odes* 3.30. After the briefest of disquisitions on the relationship of this book to conventional literary history, I give the last word to Ovid, with the assertion of immortality which closes his epic poem, *Metamorphoses*. As he foresaw, we are still reading his poetry.

New Haven, Connecticut
24 December 2000

Acknowledgements

The author and publishers are grateful to Simon Goldhill for permission to reprint 'Who's afraid of literary theory?'; W. R. Johnson for permission to reprint an extract from *Darkness Visible*; Philip Hardie and Cambridge University Press for permission to reprint an extract from Philip Hardie, *The Epic Successors of Virgil*, 1993 © Cambridge University Press; and Faber & Faber, London, and Farrar, Straus and Giroux, LLC for permission to reprint an excerpt from Ted Hughes *Tales of Ovid*, 1997 © Ted Hughes.

Chapter 1

Virgil and the meaning of the *Aeneid*

1.1   Latin literature is a big topic. It could offer many different starting points. I choose the greatest poem ever composed in Latin – Virgil's *Aeneid*, an epic poem in twelve books about the origins of Rome which was written towards the end of the first century BCE. This poem on its own, beautiful, complex and profound, is the best justification for studying Roman literature – though to say that of course raises questions about value judgements, questions which I shall return to in Chapter 3. It is also open to a rich variety of interpretations and so takes us to the core of modern critical debates about what is involved in the study of Latin literature, which I shall discuss more fully in Chapter 4. This chapter will be devoted to indicating why Virgil's *Aeneid* is, has been and should continue to be, central to our understanding of Roman culture and of western literature generally.

1.2   First, we need to know what kind of poem it is. It belongs to the genre (category of literary product) which we call epic. This name comes from the ancients' own term, *epos*. Epic was the highest form of literature in antiquity. An epic poem is a story, usually of mythical and mystical times and heroes, told expansively at considerable length and using an elevated style, chiefly through choice of metre and language. Virgil's *Aeneid* is no exception.

1.3   The poem, which is Virgil's own version of a well-established but still fluid myth, tells the story of how the hero Aeneas becomes a refugee when his home city of Troy is sacked by the Greeks at the end of the Trojan War and is commanded by the gods to found a new city in the west of the Mediterranean. We read of his wanderings through the Mediterranean as he searches for this new home and the war he is forced to fight when he reaches his fated new land in Italy. This story is announced in the opening seven lines of the poem:

> I sing of warfare and a man at war.
> From the sea-coast of Troy in early days
> to Italy he came by destiny,
> to our Lavinian western shores,
> a fugitive, this captain, buffeted
> cruelly on land and on the sea
> by blows from powers above – behind them
> savage Juno in her sleepless rage.
> And cruel losses were his lot in war,
> till he could found a city and bring home
> his gods to Latium, land of the Latin race,
> the Alban lords, and the walls of lofty Rome.

> (Virgil *Aeneid* 1.1–7, adapted
> from Robert Fitzgerald)

Literally, the story covers just one year in Aeneas' life. But through the use of flashbacks to past events and prophecies of the future and other literary distortions of time, Virgil makes his poem embrace all of Roman history. In essence, the poem is a foundation story, like the foundation stories of other nations, such as the Pilgrim Fathers in the US and the Maori tales of travellers arriving by canoe in New Zealand. This epic presents in memorable poetic form a myth about the foundation of the Roman nation by settlers from the East who through a combination of alliances and military supremacy established themselves in Italy, in obedience to the commands of Jupiter, the king of the gods.

1.4 No one would deny that this is a foundation poem, strongly teleological (i.e. looking ahead to a specific outcome) in its anticipation of the construction of the city of Rome and the Roman nation which lies in the narrative future. But beyond that, readers and critics in different places and eras have emphasized different themes in the epic. Many readings have used oppositions central to structuralist criticism, such as male versus female, order versus disorder and reason versus emotion, some of which map on to one another. Others have seen tensions between the spheres of action, variously defined as heaven and hell, East and West, future and past, epic and tragedy, collective and individual. Still others have tried to resist these polar antitheses and instead have emphasized the ambivalences built into the text. In this way the text can become a self-contained and deconstructed object which requires no reference to anything outside of itself, or an open space for the inscription of meaning by the reader. Most of these readings hinge upon the interpretation of the close of the poem, when Aeneas kills his enemy, the native Italian prince Turnus. Later in this chapter we shall examine the spectrum of interpretation applied to the end of Book 12. But first, I shall offer a slightly fuller literary and socio-political contextualization of the poem.

1.5 No poem is written in a vacuum and in the case of Roman literature it is always relevant to set it in relation to Greek literature. Roman feelings of secondariness (a mixture of indebtedness and dependency), which usually amount to an inferiority complex, will be discussed more fully in Chapter 14. For now, it is enough to note that although Rome conquered Greece in the second century BCE, as it expanded its empire through the Mediterranean, Greek literature remained the height and model of literary achievement. In the case of his epic, Virgil in his *Aeneid* makes extensive use of the Homeric poems (which we can date to the eighth century BCE), undoubtedly with the expectation that his readers, who were members of an intellectual elite who had shared the same education (see Chapter 3.5), would bring their intimate knowledge of the *Iliad* and *Odyssey* to bear. To give a couple of examples, Aeneas' romantic sojourn with Dido, the queen of Carthage, in *Aeneid* 1–4 is in some respects modelled on Odysseus' reception by the princess Nausicaa in *Odyssey* 6–12. Again, Aeneas' single combat with Turnus, the prince of the native Rutulians, in *Aeneid* 12 has close connections with the single combat between Achilles, the foremost warrior of the Greeks, and Hector, the bravest of the sons of Priam, king of Troy, in *Iliad* 22.

1.6   A further example demonstrates Virgil's adaptation of Homeric material. He makes the anger of Juno the framing motif of his poem in a clever combination of central features of Homer's epics – the anger of Achilles, which is the driving force of the plot of the *Iliad*, and Poseidon's persecution of Odysseus in the *Odyssey*. *Aeneid* 1 starts with Juno's anger against Aeneas, because of the threat he poses to her favoured city of Carthage:

> O Muse, tell me the causes now, how
> the queen of gods, galled and pained
> in her divine pride, compelled him –
> a man apart, devoted to his mission –
> to undergo so many perilous days
> and face so many trials. Can anger
> black as this prey on the minds of heaven?
> Tyrian settlers in that ancient time
> held Carthage, on the far shore of the sea,
> set against Italy and Tiber's mouth,
> a rich new town, warlike and trained for war.
> And Juno, we are told, cared more for Carthage
> than for any walled city of the earth,
> more than for Samos, even. There her armour
> and chariot were kept, and, fate permitting,
> Carthage would be the ruler of the world.
> So she intended, and so nursed that power.
> But she had heard long since
> that generations born of Trojan blood
> would one day overthrow her Tyrian walls,
> and from that blood a race would come in time
> with ample kingdoms, arrogant in war,
> for Libya's ruin: so the Fates spun . . .
> Saturnian Juno, blazing at it all,

> buffeted on the waste of sea those Trojans
> left by the Greeks and pitiless Achilles,
> keeping them far from Latium. For years
> they wandered as their destiny drove them on
> from one sea to the next: so hard and huge
> a task it was to found the Roman people.
>
> (Virgil *Aeneid* 1.8–22 and 29–33)

The poem can only conclude in Book 12 after Jupiter has mollified her anger by making some concessions to her:

> The creator of men and of the world replied
> with a half-smile: 'Sister of Jupiter
> you truly are, and Saturn's other child,
> to feel such anger, stormy in your breast.
> But come, no need: put down this fit of rage.
> I grant your wish. I yield, I am won over
> willingly. The Ausonians will keep
> their father's language and their way of life,
> and, that being so, their name. The Teucrians
> will mingle and be submerged, incorporated.
> Rituals and observances of theirs
> I'll add, but make them Latin, one in speech.
> The race to come, mixed with Ausonian blood,
> will outdo humans, outdo gods in its devotion,
> you shall see – and no nation on earth
> will honour and worship you so faithfully.'
> To all this Juno nodded in assent
> and, gladdened by his promise, changed her mind.
> Then she withdrew from sky and cloud.
>
> (Virgil *Aeneid* 12.829–42)

1.7 The dynamics of an epic narrative require an aim (in Greek *telos*, hence the word teleology) and an obstacle to that aim. In the *Aeneid* the aim is the foundation of the Roman people and the obstacle is Juno's anger (*Aeneid* 1.33): 'so hard and huge | a task it was to found the Roman people'. But Virgil's presentation of Juno's anger has a historical as well as a literary dimension. It evokes the process of the expansion of the Roman empire, emblematized in the hostility between two major Mediterranean powers, Carthage and Rome, which continued through the Punic Wars of the third and second centuries BCE until the sack of Carthage in 146 BCE. Virgil provides a vivid representation of the cause of this hostility in the curse uttered by Dido, queen of Carthage, just before she commits suicide:

> 'If necessity demands that that abomination
> find his haven and come safe to land,
> if so Jove's destinies require, and this,
> his end in view, must stand, yet all the same
> when hard beset in war by a courageous people,
> forced to go outside his boundaries
> and torn from Iulus, let him beg assistance,
> let him see the unmerited deaths of those
> accompanying him, and accepting peace
> on unjust terms, let him not, even so,
> enjoy his kingdom or the life he longs for,
> but fall in battle before his time and lie
> unburied on the sand! This I implore,
> this is my last cry, as my last blood flows.
> Then, O my Tyrians, besiege with hate
> his progeny and all his race to come:
> make this your offering to my dust. No love,
> no pact must be between our peoples, no,
> but rise up from my bones, avenging spirit!
> Harry with fire and sword the Dardan countrymen
> now, or later, at whatever time
> the strength should come. Coast with coast
> in conflict, I implore, and sea with sea,
> and arms with arms: may they contend in war,
> themselves and all the children of their children!'
>
> (Virgil *Aeneid* 4.612–29)

Virgil invites his Roman audience to see the Carthaginian general Hannibal as the embodiment of Dido's curse. This is typical of the way in which he gives his epic, set in the mythical past, a historical dimension.

1.8   This was no innovation by Virgil. Two earlier poets had shown the way, to judge from the few fragments that survive and from what ancient readers said about Virgil's literary debts. The most important name is Ennius, widely regarded as the founder of Latin poetry. Ennius had fused the Homeric and the mythical with contemporary history in his epic poem *Annals*, written in the 170s BCE. His poem embraced all of Roman history, from Aeneas and Romulus, who actually founded the first city of Rome, down to his own times. And Ennius was himself developing the precedent set by Naevius in the third century BCE, who had written an epic poem which blended ancient foundation stories with recent history. What is different about Virgil's achievement in the *Aeneid* is the way in which he builds material of historical, political and religious significance to his contemporaries into a narrative of the events of just one year set in the distant past.

1.9   This makes some awareness of the context of composition essential. The poem is the product of some ten years' work (29–19 BCE) by Virgil (who lived 70–19 BCE) under the new regime of the emperor Augustus (who lived 63 BCE–14 CE). Augustus was the adopted son and heir of Julius Caesar, who had been assassinated in 44 BCE. Though he called himself 'Caesar' before he assumed the name Augustus, our convention is to call him 'Octavian'. Octavian had been involved in a bloody civil war in the 40s–30s BCE which came to an end with his victory over Mark Antony and Cleopatra at the Battle of Actium in 31 BCE and in Alexandria in Egypt in 30 BCE. He moved quickly to consolidate his power, staged a spectacular ceremony in Rome in 29 BCE to mark his victories and the advent of peace and took the name 'Augustus' (an invented name) in 27 BCE. In this new era of stability, patronage of the arts flourished, with Augustus' un-official minister of culture, Maecenas, supporting Virgil along with Horace, another leading poet. It is to Augustus that we owe the preser-vation of the *Aeneid*, in its unfinished state: at least, the story is that Virgil's deathbed request that it be destroyed, because of his dissatis-faction with it, was overruled by Augustus.

1.10 The relationship between Virgil and Augustus is crucial to any interpretation of the poem and has given rise to the most fiercely contested readings, as we shall soon see when we look at the way it ends. In antiquity the purpose of the *Aeneid* was commonly seen as the praise of Augustus (so says Servius, the fourth century commentator on Virgil). Augustus appears in Virgil's poem both directly and indirectly. He is celebrated by Jupiter as a descendant of Aeneas at 1.286–96 and by Aeneas' father Anchises in the parade of the future heroes of Rome:

> Turn your two eyes
> this way and see this people, your own Romans.
> Here is Caesar, and all the line of Iulus,
> all who shall one day pass under the great dome
> of the sky: this is the man, this one,
> of whom so often you have heard the promise,
> Caesar Augustus, son of the divine,
> who shall bring again an Age of Gold
> to Latium, to the land where Saturn reigned
> in early times. He will extend his power
> beyond the Garamants and Indians,
> over far territories north and south
> of the zodiacal stars, the solar way,
> where heaven-bearing Atlas on his shoulder
> turns the night-sphere, studded with burning stars.
>
> (Virgil *Aeneid* 6.788–97)

A third prophetic passage is the description of the shield made by the god Vulcan for Aeneas, where Virgil reworks into an expression of Roman patriotism an episode from *Iliad* 18, the description of the shield made by the god Hephaestus for Achilles. Virgil uses this opportunity to display scenes from future Roman history, designed to inspire Aeneas in the fighting that faces him. The centrepiece on the shield is the battle of Actium, with Augustus in the starring role:

> Vivid in the centre were the bronze-beaked
> ships and the fight at sea off Actium.

> Here you could see Leucata all alive
> with ships manoeuvering, sea glowing gold,
> Augustus Caesar leading into battle
> Italians, with senators and people,
> with household gods and the great gods: there he stood
> high on the stern, and from his blessed brow
> twin flames poured upward, while his crest revealed
> his father's star.

(Virgil Aeneid 8.675–81)

Virgil explicitly aligns Augustus with Aeneas by using exactly the same phrase, 'there he stood | high on the stern', of Aeneas at 10.261.

1.11 Alongside these direct correspondences there are indirect indications too that Virgil invites us to see Augustus as prefigured in Aeneas, particularly in Aeneas' combination of military prowess and attention to religious cult and ritual observance. These two elements were central to the image of Augustus, who is depicted victorious in a later statue in Figure 1, as is demonstrated by the very close of Virgil's description of the shield of Aeneas, where Augustus celebrates his triple triumph as a military and religious leader:

> But Caesar then in triple triumph rode
> within the walls of Rome, making immortal
> offerings to the gods of Italy –
> three hundred mighty shrines throughout the city.
> The streets were humming with festal joy
> and games and cheers, an altar and a mothers'
> choir at every shrine, and bullocks
> knifed before the altars strewed the ground.
> The man himself, enthroned before the snow-white
> threshold of sunny Phoebus, reviews the gifts
> from the nations of the world, and hangs them
> on the tall portals.

(Virgil Aeneid 8.714–22)

9

FIGURE 1 Augustus wearing a cuirass, from the Villa of Livia at Prima Porta

Courtesy of Vatican Museums; Alinari/Art Resource, NY

1.12 Also important is the way in which the *Aeneid* can be seen as a story of Aeneas' development from a traditional Homeric warrior, whose first instinct is to fight to the death to defend his home city (Book 2), into one who embraces a larger vision of the future and subordinates his personal wishes and desires to the good of the collective. The qualities of courage, piety towards the gods and duty towards his family and followers which Aeneas shows are summed up in the famous phrase *pius Aeneas*, 'dutiful' or 'pious Aeneas'. It is hard to resist linking this repeated description of Virgil's hero with Octavian's choice of the name Augustus, literally 'holy' or 'revered one', for his renovation of his self-image in 27 BCE.

1.13 A wider way in which the poem can be read as praise of Augustus relates to the representation of Rome. Despite the apparent paradox that neither Aeneas nor his son Iulus actually founds the new city of Rome – this happens later with the story of Romulus and Remus – the *Aeneid* is undoubtedly a poem about Rome and a celebration of Rome. I mean that both literally and metaphorically. Literally, because Virgil revels in introducing descriptions and aetiologies (that is, explanations) of Roman places, buildings, rites and customs; and metaphorically, because it is a poem about what it is to be a Roman. This is especially evident in Book 8, when Aeneas visits the Greek King Evander, who is living on the future site of Rome beside the Tiber. Evander's settlement is described in terms that evoked familiar topographical and cultural landmarks of Rome for Virgil's readers, such as the Ara Maxima (literally, 'Greatest Altar') and Forum Boarium associated with the cult of Hercules, and the Tarpeian Rock and the Capitoline Hill. Elsewhere Aeneas' son Iulus (which gives the name Julius) gives Virgil the opportunity to look to the Roman future, for example when he leads a ceremony of equestrian manoeuvres during the funeral games in Book 5, which was revived by Julius Caesar and Augustus as a ceremony performed by noble-born boys under the name *lusus Troiae*, literally 'game of Troy'.

1.14 Above all, Virgil reflects the Roman delight in parades and catalogues, the exemplars of heroic and villainous behaviour which were held before the eyes of the Roman elite as role models to imitate and avoid, a topic to which I shall return in Chapter 2.2–5. There are two central 'parades' in the *Aeneid* – the depiction of future Roman history on the shield of Aeneas in Book 8 and Anchises' display of the future heroes of Rome when Aeneas visits him in the Underworld at the climax of Book 6. Here Anchises explains to his son the future fusion of Trojan and Italian blood to produce the Roman people. The strong teleological element of the *Aeneid* recurs with the placing of Augustus at the head of this catalogue of Romans, but Anchises also explicitly praises some of the most famous names from earlier years of Roman history, such as the Decii, the Scipiones and the Fabii. This passage is designed to evoke pride in the virtues demonstrated by these exceptional individuals from the era of the Republic and to convey a sense that these virtues constitute Romanness. This image of Romanness accorded closely with Augustus' own aspirations, seen for example on the Golden Shield (the so-called *clupeus virtutis*, *Achievements of the Divine Augustus* 34.2) which proclaimed Augustus' virtues of Courage, Clemency, Justice and Piety. In this way, both Aeneas and the Roman heroes of the future can be seen as prototypes of the ideal Roman leader, now embodied in Augustus.

1.15 By contrast with this optimistic view of the *Aeneid* as praise of Augustus, during the last century suspicion of 'propaganda' for autocratic regimes and of justifications of imperialism and warfare has brought pessimistic perspectives to the criticism of the *Aeneid*. The poem has been seen as incorporating two contrasting 'voices' in which a commentary upon the celebration of imperialist achievement by a public voice is provided by a private voice which articulates loss. Or the poem has even been regarded and rejected as the tool of a totalitarian regime. For a succinct formulation of the two schools of thought that have dominated Virgilian criticism in recent decades, I present in Appendix A some quotations from Ralph Johnson's illuminating discussion in his book *Darkness Visible*. Nowhere does this issue arise more forcefully than at the end of the poem, to which we turn now.

1.16 The climax of the *Aeneid* is the duel between Aeneas and Turnus, the prince of the Rutulians. Aeneas is cast in the role of the Homeric

Achilles, taking revenge for the death of his close friend Patroclus, whose equivalent in the *Aeneid* is the young man Pallas. Turnus is cast in the role of the Homeric Hector as defender of his native land against foreign invaders. Like Hector, he is also fighting against fate. Just as Troy was fated to fall to the Greeks, so Aeneas is fated to marry the princess Lavinia and settle in Italy. At first, Juno deploys all her powers to protect Turnus, but once Jupiter has reconciled her to fate's commands (in the passage quoted earlier) the hero faces Aeneas alone. He receives a fatal wound and pleads for some kind of mercy:

> The man brought down, brought low, lifted his eyes
> and held his right hand out to make his plea:
> 'Clearly I earned this, and I ask no quarter.
> Make the most of your good fortune here.
> If you can feel a father's grief – and you, too,
> had such a father in Anchises – then
> feel pity for the old age of my father
> Daunus, and return me, or my body,
> stripped, if you will, of life, to my own kin.
> You have defeated me. The Ausonians
> have seen me in defeat, spreading my hands.
> Lavinia is your bride. But go no further
> out of hatred.' Fierce under arms, Aeneas
> looked to and fro, and towered, and stayed his hand
> upon the sword-hilt. Moment by moment now
> what Turnus said began to bring him round
> from indecision. Then to his glance appeared
> the accurst swordbelt high on Turnus' shoulder,
> gleaming with its familiar studs, the strap
> worn by young Pallas when Turnus wounded him
> and left him dead upon the field; now Turnus
> bore that enemy token on his shoulder –
> enemy still. And when the sight came home to him,
> Aeneas raged at the relic of his anguish
> worn by this man as trophy. Blazing up
> and terrible in his anger, he called out:
> 'You in your plunder, torn from one of mine,

shall I be robbed of you? This wound will come
from Pallas: Pallas makes this offering
and from your wicked blood exacts his due.'
He sank his blade in fury deep in Turnus' chest.
Then all the body slackened in death's chill,
and with a groan for that indignity
his spirit fled into the gloom below.

(Virgil *Aeneid* 12.930–52)

1.17 The critical debate about these final lines of the poem hinges upon two things: (1) the fact that Aeneas kills Turnus and (2) the state of mind which leads him to do this. The positive view sees the killing of Turnus as an act of necessity or an act of duty or both. If we view Turnus as a villain or a hot-headed warrior, rather on the Homeric model that Aeneas himself has moved away from since the sack of Troy, it can be argued that he could have no useful role in the new world ushered in by Aeneas' alliance with King Latinus and marriage with his daughter, the princess Lavinia. To spare him would simply leave him alive to foment unrest and hostility against Aeneas later. If we recall that Aeneas had promised his ally King Evander that he would take care of his son Pallas as if he were his own son (Book 8) but that Pallas was none the less killed by Turnus (Book 10), his taking the ultimate revenge on Turnus now can be viewed as Aeneas fulfilling an obligation to Evander. A favourable interpretation of Aeneas' state of mind emphasizes his long moment of hesitation as he looks at Turnus pleading for his life (or at least for the return of his body to his father): he is clearly inclined to show mercy. It emphasizes Aeneas' recollection of the devastating grief he felt at Pallas' death. And it emphasizes the words Aeneas speaks, in which he represents Turnus' death as a ritual sacrifice to the ghost of Pallas.

1.18 The negative view sees the killing of Turnus as unnecessary, or an act of irrational frenzy, or both. This view emphasizes Turnus' courage: he explicitly says he is not asking for mercy and he clearly envisages the likelihood of Aeneas killing him. It also emphasizes the last words that Turnus speaks, in which he capitulates completely in full view of the watching Italians and surrenders Lavinia to Aeneas.

It emphasizes most of all Virgil's description of Aeneas' state of mind as 'blazing up and terrible in his anger' and views Aeneas as acting not rationally but passionately in a blind act of frenzy and cruelty. And it also might emphasize Virgil's focalization of this episode, in particular his description of the sword-belt as 'accurst', a description which invites the reader's alignment with Turnus, and more than anything else the fact that the poem closes (if this is indeed where Virgil intended to end it: see 1.9 above) not with a celebration of Aeneas' victory but with apparent sympathy for his victim, with its focus upon the discontented departure of Turnus' ghost to the Underworld. This emphasis upon the loss and destruction of fine individuals who get in the way of the foundation of the Roman people and the Roman empire, including Dido, the helmsman Palinurus, Pallas, the virago Camilla and here Turnus, is seen as a crucial theme throughout the poem. This type of reading can be seen as anti-Augustan, in contrast to the pro-Augustan type of reading which emphasizes the positive aspects.

1.19 It becomes clear that interpretation depends upon which elements in the text one chooses for emphasis. A careful study of the thumbnail sketches of the positive and negative views I have provided above indicates that the opposed interpretations are virtually complementary in the elements within the text they privilege. This takes us to the heart of the practice of literary criticism – and this applies to the criticism of any 'text' from any culture. (So, for example, this is just as valid for film criticism as it is for Shakespearian criticism or Virgilian criticism.) What critics do, in essence, is to re-state or re-present the text, highlighting the elements they believe are most important, and (if this criticism is performed properly) substantiating their views by arguments of various kinds, such as explaining how these privileged bits of the text form certain patterns or convey certain themes. Critics might appeal to other passages in the same text or the same author or the same genre to support their views. Or they might appeal to evidence from the culture that produced the text. Or they might appeal to the reception of that text in its own era or in later eras. Let us take a glance at the way this kind of material might be relevant to the close of *Aeneid* 12.

1.20 A passage from the close of *Aeneid* 6, where Anchises articulates the Roman mission in the world, is often seen as relevant to the interpretation of the close of *Aeneid* 12:

> Roman, remember by your power to rule
> the peoples of the earth, as these will be your arts:
> to pacify and to impose the rule of law,
> to spare the conquered and battle down the proud.
>
> (Virgil *Aeneid* 6.851–3)

The relevance of this passage is enhanced by the structural parallelism and by the fact that this is wisdom transmitted from father to son, which for a Roman readership endows it with absolute authority (on which see Chapter 5.25–27). But does this passage assist the positive or the negative view of Aeneas' killing of Turnus? The positive view of Aeneas justifies his action by the necessity of 'battling down the proud', while the negative view argues that he acted wrongly in not 'sparing the conquered'. That is, Aeneas is either fulfilling or disregarding Anchises' instructions.

1.21 Another kind of argument emphasizes the undoubted importance throughout the *Aeneid* of the relationship between fathers and sons. Aeneas' unflinching devotion to his father Anchises, a devotion which even enables him to undertake the terrifying journey into the Underworld (Book 6), is only the most notable example of this theme. So the way in which Turnus appeals to Aeneas in Book 12 by linking his own father Daunus with Aeneas' father Anchises might lead the reader to a negative view of Aeneas for his failure to show mercy – until, of course, thoughts of Pallas and *his* father Evander arise, at which point the reader sees Turnus and not Aeneas in a negative light. Again, it is impossible to use this evidence conclusively.

1.22 The same applies too if we turn to another relevant text (or 'intertext') to tell us how to 'read' this one. The close of the *Aeneid* evokes the episode in *Iliad* 24 when Priam makes a personal appeal to Achilles for the return of his son Hector's mutilated corpse. We could see Priam as a model for Turnus' father Daunus, which would evoke our sympathy in one direction. But we could also think of Priam as a model for Pallas' father, Evander, which would evoke an opposite sympathy.

1.23 Another approach is to appeal to the historical context in which the text was written. Here, for example, we can make a connection between Aeneas' behaviour towards Turnus and the policy of clemency (*clementia*) adopted by Julius Caesar in the years immediately preceding his assassination. During and after the civil war of the early 40s BCE, Caesar used the tactic of sparing his Roman enemies rather than having them executed. This policy can be regarded as prudent, in not inflaming extra hostilities among the Roman elite, or as a calculated measure to render his defeated opponents entirely under his sway – the mark of an absolute ruler. So in the case of Aeneas, his initial hesitation and inclination towards sparing Turnus and his subsequent killing of the suppliant Turnus can be read as a commentary upon Caesar's use of clemency. Yet again, it does not allow us to reach any firm conclusion about Aeneas.

1.24 Most recently, a number of critics have turned to the various philosophical schools of thought that were current at Virgil's time in their attempts to determine the moral and political flavour of Aeneas' action and in particular of his anger. The spectrum is provided by viewing Aeneas' anger as, at one extreme, a grave departure from the Stoic ethics that are endorsed elsewhere in the poem and, at the other, as the anger experienced by the good man at an outrage, an anger that in Peripatetic thought (the philosophical school which followed the ideas of Aristotle) is not only justified but even appropriate. Evidence from Stoic texts and from Aristotle and the Peripatetics is drafted in to support these contrasting views, and from Cynicism and Epicureanism too to support other related views, without any agreement between scholars yet achieved – and without any prospect of agreement either.

1.25 This text, then, is both suggestive and elusive: it is demonstrably capable of provoking a rich range of readings, pro-Augustan readings, anti-Augustan readings, and readings which emphasize the text's blend of positive and negative elements, held in an ambivalent and complex tension. Its richness for interpretation is visible in the sheer range of its reception and interpretation by different critics and readers throughout the centuries. The continuing intensity of the debate testifies to the relevance to our own times of the issues that Virgil raises here. Writing from my perspective at the turn of the twentieth into the twenty-first century, I see those issues as essentially concerning the nature of power: what are the expectations and the limitations and the responsibilities of seizing and wielding power and what state of mind is most appropriate for powerful people when they take action? I have deliberately framed these issues in a way that reflects the concerns of many contemporary literary critics, and historians too. I believe that it is important to draw attention to my own historical context and I view the need for self-examination and self-awareness as one of the most significant lessons of literary criticism of the late twentieth century.

1.26 The 'meaning of the *Aeneid*' is not something that can be conclusively resolved by appeal to the text itself or to evidence outside the text either. Different readers and critics make different arguments and muster different sets of evidence to support their arguments – and they will continue to do so in the future. The one small step of progress we can make for now is to be candid about the baggage that we bring to bear when we read this poem and to be honest about our own agenda. And whatever that baggage and that agenda, Virgil's status as a classic – 'the best and most renowned poet of all', according to Saint Augustine (*City of God* 1.3) – seems unassailable. As T. S. Eliot said, 'We are all, so far as we inherit the civilization of Europe, still citizens of the Roman Empire.'

Further reading and study

The secondary literature on Virgil is vast. An excellent starting point is the entry by Don and Peta Fowler in the *Oxford Classical Dictionary*, 3rd edition (edited by S. Hornblower and A. Spawforth, Oxford, 1996), along with Philip Hardie's superb survey *Virgil* in the *Greece and Rome New Surveys in the Classics* series (no. 28, Oxford, 1998: a glance at the contents page reflects the range of current critical concerns). There are several useful collections of essays: *Oxford Readings in Vergil's Aeneid* (edited by S. J. Harrison, Oxford and New York, 1990), *The Cambridge Companion to Virgil* (edited by Charles Martindale, Cambridge, 1997), *Virgil, Critical Assessments of Classical Authors* (edited by Philip Hardie, London and New York, 1999, in 4 volumes), *Reading Vergil's Aeneid: An Interpretive Guide* (edited by Christine Perkell, Norman, 1999) and *Why Vergil?* (edited by Stephanie Quinn, Wauconda, Illinois, 2000). Four important and different 'takes' on 'the meaning of the *Aeneid*' are the books by Agathe Thornton *The Living Universe. Gods and Men in Virgil's Aeneid* (Leiden, 1976), W. R. Johnson *Darkness Visible: A Study of Virgil's Aeneid* (Berkeley and Los Angeles, 1976), P. R. Hardie *Virgil's Aeneid: Cosmos and Imperium* (Oxford, 1986) and F. Cairns *Virgil's Augustan Epic* (Cambridge, 1989). The debate about the philosophical flavour of the end of the *Aeneid* has been conducted most vigorously by Karl Galinsky and Michael Putnam.

One suggestion for further study is to look more closely at the terms of this debate in, for example, K. Galinsky 'How to be philosophical about the end of the *Aeneid*' *Illinois Classical Studies* 19 (1994) 191–201 and M. Putnam *Virgil's Aeneid: Interpretation and Influence* (Chapel Hill and London, 1995) 201–45. The quotation from T. S. Eliot is from page 146 of his essay 'Virgil and the Christian world' (*On Poetry and Poets*, London, 1943, reprinted often).

Chapter 2

Role models for Roman women and men in Livy

2.1 Epic poetry, such as the *Aeneid*, which we looked at in Chapter 1, is poetry on a large scale and in the hierarchy of poetic genres it indisputably holds the top position. This was so from the beginning of Western literature: the Homeric epics were – and still are – seen as encapsulating the most important issues about human life and in Roman times readers were invited to use Homeric characters as positive and negative role models. In prose literature the top position was held by historiography – the large-scale writing of history. Ancient historiography, despite its claims to objectivity, has a strong moral agenda. In this respect it differs from modern historiography – which is not to deny the moral subtext to historical writings of all ages. If we seek a modern analogy to ancient historiography, it is perhaps found in the novel and in cinema, both of which often invite the moral engagement of the audience and stimulate us to put ourselves in the moral dilemmas of the characters.

2.2 Livy, who in the mid-30s BCE (probably) started writing his enormous 142-book history of Rome from its foundation onwards, is explicit about his moral agenda and links it closely with patriotism, when he talks in the preface about his chosen task 'of putting on record the story of the greatest nation in the world' (Livy, Preface 3):

My concern is that each reader should pay keen attention to these things: what kind of life, what kind of morals the Romans had, through what kind of men and by what means in peace and in war power was acquired and expanded; then, let him note in his mind how, as discipline tottered a little, morality began to fall apart, so to speak, then collapsed more and more, then began a downward plunge, until we have come to the present time when we can endure neither our faults nor their remedies. The especially healthy and fruitful element of the study of history is this, that you contemplate object-lessons of every type of model set up on a conspicuous monument: from these you can choose for yourself and for your state what to imitate and what to avoid, if loathsome in its beginning and loathsome in its outcome.

(Livy *From the Foundation of Rome* Preface 9–10)

Livy's imagery here is striking: history, his history, is represented as a highly visible monument which can function as medicine for the state by having us, its readers, look at the images it presents and take those images as models for our own positive behaviour and as warnings against lapses from that high standard. The key Latin word in this passage is *exempla* – the images or 'object-lessons'. Exemplarity, the presentation of precedents and patterns of moral behaviour, is a key concept in Roman historiography. This reflects the ideology of the Roman elite generally. A young man of an eminent family saw the death masks (*imagines*) of his ancestors displayed in the *atrium* (the public reception room) of his house every day and so was continually reminded of their qualities and achievements. On the occasion of a family funeral, these masks were worn by individuals impersonating the ancestors in a public procession through the streets of Rome which culminated in a speech in the Forum praising the virtues of the dead man and his ancestors. Every effort was made to encourage the well-born young Roman to conform to the positive patterns embodied in his ancestors. This was not a society that encouraged the individualism that marks modern western societies.

2.3 What about women? It is highly significant that women were not represented by *imagines* displayed in the *atrium* of a noble family, although they did feature on family trees. This conveys eloquently the ideal for women of the Roman elite: invisibility. This makes it hardly surprising that many of the women who feature in the pages of Roman historiography are represented as epitomes of wickedness, in their ambition or their lust or their appropriation of the male pre-rogatives of speech and action. Livy presents a particularly graphic example in his first book, the story of the early kings of Rome. The ambitious princess Tullia has helped her husband Tarquinius to stage a coup to overthrow her father, King Servius. This is the climax of Livy's story:

> While Servius was making his way home to the palace, stunned and without his retinue, he was caught and killed by the assassins sent by Tarquinius. It is thought that the deed was done at Tullia's suggestion – and that is not inconsistent with her other wickedness. Everyone agrees that she drove into the Forum in an open carriage, not at all overwhelmed at the crowd of men, called her husband from the Senate House and was the first to hail him as King. Tarquinius told her to make herself scarce from such a turbulent scene, so she started to make her way home. When she had reached the top of Cyprus Street and her driver was turning right to climb the Urbian Hill on the way to the Esquiline, he stopped in sudden terror and pointed to Servius' body lying mutilated on the road. An act of bestial inhumanity is said to have happened, which is commemorated in the place – it is called the Street of Crime. The story goes that the crazed woman, driven to frenzy by the avenging ghosts of her sister and husband, drove her carriage over her father's body. Contaminated and defiled, she conveyed some of her father's blood and gore on the bloody carriage to the house where she and her husband lived. The guardian gods of that house were angry at this bad start to the reign and they would ensure that it would come to a bad end.
>
> (Livy *From the Foundation of Rome* 1.48)

This is not dispassionate history – nor does Livy want it to be. In fact, he introduces this episode as 'a crime on the pattern of tragedy' (1.46, using the word *exemplum*), which alerts us to the ways in which a historian might use Greek and Roman tragedy to shape his narrative.

2.4   In Roman thought, Tullia is the archetypal negative image of woman in the way that she initiates action, is not afraid to be seen and heard in public, and, most of all, allows her own desires and ambitions to destroy the loyalty and obedience she should show to her father. To balance this negative female role model, Livy has his first book culminate in a positive female role model in the story of the rape of Lucretia. In Livy's narrative, Lucretia, the beautiful young wife of Collatinus, is introduced as an ideal wife. In contrast with the wives of the royal princes, when she is surprised late at night by her husband and the princes, she is still hard at work by lamplight upon her spinning. Her proven virtue provokes the young prince Sextus Tarquinius and he decides that he will make an assault upon her:

> A few days later Sextus Tarquinius, without Collatinus' knowledge, returned with one companion and was welcomed hospitably, since no one guessed his intentions, and, after supper, escorted to the guest-room. Here, burning with desire, he waited till the coast was clear and everyone seemed to be asleep and then he drew his sword and made his way to Lucretia as she lay sleeping. He put his left hand on her breast and whispered, 'Lucretia – not a sound! I am Sextus Tarquinius. I have a blade. Speak one word and you die!' In a terrifying awakening, Lucretia saw that death was imminent and no help at hand. Tarquinius declared his love, pleaded with her, mixed threats with prayers, used every means to conquer her woman's heart. When he saw that she was determined to resist and that not even the fear of death could bend her will, he increased terror with dishonour. He said he would kill her, then cut the throat of a slave and lay his naked body beside her, to make people say she had been killed in the act of adultery with a slave. With this dreadful threat, as if by force, his champion lust overwhelmed her resolute chastity and Tarquinius departed, exulting in his conquest of a woman's honour. Lucretia, distressed by her awful experience, wrote to her father and her husband, urging them both to come

at once, and quickly, because a terrible thing had happened. ... They found Lucretia sitting in her room, in deep distress. Tears rose to her eyes as they entered. To her husband's question, 'Is it well with you?' she answered, 'No. What can be well with a woman who has lost her honour? In your bed, Collatinus, is the mark of another man. But it is only my body that has been violated. My heart is innocent. Death will be my witness. Give me your solemn promise that the adulterer will not go unpunished. He is Sextus Tarquinius. He is the one who last night came as my enemy disguised as my guest and who armed and by force took his pleasure of me, a pleasure that will be my death – and his too, if you are men.' They gave their promise and comforted her in her distress by redirecting the blame from the victim to the one who committed the crime. They said that it was the mind that sinned, not the body: without intention there never could be guilt.

'What is due to him,' Lucretia said, 'is for you to decide. As for me, I am innocent of fault, but I will take my punishment. Lucretia will never provide a precedent for unchaste women to escape what they deserve.' She pulled a knife from under her robe, drove it into her heart and, collapsing onto the wound, fell down dying.

(Livy *From the Foundation of Rome* 1.58)

2.5 Lucretia is represented as the model Roman wife in her life and in her death. Her spinning symbolizes her devotion to the running of the household as well as her chastity, as we see from similar praise of Roman wives on their tombstones (discussed in Chapter 9.6). It is only the prospect of dishonour – Tarquinius' threat to implicate her in adultery with a slave, which would be the ultimate insult to her father and husband – that makes her yield to him. And most important of all for Livy is her motive for committing suicide: she is not prepared to allow what has happened to her to be misrepresented as an excuse or a precedent for adulterous wives. In her anxiety to avoid providing a negative role model (*exemplum*), she becomes a positive role model – a classic case of exemplarity.

2.6   This moral message might seem enough for the story of Lucretia to convey, but there is more. As I said earlier, this story is the climax to Book 1. Livy gives it a strong political charge. Lucretia's suicide and the vengeance she requests are represented as the direct cause of the end of the dynasty of the Tarquin kings of Rome and the end of the monarchy itself in 509 BCE. The consequence is the foundation of the Republic by Brutus the Liberator, which Livy makes his starting point for Book 2. When we remember that Livy started composing his enormous history in the 30s BCE, a period in which (in hindsight, at least) the Republic was in its death throes, as the triumvirate of Antony, Octavian and Lepidus gave way to a fight to the death between Antony and Octavian, the political significance of ancient Roman history becomes clearer.

2.7   The 40s and the 30s BCE were a terrible time of civil warfare, a time when eminent Romans, including Pompey and then his son Sextus, Julius Caesar and Antony, were in effect competing for sole command of the Roman world. Roman suspicion of monarchy, literally 'sole rule', seen as an Eastern institution and associated with despotism, is nowhere more obvious than in the stories about the assassination of Julius Caesar in 44 BCE. Once he had gained undisputed power, Caesar adopted the dress and insignia of the old Roman kings, but, though perhaps tempted, was wise enough to refuse the offer of the title *rex*. All the same, it was undoubtedly the unprecedented honours awarded him that led to his murder by the 'conspirators', who included Brutus, a descendant of the Brutus who founded the Republic.

2.8   In other words, it enhances our understanding of Livy's text if we attempt to situate it in the political context in which it was written. That political context not only consists of the bloody competition for supremacy mentioned above. It is also informed by centuries of political philosophy which can be traced back through Roman and Greek literature all the way to Homer. A central issue for the elites of the Greco-Roman world was what was the ideal political system and what qualities made a ruler good or bad. There was a substantial body of literature which, directly or indirectly, explored the nature of the good king and the opposite, the tyrant, including, for example, a treatise in

Greek by the philosopher Philodemus who was working in Rome from 75 BCE, entitled *On the Good King According to Homer*. Livy's history reflects a dominant strand in ancient political thought in his portrayal of the early Roman monarchy declining into a tyranny (with the classic marks of the tyrant, for example, use of a personal bodyguard) and being overthrown when it turns into a dynasty, the dynasty of the Tarquinii. According to ancient ideas, a tyrant's son was likely to be worse than his father. This is borne out by the story of Lucretia. Sextus Tarquinius, who commits the rape, is the oldest son of the king, Tarquinius Superbus, who is himself the son or grandson of an earlier king, Tarquinius Priscus. Tarquinius Superbus is presented by Livy as a tyrant, and the behaviour of his son indicates a further descent into the lawlessness associated with autocracy. It seems clear that Livy is using ancient Roman history to warn against the dangers of monarchy and to advocate the values of the Republic. The rape of Lucretia is, in effect, an assault upon Rome by a tyrant.

2.9 Livy's harnessing of history to an implicit political position might for a moment seem to be at odds with the fact that by 31 or 30 BCE, Octavian, the adopted son and heir of Julius Caesar and soon to take the name Augustus (see Chapter 1.9), had established himself as sole ruler of the Roman world. But this concern evaporates (or at least is diminished) when we recall that Octavian/Augustus took considerable trouble to emphasize that his policy was the restoration of the Republic (*Achievements of the Divine Augustus* 34.1). How we react to such a claim is, of course, another matter, perhaps one more for the Roman historian than the literary critic. For now, what is important is to observe that talk of a return to Republican values was in the air at the time that Livy was writing.

2.10 Livy's narrative of the rape of Lucretia demonstrates brilliantly, then, that 'the personal is also the political', to repeat the claim of feminists such as Nancy Miller. I have discussed Livy's text as essentially Roman in its deployment of historical figures as positive and negative role models and as essentially political in its engagement with contemporary political issues and philosophy. I now propose to finish this chapter by turning back to the text to consider it as a piece of narrative and by glancing at dominant features in the later reception of Livy's story in literature and art. This final section, then, will look briefly at ways in which theories of narrative can enhance analysis of the story, and at some issues connected with gender that are raised by the story of Lucretia and its reception in other texts, including versions by the Greek historian Dionysius of Halicarnassus, by the Roman poet Ovid, by Shakespeare, and in paintings by Titian, Artemisia Gentileschi and Tiepolo.

2.11 An important recent development in the study of ancient narrative is an approach taken from narratology (the theory of narrative) which examines the roles played by 'narrators' and 'focalizers' in texts. The pioneering work in the classical field is the narratological study of Homer's *Iliad* by the Dutch scholar Irene de Jong, *Narrators and Focalizers: The Presentation of the Story in the Iliad*. In the field of Latin literature, Don Fowler's paper on 'Deviant focalisation in Virgil's *Aeneid*' was a landmark. The topic of Fowler's paper is point of view in the *Aeneid* – but with an important modification to traditional conceptions of 'point of view'. Fowler prefers the term 'focalisation' because traditional accounts of point of view tend to confuse two distinct questions: 'Who speaks?' and 'Who sees?':

> In relation to any textual feature, the answers to these questions may be different. For the first phenomenon, we have the term 'voice', and it is helpful to have a separate term for the second; that is, focalisation. . . . [Moreover] we can easily form the agent-noun 'focaliser' to give us a partner for 'narrator' in a way that we cannot do with 'point of view'.

> (Fowler)

2.12 Let us take a look at focalization in Livy's narrative of the rape of Lucretia. A crucial element is Livy's use of direct and indirect (reported) speech. During the rape scene, Sextus' voice is the only voice we hear, in one brief speech. But this does not entail that Sextus is the focalizer. On the contrary, the narrative focalizes the event from Lucretia's perspective. We are allowed to share her thoughts: 'death was imminent and no help at hand'. Similarly, when the narrator says 'with this dreadful threat, as if by force, his champion lust over-whelmed her resolute chastity', the word 'dreadful' is not only a moral judgement on Sextus but a focalization from Lucretia's point of view. In the subsequent scene, when she has summoned her father and husband, Lucretia is again the focalizer, but in a more straightforward way: she is the only character whose words are presented in direct speech, apart from her husband's brief question. All other speech acts in these scenes are suppressed or given in indirect speech.

2.13 To clarify the degree of Livy's focalization, it is instructive to compare two other accounts of the same story. The poet Ovid, writing his *Roman Holidays* perhaps thirty years later, follows Livy's presentation of the story pretty closely, though with a greater degree of psychologization of Lucretia and Sextus (*Roman Holidays* 2.721–852). But the account in Livy's contemporary, the Greek historian Dionysius of Halicarnassus, differs significantly (*Roman Antiquities* 4.64–8), especially in the use of direct and indirect speech. In the rape scene, Dionysius gives Sextus a long speech in which he commends him-self to Lucretia. Not only does this strike us as psychologically implausible (though it is worth pausing to ask why Dionysius thought it worked and what cultural differences between then and now this indicates), it also shifts the focalization away from Lucretia and towards Sextus. In the later scene, Dionysius does not have Lucretia give an account of the outrage. This too means that the scene is not focalized through Lucretia. It looks as if Dionysius' agenda is rather different from Livy's – or that his narrative skills are less well honed. Either way, Livy's narrative is remarkable for its focalization from the female perspective.

2.14 This takes us to a final glance at some receptions of this story in later literature and art. Shakespeare in *The Rape of Lucrece* (1594) appears to follow the outline of Livy's version closely, with a similar emphasis upon the moral and political significance of the episode. His most obvious addition is his exploration of the psychology of Tarquin and Lucrece, which is probably inspired by Ovid's handling of this material but is taken much further in this much more extended version. Through a generous quantity of direct speech Shakespeare shows

Tarquin before the rape and Lucrece afterwards as experiencing deep dilemmas. Tarquin: 'Thus, graceless, holds he disputation | 'Tween frozen conscience and hot-burning will'. Lucrece: 'So with herself is she in mutiny, | To live or die which of the twain were better, | When life is sham'd and Death reproach's debtor.' One important effect of this is to alter Livy's focalization through Lucretia. Shakespeare's version, despite being dominated by Lucrece's speeches, has too many characters, each of whom takes the spotlight in turn, to maintain the narrow perspective chosen by Livy for his narrative.

2.15 More important still, in the early part of the poem, Shakespeare uses Tarquin as his focalizer by displaying the sight of Lucrece asleep in strongly eroticized terms, as seen through Tarquin's eyes. The description of her hands, face, hair and naked breasts, 'ivory globes circled with blue' veins, is presented as an incitement to Tarquin's lust and it is difficult to resist seeing this as an incitement to the reader too, even if the effect is limited and circumscribed by the strong moral framework of the poem. It appears that, for the extent of this passage at any rate, Shakespeare constructs his focalizer as male, a male eye, a male 'I'. This in turn raises the issue of the male gaze, an issue which emerges even more strongly from representations in visual art of the rape of Lucretia.

2.16 I limit myself to three examples, although there are many more, conveniently gathered and discussed by Ian Donaldson in his book, *The Rapes of Lucretia* (1982). The most striking common feature in the paintings by Titian (*c.*1570), Artemisia Gentileschi (*c.*1645–50) and Tiepolo (*c.*1745–50) (Figures 2–4) is Lucretia's nakedness and Tarquin's clothedness. As Donaldson says, 'why should Tarquin, moving from his bedchamber to Lucretia's late at night and bent upon rape, be depicted as wearing all those clothes? And why, for that matter, should the chaste Lucretia at this stage of the proceedings be in a state of total nudity? . . . Naked Tarquins . . . are rarely encountered, and never, it would seem, in the company of clothed Lucretias.' However much sympathy for Lucretia these paintings evoke, they also seem to delight in the naked female form and to invite the viewer to share that delight. For some viewers, that delight may be unproblematical. For

FIGURE 2 Titian *Tarquin and Lucretia*
Courtesy of the Fitzwilliam Museum, Cambridge

FIGURE 3   Gentileschi *Tarquin and Lucretia*
Courtesy of Stiftung Preussische Schlösser und Gärten, Berlin-Brandenburg

FIGURE 4 Tiepolo *Tarquin and Lucretia*
Courtesy of Coll. Karl Haberstock, Munich, Germany; Alinari/Art Resource, NY

others, it may be uncomfortable, not least because it seems to conflict with the moral of the story.

2.17 At the same time, it is possible to link the contrast between nakedness and clothedness with the use of light and shade in a way that counteracts the claim that Lucretia's nakedness is designed to be titillating. All three paintings use light to emphasize the whiteness of Lucretia's flesh and bed and all three throw the marauding Tarquin into the shadows. Together these contrasts can be seen as symbolizing not only innocence versus corruption but also vulnerability versus impregnability and honesty versus deception. This kind of interpretation recuperates the morality of the story by reading Lucretia's nakedness on a symbolic level.

2.18 There is one other feature common to all three paintings (and others too) which further complicates this issue. They all include in their composition a third figure, the slave that Tarquin has threatened to kill to compromise Lucretia's honour. In all three, the slave is explicitly cast in the role of voyeur, watching as Tarquin wields his dagger. We can go further: given that it is difficult to see either Lucretia or Tarquin as the focalizer, it looks as if these paintings cast us, the viewer, in a similar, voyeuristic role. Like the slave, we are holding back the curtain and spying on this secret act of rape. This is true above all of Artemisia Gentileschi's version, where the slave's perspective is closest to that of the viewer and where the slave's action in holding back the curtain actually enables the viewer to watch the rape which would be obscured behind the curtain otherwise. This demonstrates the complexity of the issue of the male eye and the male gaze. The female artist Artemisia Gentileschi seems to subscribe to the conventions for this scene established by her male predecessors such as Titian. And yet, she perhaps problematizes the issue of voyeurism more than the male artists by hinting at an assimilation of the viewer's perspective to that of the slave.

2.19 In this chapter we have studied a key text from Livy's history of Rome along with its reception in later literature and art. I hope this has demonstrated that looking at reception can be a fruitful way into the study of classical literature by offering different perspectives and commentaries on familiar material. This is particularly true of visual representations of classical material. It is easy for us to lose touch with the visuality of the role models presented by authors like Livy. It seems appropriate, then, to conclude by reiterating the image of history which Livy offers in his Preface as 'a conspicuous monument' displaying 'object-lessons of every type of model'. We come closer to understanding the Roman elite mentality if we imagine (as Kraus and Woodman invite us to) Livy's own history as a monument 'something like a Roman forum with statues arranged around and in it'.

Further reading and study

A good, accessible introduction to Roman history is provided in the *Atlas of the Roman World* by T. Cornell and J. Matthews (Oxford, 1982). On the early history of Rome see T. Cornell *The Beginnings of Rome: Italy and Rome from the Bronze Age to the Punic Wars* (London and New York, 1995) and on the period of the kings especially see Matthew Fox *Roman Historical Myths: The Regal Period in Augustan Literature* (Oxford, 1996). On the transition from Republic to Principate, the classic by Sir Ronald Syme, *The Roman Revolution* (Oxford, 1939), remains essential. Also fundamental is Paul Zanker, *The Power of Images in the Age of Augustus* (Ann Arbor, 1988). See too the collection of essays *Between Republic and Empire. Interpretations of Augustus and his Principate* (edited by K. A. Raaflaub and M. Toher, Berkeley, Los Angeles, Oxford, 1990) and *The Roman Cultural Revolution* (edited by T. Habinek and A. Schiesaro, Cambridge, 1997).

For an excellent introduction to Roman historiography including Livy see C. S. Kraus and A. J. Woodman *Latin Historians, Greece and Rome New Surveys in the Classics* (no. 27, Oxford, 1997), quotation from page 57. On exemplarity see T. Habinek *The Politics of Latin Literature* (Princeton, 1998) pages 45–59, C. Skidmore *Practical Ethics for Roman Gentlemen: The Work of Valerius Maximus* (Exeter, 1996) pages 3–27, and now Jane Chaplin *Livy's Exemplary History* (Oxford, 2000). On Roman constructions of time, including the tendency to look to the past for guidance, see the essays by Maurizio Bettini in *Anthropology and Roman Culture* (translated by John Van Sickle, Baltimore, 1991), Part II '"The future at your back": spatial representations of time in Latin' on pages 113–93, especially 'Vertical time: from the genealogical tree to the Aristocratic funeral' on pages 167–83.

Issues of Roman masculinity and femininity are discussed by Catharine Edwards *The Politics of Immorality in Ancient Rome*

(Cambridge, 1993) chapters 1 and 2, in *Roman Sexualities* edited by J. Hallett and M. Skinner (Princeton, 1997) and by Craig Williams *Roman Homosexuality: Ideologies of Masculinity in Classical Antiquity* (New York and Oxford, 1999). An important book on representations of Roman women in Latin texts is Suzanne Dixon *Reading Roman Women. Sources, Genres and Real Life* (London, 2001). On Lucretia, Ian Donaldson *The Rapes of Lucretia: A Myth and Its Transformation* (Oxford, 1982) collects an abundance of transhistorical material. On Roman ideas about female sexuality see E. Stehle 'Venus, Cybele and the Sabine women: the Roman construction of female sexuality' *Helios* 16 (1989) 143–64. For the feminist idea that 'the personal is the political' see Nancy Miller *Getting Personal* (London and New York, 1991).

Important exponents of the theory of narratology include G. Genette *Narrative Discourse* (Ithaca, 1980) and M. Bal *Narratology: Introduction to the Theory of Narrative* (Toronto and London, 1985), with helpful exposition by S. Rimmon-Kenan *Narrative Fiction* (London and New York, 1983). This theory entered classical scholarship in the work of Irene de Jong, *Narrators and Focalizers: The Presentation of the Story in the Iliad* (Amsterdam, 1987), and in Don Fowler's article 'Deviant focalisation in Virgil's *Aeneid*' *Proceedings of the Cambridge Philological Society* 36 (1990) 42–63, reprinted in the Routledge collection *Virgil* (edited by Philip Hardie, London and New York, 1999) volume 3 pages 302–23. The quotation I use occurs on the first page of the article.

Projects for further study may include a detailed compare-and-contrast exercise on Livy's account of Lucretia with the accounts in Dionysius of Halicarnassus and/or Ovid. Music fans might like to study Benjamin Britten's chamber opera *The Rape of Lucretia* (1946). It is also instructive to find other paintings depicting the rape of Lucretia and consider how they are focalized to convey conscious and subconscious messages. In general this chapter invites further thought about the production of male and female stereotypes in Roman culture and about patterns of learning, through narratives and through imitation of role models. Further stories from Livy provide highly suitable material for analysis on these lines, such as the stories of the Sabine women (1.9–13) and Mucius and Cloelia (2.12–13). Other texts which offer rich material include Sallust's depictions of the revolutionary Catiline and his fellow-conspirator Sempronia in *War with Catiline* and Juvenal's outrageous portrayal of Roman wives in *Satire* 6. A later text which sets out to demythologize Roman history by demonstrating that it was not in fact full of moral *exempla* is Augustine's *City of God*. Finally, take a look at Zbigniew Herbert's poem 'Transformations of Livy' (in *Elegy for the Departure and other poems*, translated by John and Bogdana Carpenter, Hopewell NJ, 1999), which offers a challenge to seeing Livy's history as a text of empire.

Chapter 3

What is Latin literature?

3.1   So far we have taken a direct plunge into two classic and central texts, one in poetry and one in prose, from what is usually regarded as the greatest period or 'Golden Age' of Latin literature. Virgil's *Aeneid* and Livy's enormous history of Rome were written at around the same time, under the emperor Augustus, and in some ways the two works share the same world view. This is a good enough place to start thinking about what Latin literature is – but it is essential that this is viewed only as a starting place. Before proceeding any further, we shall pause to ask what is contained under this apparently innocuous label 'Latin literature'. The answer will take us on a geographical and historical tour ranging all over the Mediterranean and through perhaps sixteen or more centuries of time. It will provoke further questions, about the people who wrote these texts and the people they wrote them for. Once we have taken this tour, we will be better able to reflect upon our preconceptions about what 'Latin literature' is as a preparation for thinking about what the study of Latin literature involves (Chapter 4).

3.2   First, deconstruction of the monolithic term 'Latin literature' invites reflection on the complexities that can be hidden by labels. Latin is the name of the Indo-European language spoken initially in

Latium (central Italy) and later, as Rome extended its power, throughout Italy, the Balkans and the western Mediterranean – and still used in the Vatican today. The earliest identifiable Latin is found on a brooch found at Praeneste (modern Palestrina, some 20 miles from Rome), dated to the second half of the seventh century BCE. This is very different from what we call Classical Latin, the written form of the Roman dialect of Latin which was used for official and literary texts, and very different again from the Latin spoken by ordinary people, which we label Vulgar Latin and which we glimpse in graffiti scrawled on walls. This last ultimately developed into the Romance languages, Italian, Romanian, French, Spanish and Portuguese. Like all languages, then, Latin changed through time and according to the place and status of those using it. Yet the Latin studied in our schools and universities is almost always Classical Latin and most of the authors studied date from the first century BCE and the first century CE, despite the fact that people continued to use Classical Latin along with its successor Medieval Latin for centuries. The Italian poet and scholar Petrarch, for instance, wrote pastoral poetry in Latin in the fourteenth century, dramatists in England in the sixteenth century wrote plays in Latin, and as late as the eighteenth century a Jesuit from Guatemala called Landivar wrote a long poem in Latin in the style of the *Aeneid*.

3.3 'Literature' too dominates the curriculum, although there are masses of other types of text in Latin which survive from antiquity, for example law codes, curses, epitaphs on graves, and inscriptions on statues and buildings. In fact, it is not clear that 'literature' forms a watertight category. How should we define Augustus' record of his achievements (*Achievements of the Divine Augustus*), which after his death was inscribed on bronze pillars outside his mausoleum at Rome, with copies displayed in the provinces of the Roman empire? Does this carefully composed text qualify as a work of literature or not? I use this example to suggest that the term 'Latin literature' may involve some arbitrary inclusions and exclusions. What is more, we should remember that modern expectations of widespread literacy, in the west at least, do not apply to the ancient world. It is clear that levels of literacy varied widely according to time and place, but what is certain is that literary sophistication was always a prerogative of the elite.

3.4 Classical Latin has been described by the linguist Robert Coleman as 'a highly artificial construct which must be regarded linguistically as a deviation from the mainstream of the language, namely Vulgar Latin'. Its very artificiality gives it a homogeneity which to some extent allows the authors who use it to transcend time and place. They seem to form a tightly-knit community of whom most are familiar with earlier Latin literature, which intensifies the impression of artificiality, a topic which will be explored in Chapter 11, especially 11.13–15. The apparent homogeneity of literary Latin is perhaps surprising given that very few of its authors came from Rome. Many of them originated in Italy – so, for example, Virgil and Livy, the authors we met in Chapters 1 and 2, came from Mantua (modern Mantova) and Patavium (modern Padua), towns in the north of Italy. The poet Catullus from the previous generation came from nearby Verona. His older contemporary, the orator and politician Cicero (106–43 BCE), came from the small town of Arpinum to the southeast of Rome. Others came from other parts of the Roman empire. Moving to the first century CE, the philosopher and dramatist Seneca and his nephew Lucan, the epic poet, came from Corduba (modern Córdoba) in Spain, while the two Plinys, the author of the encyclopedic *Natural History* and his nephew, author of the *Letters*, came from Comum (modern Como) in Cisalpine Gaul. In the second century, Apuleius, the peripatetic professor and author of the first fully fledged Roman novel, came from Madaura in north Africa. The fourth century historian Ammianus Marcellinus was born in Tyre and the epic and panegyrical poet Claudian of a generation later came from Alexandria. The few who came from Rome itself include Julius Caesar and the sixth century philosopher Boethius.

3.5 How does the homogeneity of Classical Latin sit with this geographical diversity of origin of authors? This homogeneity is largely due to the education which was shared by the male elite, centred at Rome, and disseminated throughout the empire among the provincial elites as a tool of empire. Many of the authors listed above visited the capital for shorter or longer periods or even made it their home, not least because it was the intellectual and cultural as well as the political and economic centre of the empire. The artificiality of

Classical Latin meant that it was an exclusive form of discourse. Very few women received the highest level of education and very few seem to have had the opportunity to write, or, more importantly, to perform in public, whether that meant reciting poetry or prose or delivering speeches as lawyers or orators. Those that did were certainly of the elite, for example, Sulpicia, the niece of Messalla the patron of poetry in the Augustan period, who wrote love poetry (which survives) and the younger Agrippina (15–59 CE), the mother of the emperor Nero, who wrote her memoirs (which do not survive). The status of male authors was generally high, either through their own origins or through their association with powerful men in the system of 'friendship' (*amicitia*) that pervaded Roman society. Roman history offers a number of cases of powerful men attracting an entourage of thinkers and writers, including Scipio Aemilianus in the mid-second century BCE, and of course Augustus in the late first century BCE, acting through his friend and associate Maecenas. The phenomenon of patronage will be discussed further in Chapter 7.4, 7–14, 17–19.

3.6   The informal organization of the production of literature in these circles and coteries consisting of the friends and protegés of important men is sometimes reflected directly in the way that authors assert the values of their friends and patrons. Satire is a case in point: in the second century BCE the satirist Lucilius attacks the political enemies of his friend and patron Scipio, while around a century later Horace's *Satires* can be read as a defence of his patron Maecenas and by extension the young Octavian (the future emperor Augustus). Celebration of the values of an 'in-group' can be seen in other ways too. For example, in Poem 84 Catullus, writing in the 50s BCE, attacks a man called Arrius for putting the letter 'h' in the wrong places:

> 'Hadvantages' said Arrius, meaning to say
>   'advantages' and 'hambush' meaning 'ambush',
> hoping that he had spoken most impressively
>   when he said 'hambush' with great emphasis.
> His mother, her free-born brother and his maternal
>   grandparents, I believe, all spoke like that.
> Posted to Syria he gave the ears of everyone a rest.

> They heard those same words smoothly and gently spoken
> and had no fear thenceforward of such aspirates,
>> when suddenly there came the dreadful news
> that after Arrius arrived the Ionian waves,
>> Ionian no more, became 'Hionian'.
>>> (Catullus 84, adapted from Guy Lee)

3.7   Arrius clearly doesn't have what it takes to join the 'club' of Catullus' smart set at Rome, who pride themselves on their exclusive linguistic, literary, cultural and social standards. We find a positive version of the same attitude in a poem by Statius written in Domitian's court circle towards the end of the first century CE, in which he praises a Roman born in Libya for the purity of his accent:

> Your speech is not Punic, nor your bearing;
> your outlook is not foreign: Italian you are, Italian.
> In the City [= Rome] and among the Roman knights
> there are foster-children to do Libya credit.
>> (Statius *Lumber* 4.5.45–8, adapted from
>> Kathleen Coleman)

This passage does of course reveal that there was considerable pressure for the full assimilation of provincial accents, such as Spanish and African accents, at Rome. As the professor Quintilian says in his instructions for future orators:

> If possible our voice and all our words should have the flavour of a nursling of this city, so that our speech may seem to be genuinely Roman and not just presented with Roman citizenship.
>> (Quintilian *Training of the Orator* 8.1.3)

It is no accident that the Latin word for 'sophistication', *urbanitas*, actually derives from the word *urbs*, meaning 'the city (of Rome)'. Latin writers, wherever they come from, write in a Roman voice.

3.8 So which texts, if any, fail to conform to the model of Classical Latin? It depends what standards are applied. To some ears, Livy, who came from Padua, failed the test with his north Italian Latin. He was evidently lambasted for his *Patavinitas*, his native Italian accent, by some ancient critics (Quintilian *Training of the Orator* 1.5.55–6 and 8.1.3) – his 'Paduosity', in Kraus' clever rendering. But generally the division is made according to genre and above all according to chronology. Most of the works classed as 'literature' are relatively elevated in tone. Occasionally, in genres like comic drama and novelistic-type prose we get glimpses of Latin as spoken by a wider section of the population. A good example is the chat between several freedmen (that is, men who were formerly slaves) at a dinner party in the proto-novel *Satyrica* written by Nero's courtier Petronius.

> 'Please, please,' broke in Echion the rag-merchant, 'be a bit more cheerful. "First it's one fing, then another," as the yokel said when 'e lost 'is spotted pig. What we ain't got today, we'll 'ave tomorrow. That's the way life goes. Believe me, you couldn't name a better country, if it 'ad the people. As things are, I 'ave to say, it's 'aving a rough time, but it ain't the only place. We mun't be soft. The sky don't get no nearer wherever you are. If you were somewhere else, you'd be talkin' 'bout the pigs walkin' round ready-roasted back 'ere.'
>
> (Petronius *Satyrica* 45, adapted from J. P. Sullivan)

Another might be the kinds of insults that are hurled by the characters in Plautus' comedies:

> *Calidorus*   Smother him with curses.
> *Pseudolus*   I'll tongue-twist you . . . you . . . you disgusting man!
> *Ballio*   Granted.
> *Calidorus*   You . . . wicked man!
> *Ballio*   Correct.
> *Pseudolus*   You scourgeable scoundrel!
> *Ballio*   Undoubtedly.
> *Calidorus*   Grave-robber!

> *Ballio*   Certainly.
> *Pseudolus*   Gallows-meat!
>
> > (Plautus *Pseudolus* 359–61, adapted
> > from E. F. Watling)

and so on, and on. But literary Latin mostly avoids that kind of language, even in the genre of satire.

3.9   Plautus provides us with a marvellous take on the Latin of his time – which at the turn of the third into the second century BCE was undoubtedly in its infancy as a literary language, even though it was fully-fledged as a language of politics and diplomacy. (We know of treaties in an ancient form of Latin from much earlier, such as the agreement seen by the historian Polybius (see 7.11 below) which allegedly dated from 508/7 BCE.) With fine irony, he describes the process of adapting his plays from the Greek originals like this:

> Philemon wrote the play and Plautus has translated it into barbarian.
>
> > (Plautus *Three-dollar Day* 19)

3.10   Plautus is not alone is representing himself as 'translating' from Greek originals. The first name in Latin literary history is Livius Andronicus, who is seen as the creator of Latin literature and who was probably a Greek slave freed by his Roman owners. We are told that he 'translated' the *Odyssey* into Latin, using not the hexameter of the Greek original but the native Italian Saturnian metre, and that he produced a comedy and a tragedy at the Roman Games in 240 BCE. His dependence on Greek originals is striking, but so is his use of the Italian metre. The same choice of metre is made by his contemporary, the epic poet Naevius, who composed an epic poem about the First Punic War. Unfortunately, only a tiny number of fragments of Livius and Naevius survive. This tension between Greek and Italian influences is one of the key notes of the early history of Latin literature, as we see when we glance at the second century BCE.

3.11 Naevius' combination of mythology and history was developed by Ennius (239–169 BCE) in his epic poem, *Annals*. But Ennius, who was from south Italy and spoke Greek and his local Oscan as well as Latin, broke with his predecessors in developing a Latin form of the Greek hexameter for his epic. This was no easy task, as the Latin language is not ideally suited to fit this metre. This single decision had a crucial influence on the entire future of Latin literature: it subordinated the native Italian influences to Greek influences and set Latin literature in a permanent relationship with Greek literature, as we shall see in Chapter 5 (for example, 5.8) and especially Chapter 14.

3.12 In comparison with Classical Latin, Ennius' Latin looks archaic and unsophisticated, for example, the heavily alliterative line *o Tite tute Tati tibi tanta, tyranne, tulisti!* (fragment 108) – 'Thyself to thyself, Titus Tatius the tyrant, thou tookest those terrible troubles' (in E. H. Warmington's translation). Such a judgement is, of course, unfair. Every writer should be judged by the standards of their age. Ennius was wrestling to adapt the language to his chosen forms of poetry – not just epic, but also tragedy and comedy, satire and epigram. In these different genres, he presents a range of styles. Again, we have only fragments, which makes it hard to draw firm conclusions. We can do better in the case of his contemporary, Plautus. The twenty of his plays that survive, nearly all adaptations of Greek comedies with a strong admixture of native Italian forms of drama, exhibit an astonishing range of verbal pyrotechnics, including a fair smattering of colloquial speech alongside exuberant parody of epic and tragedy. In contrast, his younger contemporary, the comic dramatist Terence, who was attached to the circle of Scipio (discussed in Chapter 7.9–16), developed a purer and more literary form of Latin for his comedies in imitation of his model Menander's Greek – and in anticipation of what we call Classical Latin. It is perhaps no surprise to learn that, although Terence claims he had some difficulties holding the audience in the theatre against rival attractions such as a tightrope walker, boxers and gladiators, his plays were used in schools as set texts from an early date, to judge from the existence of commentaries on the plays.

3.13 By contrast with comedy, satire is a genre which the Romans claimed to have invented, without any model in Greek literature. Its earliest exponents, Ennius and later in the second century BCE Lucilius, created a robust and versatile form capable of reflecting everyday speech as well as parodying elevated poetry. Prose was later to develop than verse, as in the history of Greek literature. The crucial name here is Cato the Censor (234–149 BCE), a dominant figure in the political and cultural life of Rome in the first half of the century. His major innovation was the writing of Roman history in Latin – previously Greek had been the medium – but his only work that survives is a treatise on agriculture, clearly a topic close to the heart of the Roman elite, whose wealth and leisure was essentially based upon land-ownership.

3.14 I have already indicated that our knowledge of this period and of the early literary history of Rome is severely hampered by the limited evidence that survives. So many works by so many authors that would illuminate those early stages of the development of Latin literature are lost. The same kind of limitation applies throughout the history of Latin literature. In short, it is sobering to realize that the majority of ancient literature has not survived into the modern age. How do we know this? From ancient works in which authors are listed and evaluated. For example, in a fragment from the first century BCE, a writer called Volcacius Sedigitus gives his top ten comic dramatists (preserved by Gellius, *Attic Nights* 15.24), as follows: in first place Caecilius Statius, then Plautus, Naevius, Licinius, Atilius, Terence, Turpilius, Trabea, Luscius and in tenth place Ennius, 'because of his great antiquity'. Of these, we have complete plays only by Plautus and Terence.

3.15 A quotation from the famous ideal school curriculum for the trainee orator laid down by the professor of rhetoric, Quintilian, at the end of the first century CE is similarly revealing. After asserting the pre-eminence of Virgil among Roman epic poets he continues:

> All our other poets are a long way behind. Macer and Lucretius are definitely worth reading, but not for the formation of style,

the substance of eloquence. Both handle their themes with elegance, but Macer is uninspiring and Lucretius difficult. Varro of Atax gained his reputation through a translation but should not be despised, although his language is not rich enough to develop powers of eloquence. Let us revere Ennius like those groves which are sacred because of their age, where the huge ancient trees do not so much possess beauty as inspire awe. Other poets are closer in time and more useful for our purposes. Ovid is playful even when he writes epic and is too much in love with his own talent, but still deserves praise here and there. On the other hand, Cornelius Severus, even though he is a better versifier than poet, could have claimed second place rightfully if he had written the whole of his 'Sicilian War' in the same style as his first book. Premature death prevented Serranus from reaching his peak, but his youthful works show enormous talent and devotion of the right kind amazing in someone so young. Our recent loss in Valerius Flaccus is considerable. Saleius Bassus' talent was spirited and creative, but it did not mature with age. Rabirius and Pedo are not unworthy of attention if one has the time. Lucan is fiery and passionate and extraordinary for his epigrammatic phrases and, to express my true feelings, more suited for imitation by orators than by poets.

(Quintilian *Training of the Orator* 10.1.87–90)

Those of the names he mentions whose poems survive are Lucretius, Ovid, Valerius Flaccus and Lucan. Of the rest we have only fragments (as in the case of Ennius) or nothing at all. Yet this is Quintilian's overview of the important names. This realization should lead us to reflect on the hazards that faced ancient texts.

3.16 Their survival was dependent upon the process of transmission from antiquity to the modern world, a process which was in turn governed by a combination of more or less conscious selection and chance. Before we can survey the hazards involved in the transmission of ancient texts, it is important to understand the physical nature of a 'book' in antiquity along with the means of 'publication'. In the time of Catullus or Virgil or Livy, a book did not closely resemble what we call a book today. It consisted of a long roll of papyrus with writing in columns, which was held in both hands and rolled horizontally from right to left. In the first century CE the modern form of book was invented. This was the codex, made from sheets of parchment fastened together at one edge. Initially these were just used as notebooks, but the adoption of the codex by Christians from the second century onwards guaranteed that it would become the standard form for the book and, by the fourth century, the vast majority of literary texts were in this form. They were, of course, all written by hand – which explains our term, manuscript. Until the (western) invention of the printing press in 1440, 'publication' of a text involved the creation of multiple copies. Slaves were set to work on this task, either by the author himself or by 'publishers' and 'booksellers'. In later centuries, the task of copying fell to the monks in the monasteries where the manuscripts were housed. The physical aspects of the book turn out to be highly relevant to questions of survival from antiquity.

3.17 Survival depended partly upon the physical state of the text. A text could easily be damaged – the beginning and end of the papyrus roll were particularly vulnerable, for example. Or, if a text was written on an expensive piece of parchment, it ran the risk of being washed off so the parchment could be reused. It could be affected by mould, by bookworms, by water and above all by fire. Many texts that we would have treasured were lost when the libraries which housed them burned down and when the monasteries where they were later kept and copied went up in flames during the depredations of the sixth to eighth centuries, the so-called Dark Ages. But survival also depended upon questions of choice and taste.

3.18 Copying a manuscript was a slow and laborious business and would only be undertaken for a good reason. At every period, there were reasons why a text might not be re-copied. Some texts, like Virgil's *Aeneid* and the plays of Terence, were valued more or less consistently for their own sake or as pedagogic tools or both. This is proved by the existence from early times of scholarly commentaries written to illuminate these texts, such as the fourth century commentaries on Terence and Virgil by Donatus and Servius and the commentary by Macrobius on Cicero's story of the dream of Scipio (discussed at Chapter 5.26) which closes his *On the Republic*, a commentary which ensured the preservation of that text. Others rose and fell in favour, with some falling so far that they disappeared completely. This is a story of a series of bottlenecks. I have already mentioned the change from papyrus roll to codex form: this was the first major bottleneck and not all texts made it. Then came the radical shift brought about by the rise of Christianity in the fourth and fifth centuries. Some of the 'pagan' texts of Latin literature, those which could be recuperated by Christianity, for example the *Aeneid*, survived, while others, such as some erotic poetry, did not. Another bottleneck occurred during the Dark Ages of the sixth to eighth centuries on continental Europe, when the political, economic and cultural situation meant that few new copies were being made and when parchment was so precious that it was reused. At such a time, religious texts took priority over pagan or secular texts. The so-called Carolingian revival under the emperor Charlemagne (768–814 CE) saw the establishment of schools attached to monasteries and the preservation (i.e. copying) of much of extant Latin literature, but the fragmentation of the empire in the ninth and tenth centuries again posed a renewed threat. The humanistic values of the Renaissance finally shifted secular literature out of the hands of the church, but even after the advent of printing – Latin texts appeared in print from the 1470s on – manuscripts were still being lost.

3.19 It is worth pausing for a moment to review a few of the losses – whether from chance or design – that we know of. First, authors of whom nothing survives: Pollio's tragedies would illuminate Seneca's dramas and if the empress Agrippina's memoirs had been preserved, they would have shed a fascinating light upon the events of the reigns of Claudius and Nero presented so negatively by Tacitus. Then, 'missing' works by extant authors: the polymath Varro's encyclopedic treatise on ancient Roman customs and religious observance is probably the most lamented lost work of Republican prose, while in verse Ovid's tragedy *Medea* would feature on many wish-lists. Then there are texts that survive only in fragmentary form, either by being cited by later writers or because the text is literally fragmentary. Much of early Latin poetry survives in the form of brief quotations in later grammarians, often chosen to illustrate an abnormal Latin usage and always isolated from their original context. This applies to Ennius' epic poem, *Annals,* and to his tragedies and comedies and to the satires of Lucilius, for example. In the case of Gallus, the friend of Virgil and creator of the genre of love elegy, all that survives (apart from one pentameter cited by a geographer) are a few lines on a papyrus from the sands of Egypt dating from perhaps the 20s BCE. More fragments may yet come to light from Egypt and from papyri from the libraries in Herculaneum in the Bay of Naples through the careful work of experts that is currently in progress.

3.20 Sometimes, complete manuscripts seem to have been partially damaged at a later stage. So, what we have of Petronius' proto-novel, *Satyrica*, probably consists of Book 15 with parts of Books 14 and 16: only a small proportion of the whole, which may have been twenty books or more. In the case of the imperial historian Tacitus, the absence of the later books of his *Histories* and the middle books of his *Annals* is much lamented. In a few cases, we know enough about the history of a text – about which manuscripts were in existence and where (we know this from the catalogues of holdings in monasteries) – to appreciate how precarious its survival was. A case in point is the poetry of Catullus, which was virtually unknown during the Middle Ages and in 1300 may have existed on a single copy. A similar story applies to the love poet Propertius. A copy of Cicero's important philosophical essay *On the Republic*, designed as a Roman response to Plato's *Republic*, survived complete only until the seventh century, when the text was washed off so the codex could be reused for Augustine's commentary on the Psalms. Modern scholars have been able to recover some of Cicero's work from this palimpsest (which means a parchment 'scraped again').

3.21 This brief glimpse of the hazards facing Latin texts in the process of transmission from antiquity to the era of the printing press might make it seem miraculous that so much has survived, more or less intact. But in the era of printing too we see similar principles of selection at work. Some texts are in vogue for decades or more, while others go for years without receiving attention from scholars and almost disappear from view, although the fact that there are numerous copies ensures their survival until periods when they are appreciated again. So for example, Valerius Maximus' collection of *Memorable Acts and Sayings* (first century CE), an immensely popular work throughout the Middle Ages and later, received no modern translation into English until the recent edition for the Loeb Classical Library. Different intellectual climates and educational priorities in different places value different texts. Currently, the narrowest focus is perhaps in England, where it is unusual to study any texts outside the period 90 BCE–120 CE. By contrast, students in continental Europe regularly study the *Consolation of Philosophy* which Boethius wrote in prison in the early sixth century.

3.22 New technology does not necessarily help. It is a wonderful fact that much of Latin literature is now available on CD-ROM and on the Internet, so making a whole library available at home to anyone interested, but this alone cannot supply new readers if Latin is out of fashion. Academics and the academic presses make decisions about which texts are suitable as set texts and merit attention. Editions and translations of these are commissioned, while other texts languish. Fashions change and even the canon of 'classic' texts changes. This might invite us to think hard about the texts that we study under the rubric of 'Latin literature' and about the concept of 'the classic', a concept enshrined in the ideology of the Great Books course taught in some US universities. The canon can be regarded 'at one extreme as a conspiracy of the ruling elite (seen as the self-perpetuation of the DWEMs – Dead White European Males) and at the other as a collection of masterpieces that transcend history', to quote from Charles Martindale's discussion of 'the classic of all Europe' – namely, Virgil. We would do well to ask who makes judgements and selections of 'classic' status, on what criteria and with what agenda, conscious and subconscious. It should by now be obvious that the creation of any canon of 'classic' texts, recommended texts, set texts, is fraught with hazard for the texts that are excluded. It is only recently that the prejudice that values texts from the so-called Golden Age of Latin literature (basically the Augustan period) over the 'Silver Latin' texts of the early empire has been challenged, with the rehabilitation of authors like Lucan and Statius. And yet Dante in the fourteenth century admired Lucan and Statius as among the best of the Latin poets. At any rate, I hope it is safe to predict that questioning the validity of the canon will remain an important strand of scholarship in Latin literature in the twenty-first century.

Further reading and study

For an overview of the development of the Latin language see the article 'Latin language' by R. G. Coleman in the *Oxford Classical Dictionary*, 3rd edition; L. R. Palmer *The Latin Language* (London, 1954) provides a full discussion. On literacy and writing in the Roman empire see W. V. Harris *Ancient Literacy* (Cambridge, Mass., 1989), and *Literacy in the Ancient World* (edited by Mary Beard, Ann Arbor, Michigan, 1991; *Journal of Roman Archaeology* supplement 3). On the social aspects of Latinity see W. M. Bloomer *Latinity and Literary Society at Rome* (Philadelphia, 1997) and on perceptions of the Latin language across the ages see Joseph Farrell *Latin Language and Latin Culture: From Ancient to Modern Times* (Cambridge, 2001). On the concept of sophistication, see E. S. Ramage *Urbanitas: Ancient Sophistication and Refinement* (Norman, 1973).

On the homogeneity of education and its role in socializing the Roman male elite see Elizabeth Rawson *Intellectual Life in the Late Roman Republic* (London, 1985), especially Part I, T. Morgan *Literate Education in the Hellenistic and Roman Worlds* (Cambridge, 1998), A. M. Keith *Engendering Rome: Women in Latin Epic* (Cambridge, 2000) chapter 2, and on women and education see E. Hemelrijk *Matrona Docta: Educated Women in the Roman Elite from Cornelia to Julia Domna* (London and New York, 1999). On the interconnection between culture and power see T. Habinek *The Politics of Latin Literature* (Princeton, 1998) especially chapter 5. On Roman education as the key to the assimilation of provincial elites see Peter Brown *Authority and the Sacred* (Cambridge, 1995) 29–54.

For a full account of Latin literary history see the *Cambridge History of Classical Literature* volume on Latin Literature edited by E. J. Kenney and W. V. Clausen (Cambridge, 1982), which includes a discussion of books, readers and education by E. J. Kenney in chapter 1. G.-B. Conte's *Latin Literature: A History* (translated by Joseph Solodow, revised by Don Fowler and Glenn Most, Baltimore, 1994) is indispensable on individual authors. On the circumstances of literary production in Rome see Elaine Fantham *Roman Literary Culture: From Cicero to Apuleius* (Baltimore, 1996).

The best introduction to the transmission of texts from antiquity is L. D. Reynolds and N. G. Wilson *Scribes and Scholars* (3rd edition, Oxford, 1991). A striking dramatic treatment of aspects of nineteenth and twentieth century textual scholarship is presented by Tom Stoppard in his play about A. E. Housman, *The Invention of Love* (London, 1997).

Questions about the canon are raised by e.g. Charles Martindale *Redeeming the Text* (Cambridge, 1993) pages 23–9 'Firing the canon – tradition or treason?' and in his introduction to the *Cambridge Companion to Virgil* (Cambridge, 1997) especially pages 1–6; similar issues are raised on a larger scale in Italo Calvino's recent book *Why Read the Classics?* (translated by Martin McLaughlin, London, 1999).

Most of classical Latin literature is available on the Packard Humanities Institute CD-ROM and much of it at http://www.perseus.tufts.edu/.

A suggestion for further study is to read Tom Stoppard's play *The Invention of Love* and to research its background in terms of what it reveals about the priorities and preferences in the study of Latin literature in the nineteenth and twentieth centuries. Another is to investigate the origin and use of the term 'classic', using the *Oxford English Dictionary*. Another is to make up your own list of the canon of, say, ten classic texts of Latin or English or American literature and to see how your list differs from those of other people. This is a good moment to have an argument about what makes a text a 'classic'.

Chapter 4

What does studying Latin literature involve?

4.1   Just as canons change through time and place (as indicated in Chapter 3.18–22), so favoured methods of study and interpretation change. Roman schoolboys studied set texts and learned them by heart, chanting them over and over, first sitting down, then standing up, as we learn from a complaint about the 'rehashed cabbage' that kills the poor teachers in Juvenal's *Satire* 7 (lines 152–4). Something like the same thing was still happening in England a hundred years ago, in the classrooms at schools like Eton. Since then, things have changed. Most modern students are likely to meet Latin texts through the medium of English translation and are certainly not expected to learn them by heart.

4.2   There is a huge divide between, on the one hand, scholars who believe that it is essential to study in the original language and that everything else is second class and second rate, and, on the other hand, scholars who believe in the value of studying texts through the medium of English translation either in their own right or as a window on to Roman society or both. The two modes of meeting Latin texts involve different kinds of study and require different kinds of teaching too. Generally speaking, the first group of scholars promote linguistic skills and the exploration of what we can call the philological background, including the explication of grammar, syntax, vocabulary and metre. The second group focus on the structure and content of texts and encourage skills that involve understanding of the context(s) that affected the formation and the reception of the text. 'Generally speaking,' I said, because there are dangers of drawing too sharp a dichotomy here, although that has been how many of the scholars concerned have situated themselves. Most teachers, after all, whether the text is encountered in English or in its original Latin, attempt to set that text in *some* kind of context. So the big question is *how* to define that context.

4.3   The material presented in Chapters 1 and 2 is designed to introduce a range of the possible contexts without an overload of scholarship, theory or jargon. Chapter 1 introduces two basic kinds of analysis, the diachronic and the synchronic, of which (1) the diachronic approach sees a text as shaped by earlier literary history and (2) the synchronic approach focuses upon a text at its moment of production. In this case, (1) involves looking at Virgil's relationship to earlier works in the epic genre, both Greek and Latin, while (2) involves situating Virgil at a particular moment of Roman history. The second category has complex ramifications, which include (3) the socio-economic context of the production of literature, here seeing Virgil as a recipient of support from his patron Maecenas; (4) the political context of literature, here analysing the *Aeneid* as promoting a favourable image of Augustus and of Augustan ideology, or not; and finally (5) the philosophical context, here reading the dilemma facing Aeneas at the end of the *Aeneid* in terms familiar to Virgil's elite readership from contemporary philosophical thought.

4.4   Chapter 2 introduces the following approaches: (1) explanation of important features of a text by reference to national character, here in terms of the moral dimension of Roman historiography, particularly its interest in exemplarity, that is, the display of positive and negative role models for men and for women; (2) exploration of the political and philosophical context (again), here in terms of how ideas about good and bad rulers emerge in this text; (3) the borrowing of ideas and terminology from narratology (the study of narrative) to highlight

Livy's presentation of the story of the rape of Lucretia from a narrow, highly focalized perspective (that of Lucretia), which becomes clearer through comparison with other versions of the story, contemporary and later; and (4) the reception of classical material at later times in literature and in art, which in turn raises important questions about the gendering of texts and paintings. I have tried to do this without burdening my text with scholarship, with footnotes or with the names of scholars, while giving some sense of the range of approaches and the intensity of scholars' disagreements. After the preparation provided by Chapters 1 and 2 and by Chapter 3, with its invitation to think about 'Latin literature', this chapter offers the opportunity to get more explicitly theoretical, to examine what the study of Latin literature does or can involve.

4.5   Classics is no stranger to fierce debate. Just think of the furore about *Black Athena* or, more recently, the reaction in the USA (but nowhere else) to the controversial book *Who Killed Homer?*, which has sold many thousands of copies with its attack on theorists and also on philologists of recent years for losing touch with the values of the Greeks. But in the specific field of Latin literature, the debate has not usually been conducted quite so publicly. To illuminate the terms of the debate, I shall take as my starting point three items published in the early 1990s, whose relevance throughout the English-speaking world is undiminished today, because there is still not enough genuine dialogue between the different sides.

4.6   First is a 1991 article by Tony Boyle, a Latinist who has studied and worked in the UK, Australia and the USA, in which he takes the occasion of the twentieth birthday of the journal *Ramus* to look backwards and forwards at the state of literary studies. In 'Intellectual pluralism and the common pursuit', he expresses qualified optimism for the future, glossing that as follows:

> Not all departments are pluralistic. There are blinkered textual critics and self-proclaimed 'philologists' who show intolerance of cultural and literary historians, and blinkered 'theorists' (also often self-proclaimed) who show intolerance of papyrologists,

textual critics and language specialists. There seems also a more active resistance to intellectual pluralism on the Latin side than on the Greek, where the current focus on gender, sexuality and power, for example, is reflected widely in departmental curricula and figures strongly in 'mainstream' contemporary debate. And where such resistance or intolerance becomes an issue of professional power . . . , where appointments are made, grants allocated, fellowships awarded, and articles and books accepted prejudicially, it becomes a matter which members of the classics profession must address.

In this quotation, Boyle depicts graphically the tendency to polarization between the 'theorists' and the 'traditionalists' and succinctly explains why awareness of how we and others approach texts matters.

4.7   In an effort to overcome this polarization, the editors of the *JACT Review* (a publication of the Joint Association of Classical Teachers in the UK, aimed at teachers of Classics in schools and universities) commissioned an article by Simon Goldhill of Cambridge University, which is entitled 'Who's afraid of literary theory?' (reproduced here as Appendix B). This is a lucid and spirited defence of the value of literary theory or theories in the study of Greek and Latin literature and culture. Goldhill starts with a quotation from Terry Eagleton, whose name is synonymous with the explication of literary theory in the field of English literature:

Without some kind of theory, however unreflective and implicit, we would not know what a 'literary work' was in the first place, or how to read it. Hostility to theory usually means an opposition to other people's theories and an oblivion of one's own.

Goldhill glosses this by saying:

'Theory' isn't something one tacks on to reading. It's what makes reading *possible*. It's there already. Always. The question is how explicit to make it and how to make it explicit. . . . What literary theorists do is to try to understand the process of reading. What we do to books and books do to us.

That is, he sees reading as a process, involving readers (us, for example) actively, even when we think we are being passive.

4.8   My last item is Don Fowler's provocative picture of the state of Latin studies in his final review of recent books on Roman literature for the journal *Greece and Rome* in 1993, written from his isolated position as a 'theorist' in Oxford. This review encompasses such contrasting offerings as the volume edited by Woodman and Powell on *Author and Audience in Latin Literature* and the three volumes launching the Cambridge series edited by Feeney and Hinds, *Roman Literature and its Contexts*, by Hardie, Kennedy and Martindale, as well as books by what we might call quintessential products of Oxford (Hutchinson) and Cambridge (Gowers). Fowler does not mince his words:

> In the modern quarrel of ancients and moderns, the major weapons of the conservatives are common sense and tolerance. They like to image themselves as charming middle-aged men puffing on a pipe before a cosy gas-fire and accepting the world with a warm smile, while their opponents are strident bolshie young prigs, some of them even women, who arrogantly think they know better than anyone else. But an appeal to common sense only works if there is real commonality: if there isn't that sense of sharing, the move from personal opinion to universal claim that 'common sense' embodies merely makes one angry at missing the party. Common-sense statements conceal their agenda and their will to power through systematic ambiguity. It is simply common sense to me, for instance, that we construct our own readings of antiquity: I don't see how anyone could deny this (it sure ain't the Klingons or the archangel Gabriel who do it for us). But in my word 'construct', of course, is a whole postmodernist agenda I'm trying to con people into buying.

Later, he goes still further: 'Batting for the opposition (i.e. youth, progress, truth, beauty, and life) are the first three heroes of the new Cambridge series.' I do not believe that Fowler intended his review to be as offensive as it was taken to be in some quarters. But the reaction that he provoked by this rigid drawing up of the battle lines unfortunately seems to have reinforced and entrenched the stark polarization that he, Boyle and Goldhill all remark upon – and it is not clear that things have changed that much since the early 1990s. That is why it is important to know about the existence and the terms of this debate.

4.9 Fowler's starting point in his review is the discussion by Woodman and Powell of the author's intention and authority, in the epilogue of their volume. This is a useful starting point for us too. Woodman and Powell assume that recovering 'the author's probable intentions' is a central aim when reading literary texts. Fowler challenges that. He doesn't say (although he might have) that even if we could recapture an author's original intention, it is not clear that this would be all that useful. Instead, he draws attention to the context in which literature is written and the audience it is written for – and asserts that these are not fixed and certain but have to be argued about. This, roughly speaking, is the 'death of the author' that the French literary critic Roland Barthes made so famous (or infamous). The central idea here is that many factors shape the production and the interpretation of a literary text and that the most valuable thing we can do as readers and critics is to focus upon those factors. The value of the kinds of approach labelled (or dismissed) as 'theory' is that they illuminate the factors that might be relevant to understanding a literary text in its context(s) and for its audience(s).

4.10 I offer another quotation from Terry Eagleton which insists upon our situatedness and responsibility as readers:

> Some literary students and critics are likely to be worried by the idea that a literary text does not have a single 'correct' meaning, but probably not many. They are more likely to be engaged by the idea that the meanings of a text do not lie within them like wisdom teeth within a gum, waiting patiently to be extracted, but that the reader has some active role in this process. Nor would many people today be disturbed by the notion that

the reader does not come to the text as a kind of cultural virgin, immaculately free of previous social and literary entanglements, a supremely disinterested spirit or blank sheet on to which the text will transfer its own inscriptions. Most of us recognize that no reading is innocent or without presuppositions. But fewer people pursue the full implications of this readerly guilt.

'Theory' is helpful for thinking about the forms that our situatedness takes.

4.11 A catalogue of the names of thinkers who have shaped anew our sense of classical literature in relation to its contexts and audiences, though few of them set out to do this, would include Sigmund Freud, Ferdinand de Saussure, Claude Lévi-Strauss, Roman Jakobson, Mikhail Bakhtin, Vladimir Propp, Simone de Beauvoir, Northrop Frye, Harold Bloom, Gérard Genette, Roland Barthes, Michel Foucault, Pierre Bourdieu, Jacques Derrida, Jacques Lacan, Julia Kristeva, Hélène Cixous and doubtless others. (To formulate a catalogue like this is, of course, to invite disagreement.) This list of thinkers, mainly European and mainly working in a language other than English, represents the pioneers in fields such as psychology, linguistics, anthropology, sociology, philosophy, as well as literary criticism, during the twentieth century. They are the names associated with some of the -isms so prominent in recent and contemporary criticism of classical literature – formalism, structuralism, post-structuralism, postmodernism, deconstruction, New Historicism, reception theory, psychoanalysis, feminism and dialogism. This is not the place to explore these -isms in their own right. There are books such as Terry Eagleton's *Literary Theory. An Introduction*, Jonathan Culler's *The Pursuit of Signs* and Toril Moi's *Sexual/Textual Politics: Feminist Literary Theory* which do that lucidly and which provide plenty more bibliography. What is important is to understand that some classical scholars have taken the insights of these thinkers, sometimes treating them as gurus and sometimes treating them more critically, and applied them to classical culture and classical texts. The result is that we now have a much wider range of ways of reading ancient texts than a hundred years ago.

4.12 Whether or not that is a good thing is of course hotly debated. One thing that is at stake here is our relationship to the texts of Latin literature and to the ancient Roman culture that produced them. Some of us see our culture as a continuation of that of the ancient world and the study of the classics as the study of our own past. Others of us regard the ancient world as an alien place and its literature as something of an enigma that needs to be resolved. In that case, anything that helps us to think ourselves out of our own preconceptions and prejudices about literature, its contexts and its audiences, will be helpful. That explains why classicists, including scholars studying Latin literature, turn to these ideas to illuminate texts that predate these ideas by many centuries.

4.13 It should by now be clear that I believe that both approaches are valuable. I do not believe that we should be forced into an unmitigated choice between these two perspectives. There will be moments when the assimilating perspective, that sees a continuity between antiquity and the modern world, will be more useful as a tool of literary criticism – and moments when the dissimilating perspective, which emphasizes the differences, will be superior. But what is needed is a greater level of mutual tolerance between practitioners of both kinds of scholarship.

4.14 What is more, to posit a stark conflict between the 'traditionalists' and the 'theorists' is to neglect the process by which texts have come down to us. I am not here talking about the process of transmission outlined in Chapter 3 so much as the process of reception through the ages. The thinkers of the twentieth century do not have a monopoly on the interpretation of ancient texts. The worship of the modern should not obscure the fact that people have been reading these texts and reacting to them – as scholars and as poets – since they were written, 2,000 years ago, and that those readings and reactions have shaped the history of those texts. This is the argument eloquently made in an important 1993 book by Charles Martindale, *Redeeming the Text: Latin Poetry and the Hermeneutics of Reception.* Following this argument, it is illuminating to ask what poets and scholars of the intervening centuries thought of the texts of Latin literature. So, for example, Martindale argues that our view of the Latin epic poets Virgil, Ovid, Lucan and Statius is, or might be, mediated or somehow affected by the views of Dante, Milton and Dryden, who translated or reworked or interacted in other ways with their Latin predecessors in the epic genre. In prose, I suppose a similar argument could be made about Gibbon and Tacitus. It is likely, after all, that more people have dipped into Gibbon's *The Decline and Fall of the Roman Empire* than have opened the pages of Tacitus' *Annals* or *Histories*, which give *his* view of the decline of the Roman empire.

4.15 This kind of approach also legitimises the study of the reception of Latin literature by scholars as well as poets. So, for example, the way that, in the fourth and fifth centuries CE, Servius, the grammarian and schoolteacher, interprets Virgil's *Aeneid* in his commentary and Augustine, the orator and, later, Christian convert, interprets Apuleius' novel *Metamorphoses* have their own value. For sure, their comments may strike us as jejune and unsophisticated. But it is undeniable that those comments emanate from a culture that was far closer than ours is to the culture that produced the texts – and that in itself presents us with the challenge of trying to understand the factors that shaped the reception of Latin literature in different contexts and by different audiences.

4.16 New developments in criticism can, in turn, have an impact on the canon, by awakening interest in texts which had previously been neglected or marginalized. One example of the effect of scholarship on the types of text we study is the recent 'discovery' of the ideas of Mikhail Bakhtin, a Russian linguist, philosopher and literary theorist writing in the late 1920s. Bakhtin's work has yielded two important ideas which have been taken up by classical literary criticism in recent years. The first is dialogics – an emphasis on the interactive nature of language and of texts – and in 1993 this interest generated an entire volume of the ground-breaking US journal *Arethusa* devoted to classicists' use of Bakhtin's approach. The second is the idea of the carnivalesque, by which is meant the inversion of social and intellectual norms as represented and enacted in texts. This includes a focus upon the body and bodily functions. Bakhtin originally explored the realm of bodily discourse in his study of Rabelais and his novel *Gargantua*. Classical scholars have applied the same approach to what we might call Rabelaisian texts from the classical repertory, in particular the novel and comedy and satire, for example J. K. Newman in his 1990 book on Catullus and Emily Gowers in her 1992 book on food in Roman literature. One effect of this recognition of the value of Bakhtin's ideas is the validation of the study of certain texts which were previously relegated to the margins. Where the canon previously consisted of the 'higher' genres such as epic, readjustments are now being made so that texts whose richness is best appreciated through a Bakhtinian lens – texts such as the novel and comedy and satire – can have their candidacy for admittance to the canon taken seriously.

4.17 I conclude this discussion with an extensive quotation from one of the finest critics of Latin literature, Philip Hardie. Hardie develops ideas about the origins and function of sacrifice from René Girard's studies of the anthropological and mythological dimensions of Athenian tragedy and demonstrates how these ideas illuminate the narrative patterns of the *Aeneid* and above all the final scene of the *Aeneid*, which we met in Chapter 1.

> Sacrifice operates through substitution and exchange; the victim is offered in exchange for benefits or in payment of a negative balance incurred through earlier crimes. The victim itself has a symbolic value, standing in as a surrogate for those who offer it. The Palinurus episode reveals a chain of such substitutions and exchanges. He is the price exacted in return for the safe arrival in Italy of the rest of the Trojans. But substitution also extends to disguise and role-playing: the god of sleep, Somnus, disguised as, or playing the part of, the human Phorbas, offers himself deceptively as a substitute helmsman while Palinurus takes on the part of sleep (5.846 'I myself will carry out your duties on your behalf for a while'). Sleep, as we know, is the close brother of Death, and here is another disguise, for what Somnus really offers is not forty winks but the forgetfulness of death. Palinurus himself functions as a kind of twin of Aeneas;

his death is a substitute for the latter's death and precondition for his fated success (as the success of Romulus arose out of the death of his twin). When Palinurus has fallen overboard his place and office are taken by Aeneas (5.868): 'he himself (ipse) steered the ship over the waves through the night,' as if through this chain of substitutions we finally arrive at a halting-place, the man 'himself' (ipse vir).

The shifting identifications in the death of Palinurus provide a model for a reading of the final 'sacrifice' of the poem, a play of substitution in which neither the victim Turnus nor the slayer is wholly himself. Turnus loses his life because he is wearing another man's armour, the swordbelt of Pallas; and by doing so he transfers to himself the symbolism of the ephebe cut down on his wedding night contained in the swordbelt's scene of the Danaids. In reminding Aeneas of what is most dear to him this has the effect of alienating Aeneas from himself, both in the sense, often noted, that he loses control of his emotions, and through his appropriation of another's name for his decisive action (12.947–9): 'Are you, wearing the spoils of my friends, to be snatched from me? Pallas sacrifices you, Pallas [not "Aeneas"], with this wound.' . . . These substitutions have their Iliadic background: Pallas plays the role of (is a Virgilian substitution for) Patroclus, the companion of Achilles who goes into battle wearing the armour of Achilles. Patroclus is an alter ego of Achilles who dies in his stead (and whose death is also a prefiguration of Achilles' own death), and it is probable that in Homer the literary motif of the alter ego conceals an older practice of the ritual substitution of a human victim for the king who should die. Furthermore the use here of the name Pallas is itself a Virgilian appropriation of an Iliadic passage that talks of surrogate action and compensation: at Iliad 22.270–2 Achilles tells Hector 'There is no longer any escape for you; Pallas Athene will straightway conquer you with my spear, and now you will pay back all the deaths of my companions whom you killed with the spear in your battle rage.' Through the homonymy of the name Pallas, Virgil substitutes a mortal youth for the warrior goddess; but this is a substitution that also operates within the text of the Aeneid itself, for, if the poem ends with the hero killing his enemy in the name of Pallas, it had begun with Aeneas' enemy Juno's wish that she could kill him in a repetition of the punishment of Oilean Ajax – by none other than Pallas (Athena), 1.39.

Virgil sharpens the Homeric model and gives it greater emphasis by choosing to end his epic in a hall of mirrors where identity is split. This last scene of the Aeneid pulls in (at least) two directions at once. On one level the final encounter of Aeneas and Turnus is the most personal episode in the poem. The dispute has been resolved on the divine level, and the one remaining divine actress, Juturna, has been pulled out; we are left with the individual Aeneas facing the individual Turnus. But both humans are acting out other roles than their own, wearing other disguises and masks, Aeneas above all as an ersatz-Achilles to Turnus' Hector; as vicariously performing the will of Jupiter; and, by his own words, as the re-embodiment of the dead Pallas. Instead of Aeneas facing Turnus we might see this as two versions of Pallas opposing each other, Aeneas as the agent of Pallas' revenge and Turnus as the young warrior who, by foolishly dressing in the sword-belt of Pallas, has consigned himself to the same premature and pathetic death in battle as his victim. Once more the collapse of distinctions that results from the play of literary models seems to coincide with a feature of sacrifical practice as analysed by Hubert and Mauss in their chapter on 'Sacrifice of the God': (p. 85) 'the priest can be an incarnation of the god as well as the victim: often he disguises himself in the god's likeness'; (p. 88) 'Priest or victim, priest and victim, it is a god already formed that both acts and suffers in the sacrifice.'

In the final fulfilment of his mission in Italy, and when he should be most true to himself, Aeneas as sacrificer is caught up in a logic of sacrificial substitution. This is disturbing if a central subject of the Aeneid (as of the Odyssey) is 'the man (himself)' (virum, Aen. 1.1); the epic will set about defining that man, its hero, but ends only by placing his identity in doubt. 'Who is Augustus and what does he stand for, and what indeed is his name?' were the questions that pressed on Virgil's contemporary audience, and the definition of the emperor was to remain problematical.

On the literary–historical level, epic closure is thwarted, allowing for the possibility of an indefinite series of replays in epics after the Aeneid as the Roman epic hero constantly seeks to define his own identity through the impersonation of earlier historical and literary models; perhaps as each successive Roman emperor sought the appropriate self-representation, defining his own closeness to, or distance from, the first emperor Augustus.

(Hardie *The Epic Successors of Virgil*, pages 32–5)

Hardie not only synthesizes a vast tract of ancient literature – ancient epic – but uses the tools of modern literary criticism to demonstrate the patterns of narrative and ideology articulated in his chosen text. This is not, of course, the last word on this text – but it makes instructive, provocative and profitable reading.

4.18 I shall close this chapter by offering a justification of the organization of material in this book. It would have been relatively straightforward to present a series of chapters devoted to various -isms in turn – formalism, structuralism, post-structuralism, deconstruction, reception theory, feminism, psychoanalysis, dialogism and so on. Each chapter would have focused upon one or two texts that appeared to lend themselves to such a model and upon the scholars who had pioneered the reading of Latin texts in the light of their chosen -ism. But, however interesting the individual chapters might have been, I do not believe that the result would have amounted to an adequate overview of Latin literature. As President Eisenhower allegedly said, 'All -isms are wasms'. So instead, I have chosen a number of topics or 'collecting points' which cumulatively will facilitate an understanding of Roman literary culture. In each of these chapters a range of texts will be discussed along with a range of critical interpretations. In this way, I hope to avoid the tyranny of the -isms while reflecting the exciting range of the criticism of Latin literature.

4.19 My basic organizing principle is the opposition between public and private, an opposition influenced especially by the work of French scholars such as Michel Foucault and Paul Veyne, who argue that the public/private antithesis was constructed differently in the ancient world(s) from how it is in our contemporary culture(s). A further organizing principle is one that privileges the idea of textuality in terms of surface and depth, especially in the relationships that texts have with other texts and with their audiences. Finally, I make some concession to the idea of literary history by offering a brief look at the past, present and future of Latin literature and its reception.

4.20 Accordingly, I start with three chapters that reflect the public face of Latin literature. Since much of Latin literature was written by the Roman elite for the Roman elite, it is not surprising to find literature as the mirror and the agent of the formation of Roman identity. In Chapter 5, I emphasize the way literature reflects the militaristic aspect of Roman society. It is readily used as a vehicle of patriotism, of morality, of forging and reinforcing an approved national identity and celebrating the idea of Rome. Hand in hand with this agenda comes the awareness that literature is an occasion of performance: Chapter 6 brings together a range of texts which epitomize the performance of Romanness and especially of Roman masculinity in front of an audience which surrounds the performer. The idea of circles is picked up in the next chapter with a focus upon the organization of the production of literature in groups, cliques and circles, including court circles: here I shall examine the resulting relationship between patronage, panegyric and freedom of speech (Chapter 7).

4.21 The next three chapters counterbalance the focus on literature as public discourse with a focus upon the treatment of private life and private lives in Latin literature. So Chapter 8 examines the loss of Roman identity involved in being exiled and in being enslaved by love as represented in at times militantly unofficial voices by lovers and philosophers. Chapter 9 demonstrates the difficulties in trying to recuperate 'real' lives from the kind of evidence available – biographies, epitaphs, letters and confessions – and Chapter 10 investigates texts from epic, tragedy and satire which explore individual identity and invite introspection.

4.22   The next three chapters shift the focus from the text as a vehicle to the surface of the text itself. Literary texture and intertextuality is the subject of Chapter 11. Chapter 12 deals with the ruptures of the surface of the text involved in metapoetics, a process of self-referentiality that occurs in narrative and in drama. Chapter 13 presents a brief discussion of allegory, a phenomenon which need not disrupt the surface of the text but which adds layers of interpretation.

4.23   The book closes with two chapters which offer a broader diachronic overview of some of the central issues in the history of Latin literature. I devote most of Chapter 14 to a discussion of its inferiority complex to Greek literature and conclude with consideration of implications of the concepts of genre and generic boundaries that are so often used to analyse Greco-Roman literature. In Chapter 15 I link Latin literature with the physicality of the city of Rome as part of my argument that it eventually shrugs off its indebtedness to Greek literature. At the moment when Latin literature comes of age I prefer to label it not Latin but Roman literature: in this chapter I look at three texts which articulate immortal ambitions for Rome and Rome's poets. I also reflect for a moment on the demands of writing a literary history and I offer a brief justification for the unconventional organization of this book, with the intention of emphasizing that readers of this book are hearing a personal voice with which they are invited to debate and disagree.

Further reading and study

On Classics at Eton in the late nineteenth century see Chris Stray *Classics Transformed: Schools, Universities and Society in England, 1830–1960* (Oxford, 1998) chapter 3.

   Black Athena: the Afroasiatic Roots of Classical Civilization by Martin Bernal (New Brunswick, vol. 1 1987, vol. 2 1991), arguing for an African dimension to classical culture, generated multiple responses, including 'The challenge of Black Athena', a special issue of the journal *Arethusa*, Fall 1989. V. D. Hanson and J. Heath's *Who Killed Homer?* (New York, 1998), a contribution to the 'Culture Wars' raging in the USA during the 1990s, was an all-out attack on modern ways of teaching Classics which provoked an impassioned response within the USA but made no ripples in the UK or the rest of Europe. The Winter 1999 edition (6.3) of the journal *Arion* published reactions by Willett, pages 84–102, Martindale 103–21 and Green 122–49 and a response by Hanson and Heath 150–95. The Fall 1999 number (7.2) has a reply by Martindale to Hanson and Heath 174, with further thoughts by Green 175–8, Hanson and Heath 179–80 and Steinmeyer, working in Sarawak, 181–4.

The passages quoted are from A. J. Boyle 'Intellectual pluralism and the common pursuit' *Ramus* 20 (1991) 113–22, quotation from 120; Simon Goldhill 'Who's afraid of literary theory?' *JACT Review* 10, Autumn 1991, 8–11, also in Appendix B below; and Don Fowler *Greece and Rome* 40 (1993) 226–36. The six books reviewed by Fowler are: Tony Woodman and Jonathan Powell (editors) *Author and Audience in Latin Literature* (Cambridge, 1992); the three volumes launching the Cambridge series *Roman Literature and its Contexts*, edited by Denis Feeney and Stephen Hinds in 1993 – Philip Hardie *The Epic Successors of Virgil: A Study in the Dynamics of a Tradition*, Duncan Kennedy *The Arts of Love: Five Studies in the Discourse of Roman Love Elegy* and Charles Martindale *Redeeming the Text: Latin Poetry and the Hermeneutics of Reception*; and books by what we might call quintessential products of Oxford (G. O. Hutchinson's *Latin Literature from Seneca to Juvenal*, 1993) and Cambridge (Emily Gowers' *The Loaded Table: Representations of Food in Roman Literature* (but actually published by Oxford University Press, 1992)).

A painless way into literary theory is provided by Terry Eagleton *Literary Theory. An Introduction* (Oxford, 1983) – the quotation at 4.10 is from page 89; Jonathan Culler *The Pursuit of Signs* (London, 1981); and my favourite, Toril Moi *Sexual/Textual Politics: Feminist Literary Theory* (London and New York, 1985).

An eloquent argument for the importance of the process of reception is offered by Charles Martindale in *Redeeming the Text* (above). On Bakhtin and Classics see 'Bakhtin and ancient studies: dialogues and dialogics', *Arethusa* 26.2, Spring 1993; J. K. Newman *Roman*

Catullus and the Modification of the Alexandrian Sensibility (Hildesheim, 1990); Emily Gowers *The Loaded Table* (above). For the application of French anthropological approaches to Latin literature see Philip Hardie *The Epic Successors of Virgil* (above).

On the public–private antithesis see M. Foucault *The History of Sexuality* (3 vols, translated by R. Hurley, New York, 1978–86) and P. Veyne *Roman Erotic Elegy: Love, Poetry and the West* (translated by D. Pellauer, Chicago, 1988). It is interesting to note that Veyne was a colleague of Foucault in Paris. See also Maria Wyke's review article 'In pursuit of love, the poetic self and a process of reading Augustan elegy in the 1980s' in *Journal of Roman Studies* 79 (1989) 165–73.

Any of the debates sketched here – about *Black Athena*, about *Who Killed Homer?* and about what Latinists think they are and should be doing – provide ample opportunities for further discussion.

Consider the idea that 'The past is a foreign country' (the opening words of L. P. Hartley's 1953 novel, *The Go-Between*) as it relates to the study of Latin literature.

Chapter 5

Making Roman identity: multiculturalism, militarism and masculinity

5.1 An idea that is central to any understanding of Latin literature can be encapsulated in the word *Romanitas*, 'Romanness'. This word does not actually occur in any classical Latin text (the first time is in Tertullian in the early third century CE), rather as 'Americanness' and 'Englishness' and 'Australianness' do not trip off the tongue. All the same, it expresses one important preoccupation in Latin literature – the definition of Roman identity and encouragement to conform to that definition, a tendency we have already met in our study of exemplarity in Livy's history (Chapter 2.2).

5.2 This feature of Latin literature is inseparable from the early history of Rome. In the early days, Rome was just one of many city states in the Mediterranean. It rose to power through its phenomenal military success, against a very diverse cultural backdrop. The Romans seem always to have been good at assimilating the best of what they found in other cultures, for example, in matters of religious cult, technology and military tactics, although this assimilation went hand in hand with the destruction of other features. It usually operated through inviting the members of local elites to participate, at some level, in Roman power. This technique of co-optation (voluntary participation) was effective in the case of culture too. The Romans were never shy of harnessing the finest talent of outsiders for Rome (as we saw in our glance at the origins of writers of literature in Latin in Chapter 3.4).

5.3 This phenomenon is highly visible in the early days of Latin literature. According to the ancient tradition, the first poetry in Latin was written by Livius Andronicus, a Greek or half-Greek freedman (i.e. ex-slave) from Tarentum in South Italy, in the period when Rome was taking over this area. In the year 240 BCE he is said to have put on a comedy and a tragedy at the Roman Games. He also wrote a translation of Homer's *Odyssey* using not the Greek dactylic hexameter metre but an Italian metre called the Saturnian. Even this snippet of information demonstrates the interaction of the Greek and the native Italian cultures in the formation of Latin literature. The same kind of complexity emerges from a glance at another author from the next century. The comic dramatist Terence is said to have been born at Carthage, on the coast of north Africa, and to have come to Rome as a slave, where he was freed by his owner. He gained the patronage of prominent Romans including Scipio Aemilianus, a leading politician and general, who attracted a 'circle' of intellectuals and writers who were all advocates of Greek culture at Rome (see Chapter 7.9–16 on 'circles' and Chapter 14 for a fuller discussion of the interrelationship between Greek and Latin literature). Terence's plays are closely based on Greek originals, mainly by the Athenian playwright Menander. They reproduce the effect of Menander's pure Greek with a purity of Latin that gave Terence's plays a central place in the European school curriculum from antiquity down to the nineteenth century. It says something significant about Roman literary culture that such landmarks and classics came about from the genius of men for whom Latin was not their first language.

5.4 After a glance at the multicultural backdrop, this chapter, then, will be devoted to some of the definitions and explorations of *Romanitas* in Latin literature. The multicultural backdrop cannot be separated from the idea of *Romanitas*. Definition of identity is so often formulated by contrast with what that identity is not. This makes it important to appreciate the variety of literary cultures which did impact and might have impacted upon Latin literature.

5.5   Greek literature was a ubiquitous presence for the Romans. But that term is too vague to be useful. When we say 'Greek' we so often mean 'Athenian' and not 'Spartan' or 'Corinthian' or any of the other cities of the Greek world. As in the later case of Rome, Athens' political and military domination went hand in hand with cultural domination. One exception might seem to be the Homeric poems, which originated long before Athens' supremacy as oral poetry in Ionia (the west coast of Asia Minor) where a dialect of Greek which we call Ionic was spoken. But even in this case, these poems were (probably) first written down in roughly the form in which we have them today at the command of the ruler of Athens in the sixth century BCE, a tyrant called Peisistratus. It was the fifth century BCE that saw Athenian literature flourish, in the form of tragedies and comedies written for performance at religious festivals, poems of praise and lament written for other public occasions, historiography and (into the fourth century) oratorical speeches and philosophical dialogues. All of these types of literature feature in Latin literature too.

5.6   After the fall of the Athenian empire, the next major concentration of power in the Mediterranean was the empire of Alexander of Macedon (356–323 BCE), known as 'Alexander the Great'. After his death his enormous empire was divided up by his generals, including Ptolemy, who took the kingdom of Egypt and established his court at the city of Alexandria, where the Nile flows into the Mediterranean. He and his son, Ptolemy II, developed Alexandria as a centre of artistic and cultural life by building the famous Library (to hold the extensive and ever-growing royal book collection) and the Museum (literally, 'House of the Muses'), a focus for lectures and scholarship. The resulting concentration in Alexandria of poets and scholars from all over the Mediterranean had a huge and lasting impact on the development of western literature. This period, often called the Hellenistic Age, saw the emergence of the scholar-poet. The classic example is Callimachus – and he with others of the same outlook had an enormous influence on Latin literature. Theirs was poetry written by and for intellectuals. In the hands of the 'Alexandrian' poets, poetry lost its original roots in communal life and receded into the more refined air of the ivory tower.

5.7   Latin literature invariably exists in some kind of relationship with Greek literature, then, whether the archaic literature of the Homeric poems, the literature of the classical age of fifth and fourth century Athens or the evolving intellectualized form of literature that emerged in Alexandria during the third century BCE. In fact, the relationship with Greek literature so dominates our Latin sources that it would be easy to neglect other influences, some of them closer to home. In Italy, there were clearly forms of pre-literary or sub-literary 'literature' which do not survive. We know, for example, of sub-literary (i.e. too low in status to have been recorded) forms of drama, such as Atellan farce, named after a town in Campania (west central Italy) and associated with the Oscans who originally inhabited that part of Italy. It seems highly likely that this form of drama influenced the comic dramatist Plautus, writing at the turn of the third into the second century BCE, in his Latin adaptations of Greek comedies. Perhaps, too, the invention of satire by the Romans – there is no Greek equivalent – reflects a strand of pre-literary or sub-literary Italian culture. In any case, it is clear from visual representations that the indigenous cultures, such as the Etruscans who ruled much of Italy prior to the Romans, had their own narratives celebrating their mythology and their local heroes, despite the fact that none of this tradition survives in written form, erased by the domination of Rome. Elsewhere in the Mediterranean too, the arrival of Roman rule obliterated cultures with a high level of literary achievement, such as Punic literature from Carthage.

5.8   The uneven survival of these possible influences on Latin literature makes it hard to gauge their impact. But we gain a glimpse of the multiculturalism that essentially underpinned the Roman achievement in Latin literature when we look at the figure of Ennius (239–169 BCE), who is often regarded as the creator of Latin poetry. Ennius came from Calabria in south Italy, where Greek culture was dominant, and he spoke Greek, Oscan (the local Italian language) and Latin (the language of Rome). He went to live in Rome in 204 BCE, associated with members of the Roman elite including Scipio Africanus (grandfather of Scipio Aemilianus mentioned above), travelled with his patron Fulvius Nobilior on military campaign and was awarded Roman citizenship in 184 BCE (see Chapter 7.7 for more details). He wrote in the genres of tragedy, comedy, satire, epigram and philosophical prose. But most important was his epic, *Annals*, which he wrote in the 170s. In the *Annals*, Ennius presented the history of Rome from its origins, starting with the stories of Aeneas and Romulus and Remus, down to his own times. Although only fragments survive, it is clear that Ennius' *Annals* was an encapsulation of Romanness in terms of history, traditions, customs and above all morality. At the same time, Ennius presents himself as Homer reincarnate, but also reflects the influence of the Hellenistic scholar-poet Callimachus. The fact that the poet who is credited with the invention of Latin poetry and who offered the seminal articulation of *Romanitas* was one who was not from Rome, for whom Latin was perhaps his third language and who was clearly influenced by various kinds of Greek literature, speaks volumes. It is a graphic demonstration of how the Romans forged a literature of their own to express their national identity.

5.9   What, then, does Roman identity consist of? First and foremost, Rome was a military power, constantly at war somewhere in the Mediterranean. This was symbolized in ritual: the gates of the temple of Janus in the Forum were kept open except in times of complete peace. When Augustus closed the gates in 29 BCE this was the first time for more than two hundred years and only the third time in Roman history that this had happened. Consequently, Roman society was a militaristic, 'macho' society which rewarded high achievers in warfare with status, political clout and material benefits. This means that the representation of warfare and of military achievement in Latin literature is at the other end of the spectrum from the doubts about warfare often articulated in the west since the First World War and especially in the light of the conflicts in Korea and Vietnam. The widespread modern prejudice against war is a major stumbling block for many of us in our understanding of Latin literature.

5.10 A considerable proportion of Latin epic poetry is devoted to the description of battles and warfare, but this is not reflected at all adequately in the discussions of these poems in the scholarly literature. For example, Virgil devotes the second half of his *Aeneid* to the war that Aeneas fights in Latium and he characterizes this as his 'greater task'

(*Aeneid* 7.45), greater, that is, than the travels he describes in the first half of the poem. Yet you could not guess this from the critical literature. This immediately demonstrates a difference in sensibility ancient and modern. Ennius asks, 'Who can unroll this great war from end to end?' (*Annals* 173) and his question is closely echoed by Virgil who seeks the assistance of Calliope and the other Muses to 'unroll with me this great war from end to end' (*Aeneid* 9.528). So one important problem that we face right away when we read Latin literature is to understand why these authors include so much warfare.

5.11 A passage from the epic poem on Rome's conflict with Carthage back in the third century BCE written by Silius Italicus at the end of the first century CE is a good starting point:

> I cannot hope to tell of all these countless deaths
> and awful deeds in a manner worthy of the theme's
> > renown
> or find words to match the ardour of the warriors.
> But grant me this, Calliope, for my toil –
> to hand down to long ages a great man's noble deeds,
> > too little known,
> and to crown a poet with the honour he deserves.
> Ennius, from the ancient family of king Messapus,
> was in the front line and his right hand was distinguished
> by the Latin vine-staff, that badge of pride. He came
> from the rugged land of Calabria, a son of ancient Rudiae,
> Rudiae which now owes all her fame to this her child.
> > (Silius Italicus *Punic War* 12.387–97)

5.12 Silius makes it clear that the epic poet's task is to record for posterity the noble deeds of warriors – and with a piquant twist he celebrates the noble deeds in war of Ennius, his predecessor in the epic genre, here depicted as a soldier. He implies that Ennius' fame replies solely on his poetry and seeks to rectify the situation. A hundred and fifty years earlier, in a legal speech which involved defending the value of poets to society, the statesman and orator Cicero had praised Ennius for celebrating not just individuals but the Roman people:

Our Ennius was a close friend of the elder Africanus and that is why, as is thought, a marble statue of him was set up in the tomb of the Scipios. But his verses of praise surely celebrate not only the person praised but also the name of the Roman people. Cato, ancestor of Cato here, is extolled to the skies; this brings with it great honour for the history of the Roman people. In short, all those great names – the Maximi, Marcelli, Fulvii – are magnified by praise which is shared by all of us. That is why he who had done this, a man of Rudiae, was welcomed by our ancestors into Roman citizenship.

(Cicero *For Archias* 22)

5.13 Fragments of the *Annals* illustrate how Ennius uses battle scenes to present noble conduct, worthy of record and worthy of imitation, by warriors. A classic example occurs in a battle fought in the early third century BCE in which Decius Mus offers himself to the Roman gods as a sacrifice on behalf of the entire army, in a practice called *devotio*, with these words:

Gods, spare a moment to hear this prayer of mine
as I dismiss the life from my body, with full knowledge and
determination,
in warfare and in battle, for the sake of the Roman people.

(Ennius *Annals* 200–2)

Another fragment celebrates the strong sense of competition in valour felt by Roman warriors:

A powerful desire is mine to equal the deeds of my
heartfellows.

(Ennius *Annals* 131)

5.14 A typical scene of fierce fighting in Latin poetry might go like this:

Each army's total strength was now engaged,
all Latins and all Trojans, every man:
Mnestheus and fierce Serestus, Messapus

> the horse-tamer, valiant Asilas, the Tuscan
> squadron, Arcadians of Evander,
> each putting all he had into the struggle,
> never a let-up, never a breathing-spell –
> in the vast combat every man fought on.
>
> (Virgil *Aeneid* 12.548–53,
> adapted from Robert Fitzgerald)

Such passages tend to make difficult reading for us, especially if we are struggling to identify the names. It is perhaps helpful to view these passages on a cinematic model, as crowd shots from an overhead perspective which depict the general context before the camera zooms in on one individual. Epic, like cinema, enjoys portraying individual heroism. There is even a semi-technical term for the depiction of an individual warrior's exploits in epic – his or her *aristeia* (a Greek word, literally, 'best moment'). Following Homeric precedent established in the *Iliad*, Virgil includes an *aristeia* of Turnus, Aeneas' Rutulian enemy (Book 9), of Pallas, the son of Aeneas' Greek ally Evander (Book 10), of Camilla, the leader of the Volscians and ally of Turnus (Book 11), and of Aeneas himself in Book 12.

5.15 The cinematic analogy works for a passage like this, from the *aristeia* of Turnus:

> Turnus spoke and rose to full height, sword in air,
> then cleft the man's brow square between the temples
> and cut his head in two – a hideous gash
> between the beardless cheeks. The earth resounded
> quivering at the great shock of his weight
> as he went tumbling down in all his armour,
> drenched with blood and brains; in equal halves
> his head hung this way and that way from his shoulders.
> Trojans, aghast, turned round in a stampede,
> and if the thought had come to the warrior
> to break the gate-bars, to admit his friends,
> that would have been the last day of the war,
> last for the Trojans. But rage and mindless

> lust for slaughter drove the man ablaze
> against his enemies.

(Virgil Aeneid 9.749–61)

The graphicness of this description is liable to make our stomachs turn, although it finds its modern analogies, for example, in the movies of Quentin Tarrantino and in attempts to depict the bloodiness of war in *Saving Private Ryan* (1998) and *The Thin Red Line* (1998). The Romans, by contrast, were evidently much less squeamish than we are – which is perhaps not surprising for a society in which a fair number of the elite, during the Republic at least, saw military action and in which the slaughter in the gladiatorial arena became a familiar sight under the Principate. The attempt to read such a passage as a Roman might have done is a real challenge.

5.16 Virgil's graphic descriptions of warfare are not simply descriptions. Often, there is a moral. Here, Virgil indicates clearly that Turnus' blood-lust leads him to squander the strategic advantage he has gained through his military prowess. In another case, in his description (as portrayed on the shield of Aeneas: see Chapter 1.10) of the battle of Actium in 31 BCE at which Octavian defeated Antony and Cleopatra, Virgil moralizes the battle by lining up the gods on both sides:

> The queen amidst the battle called her flotilla on
> with her Egyptian sistrum's beat,
> not yet turning her head to see
> twin snakes of death behind, while monster forms
> of gods of every race and the barking
> dog-god Anubis held their weapons up
> against our Neptune, Venus and Minerva.
> Mars, engraved in steel, raged in the fight
> and from high air the dire Furies came
> with Discord, taking joy in a torn robe,
> and on her heels, with bloody scourge, Bellona.
> Overlooking it all, Actian Apollo
> began to pull his bow. Frantic at this sight,
> all Egypt, Indians, Arabians, all

Sabaeans put about in flight, and she,
the queen, appeared crying for winds to shift
just as she hauled up sail and slackened sheets.

(Virgil *Aeneid* 8.696–708)

Although – or perhaps because – this battle had taken within the past ten or twelve years at the time that Virgil was writing and must have been vivid in the memory of his readers, he chooses not to describe the battle literally but to endow it with symbolic and moral significance.

5.17 The description of the shield of Aeneas closes with a picture of Augustus celebrating his triple triumph in Rome in 29 BCE (quoted in Chapter 1.11). The award of a triumph was undoubtedly the height of achievement for a Roman general under the Republic and the ceremony assimilated him to a god for the day. As the Augustan poet Horace says, referring to the triumph ceremony, 'To do deeds and parade prisoners before the people – | that is to touch the throne of Jupiter and mount to heaven' (*Epistles* 1.17.33–4). A triumph was a privilege awarded by the Senate and People (SPQR) to a high-ranking general (that is, one holding high political office) for a victory over a foreign enemy in which at least 5,000 of them were killed and the war was terminated. The ceremony meant a holiday for everyone in Rome and people gathered in the streets to watch the procession, which entered through the Triumphal Gate and advanced by a circuitous route to the Capitoline Hill where sacrifices were offered at Jupiter's temple, as indicated on the sketch map at Figure 5. The triumphing general (*triumphator*) rode in a four-horse chariot, dressed in purple, wearing a laurel wreath, perhaps with his face painted red to resemble Jupiter, and he was escorted by his troops and eminent captives, by treasures seized in the victory and by paintings of cities and rivers captured or of the battles fought. Perhaps the fullest description of a triumphal procession in Latin poetry is provided by Ovid in *Sorrows* 4.2, a poem he wrote from exile on the Black Sea coast of Romania in 12 CE (discussed in Chapter 8.4–5). Not surprisingly, there was intense competition for the award of a triumph during the late Republic, which explains why, under the Empire, the triumph became an imperial prerogative and monopoly, limited to members of the imperial family.

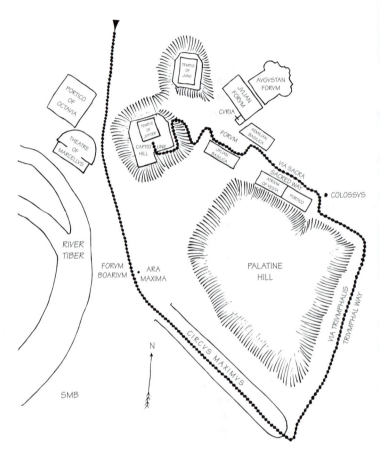

FIGURE 5 Sketch map of the triumphal route through Rome

5.18 The triumph ceremony plays a large role in the literature of this period, which we can conveniently call Augustan literature. It appears both literally, in contexts of victory in warfare past, present and future, and figuratively, that is, as a metaphor, in contexts of victory in love affairs and in poetic achievement. This indicates how deeply the militaristic mentality of Roman society runs: it seems difficult for Romans to think without recourse to images of fighting and triumphing (as we shall see in Chapter 8.15 and 17).

5.19 To demonstrate how pervasive the triumph is in poetry of this period we need look no further than another important text which, like *Aeneid* 8, celebrates Octavian's victory at the battle of Actium. Horace's *Odes* were innovatory adaptations of Greek lyric poetry, that is, the short personal poems written by Alcaeus and Sappho among others on a range of topics including love and friendship, poetry and politics. With the support of Virgil and despite fighting on the losing side in the civil war, Horace had gained the patronage of Maecenas, Octavian/Augustus' promoter of the arts, during the 30s, and in 23 BCE he published Books 1–3 of his *Odes*, which represent a major vindication of Augustus' policies. In *Odes* 1.37 Horace imagines himself as master of ceremonies on the day the good news about Actium reaches Rome:

> It's time for drinking, time with feet unfettered
> to beat the ground in dances, high time today
>   to furnish the Gods' cushioned couches
>   with Salian banquets, comrades.
>
> From their ancient bins it was sacrilege
> till now to bring out Caecuban wine, while the queen
>   was plotting mindless ruin for the
>   Capitoline and an end to Empire,
>
> among her pervert company of disease-
> polluted 'males', intemperately nursing
>   wild hopes, and drunk upon her sweet
>   good fortune, but madness was checked when
>   hardly
>
> a single ship escaped the consuming flames,
> and Caesar brought back fearful reality
>   to a mind deranged by Mareotic wine,
>   while she fled Italy,

by chasing her with his oared galleys, as sparrowhawk
pursues the gentle dove or brisk hunter
    the leveret on plains of snowy
        Thessaly, so he could load with fetters

the deadly deviant. She, though, determining
to die more nobly, neither was terrified
    as women are by sword nor changed course
        with her swift fleet for some hidden refuge,

but dared go see her palace in its collapse
with brow serene, and handle courageously
    her angry serpents so that she could
        drink with her body their blackest venom,

the more defiant having resolved to die,
and loth, no doubt, that barbarous Liburnians
    should bring her here dethroned for pompous
        triumph, a woman but not submissive.
        (Horace *Odes* 1.37, adapted from Guy Lee)

If it was the supreme achievement for a Roman to celebrate a triumph, then to be paraded in a triumph was the ultimate humiliation. The visible loss of autonomy entailed a loss of face (on which see Chapter 6) and so a loss of masculine identity. Horace demonstrates this central feature of Roman ideology in this text by praising Cleopatra, the ruler of Egypt, for committing suicide instead. That is, he creates a paradox: he takes the example of someone who is in some ways the antithesis of a member of the Roman elite – a woman, a foreigner, a 'deviant' surrounded by the eunuchs of her Egyptian court – and uses it to set the standard for proper masculine and Roman behaviour.

5.20 Cleopatra clearly shows great courage in not shirking the dagger 'like a woman' would. But she is very unusual. The Romans saw a rigid demarcation between masculine and feminine behaviour. Perhaps only a queen – that is, a woman in the position of a (usually male) ruler – could transgress these gender boundaries. Significantly, the

Latin word for courage is *virtus* – that is, the quality of being a man, *vir*. The word itself declares that 'courage' is a male prerogative and primarily a military concept, a long way from the Christian overtones that the word 'virtue' has acquired since Roman antiquity. (This failure of abstract concepts to map neatly on to one another in different languages and cultures explains why it is sometimes desirable to leave words in the original Latin.) Militarism, masculinity and morality are inseparable in Roman thought.

5.21 But Roman morality and *Romanitas* consist of more than just courage (*virtus*). Augustus' Golden Shield (mentioned at Chapter 1.14) sets his Courage alongside his Clemency, Justice and Piety. Other texts add many other possible Roman 'virtues', including Goodness, Fairness, Consistency, Reliability, Strictness, Freedom from Corruption and many forms of Self-control. Like courage, these 'virtues' are masculine prerogatives, because they belong to the public spheres of action, in military, political, judicial, religious and social matters. Chastity, a virtue which can be attributed to women and young men, is perhaps the chief exception to that rule. Otherwise, the concern with the formation of the ideal Roman is focused upon the Roman *man*.

5.22 And yet the Latin language produces the paradox that these abstract nouns for the 'virtues' are, virtually without exception, all feminine nouns and thereby capable of being represented in iconography, for example, on coins and in sculpture, by female personifications. This paradox finds its literary expression in a Latin epic poem by Prudentius dating from the fourth century CE called *Soul-Battle*. Here, Prudentius depicts the virtues as female warriors fighting it out against the vices, like epic heroes, in the first wholly allegorical poem in Latin (see Chapter 13.16–18).

5.23 We have already seen from the case of Livy in Chapter 2 how the Romans inculcated the appropriate virtues through the use of *exempla* – narratives presenting positive and negative role models. Many if not most other texts of Latin literature do the same thing. A classic case is Horace *Odes* 3.5, one of the poems conventionally called the 'Roman Odes' at the start of Book 3 in which Horace's political engagement is overt and sustained. In these poems Horace styles himself 'the priest of the Muses' (*Odes* 3.1.3) to claim high status for his voice. *Odes* 3.5 is designed to provide a model of patriotism – of putting your country above your own survival. This message is conveyed through the story of Regulus who, as a prisoner of war in the First Punic War (264–241 BCE), was sent to negotiate peace with Rome on condition that he would return if the negotiations failed. But in fact, he advised the Romans to continue the war and honourably returned to Carthage where he was tortured to death. In Horace's words, he 'refused a base peace | And spurned the precedent | That would have brought the unborn age no good' (14–16).

5.24 The Roman habit of thinking by means of role models emerges nowhere more clearly than in the pages of Valerius Maximus, an author who was immensely popular from antiquity through to the Middle Ages but who has fallen from favour since then (see Chapter 3.21), to the extent that only very recently has an English translation become available (Shackleton Bailey's *Loeb Classical Library* edition). Valerius' *Memorable Acts and Sayings*, written under Augustus' successor the emperor Tiberius (14–37 CE), is a compendium of narratives which illustrate virtues and their opposites among other phenomena, organized under headings such as 'On bravery', 'On endurance', 'On military discipline', 'On cruelty', 'On generosity' and so on. Valerius' first choice of illustrations is always members of the Roman elite, but he also includes cases of foreigners and even of women if they embody the qualities he is discussing, perhaps as exceptions that prove the rule. All the same, there can be no doubt that the formation and the performance of Roman morality is primarily an issue for men, as we shall see in Chapter 6.

5.25 That is why the relationship between fathers and sons is so important in Latin literature. The ideal way for a son to learn Roman morality, Roman masculinity, *Romanitas*, was at his father's side, by accompanying him through his daily round of meetings and business. This is the model picture presented by Pliny the Younger, writing at the turn of the first and second centuries CE, in one of his *Letters*:

In ancient times it was the custom for us to learn from our elders by watching as well as listening and so acquire the principles that would govern our own behaviour and which we could hand down in turn to our descendants. ... Everyone was instructed by his father, or, if he was fatherless, by some important older man who took his father's role. And so men were taught by example, the surest method of instruction.

(Pliny *Letters* 8.14.4–6)

And this is precisely the picture presented by Horace in a poem where he asserts his own morality to refute people who claim that his satire is malicious:

> Yet if I'm a little outspoken or perhaps
> too fond of a joke, I hope you'll grant me that privilege.
> My good father gave me the habit; to warn me off,
> he used to point out various vices by citing examples.
> When urging me to practise thrift and economy and to live
>   content
> with what he himself had managed to save he used to say:
> 'Notice what a miserable life young Albius leads and how Baius
> is down and out – a salutary lesson not to squander
> the family's money.'

(Horace *Satires* 1.4.103–11, adapted from Niall Rudd)

5.26 The classic father–son relationship in Latin literature is that of Anchises and Aeneas, above all in Book 6 of the *Aeneid*. As we saw in Chapter 1, Anchises instructs his son in morality and in the future history of Rome. He also explains to Aeneas the workings of the cosmos (the relationship of gods, humans and nature) and what happens after death. Virgil's idea of having a son instructed by his deceased father in morality and metaphysics and eschatology was inspired by another classic text, the so-called 'Dream of Scipio' with which Cicero closes his treatise of political philosophy, *On the Republic* (itself inspired by Plato's *Republic*: see Chapter 3.20), written in 54–51 BCE. Cicero presents the fictional dream of Scipio Aemilianus (185–129 BCE, discussed further in Chapter 7.9; see too 3.18) in which his adoptive grandfather, Scipio Africanus, appears to him and explains how souls escape from the prison of their bodies into the only true life, life after death. Next Scipio's natural father, Aemilius Paullus, appears and explains to him how he should live:

> 'But you, Scipio, as your grandfather here did, and as I who begot you have done, must practise justice and do your duty: your duty which is great towards parents and family, but greatest of all towards your country. Living like this is the way to heaven, into this gathering of those who have lived their lives and who, now freed from the body, inhabit that place which you see –' (this was a circle of brilliant whiteness, shining out and surrounded by flames) '– which you have learnt from the Greeks to call the Milky Way.'
>
> (Cicero *On the Republic* 6.16, adapted from Jonathan Powell)

Then Africanus explains to his grandson the arrangement of the planets and the 'music of the spheres'. He emphasizes the fragility of earthly glory and of Roman activity in the world before talking about the immortality of the soul. In a strongly Roman and patriotic finale, he asserts that the best life for the soul while on earth is to work for the preservation of one's country.

5.27 This text demonstrates clearly that for the Romans, fathers and ancestors represented the ultimate authority figures. For a son to learn from his father like this was the quintessential mode of learning. In part, this reflects the legal reality of Roman society, in which a son, whatever his age and social status, did not come into full legal autonomy until the death of his father. But it also reflects a huge psychological gulf between modern western societies and Roman antiquity. While we may embrace change, challenges and innovation, Roman society was a society which valued authority and conformity. The idea of tradition, of doing things the way they had always been done – an idea which is neatly encapsulated in the Latin phrase *mos maiorum* (literally 'the ways of our ancestors') – is the essence of *Romanitas*.

Further reading and study

For an account of Rome's acquisition of empire see *Cambridge Ancient History* 2nd edition vol. 7 part 2 *The Rise of Rome to 220 BC* (Cambridge, 1989) and vol. 8 *Rome and the Mediterranean to 133 BC* (Cambridge, 1989). E. Gruen *The Hellenistic World and the Coming of Rome* (2 vols, Berkeley, 1984) demonstrates how essential it is to understand the rise of Rome in the context of the Hellenistic world. On the interaction with Greek culture see too A. Momigliano *Alien Wisdom. The Limits of Hellenization* (Cambridge, 1975), E. Gruen *Culture and Identity in Republican Rome* (Ithaca, 1992), E. Gruen *Studies in Greek Culture and Roman Policy* (Leiden and New York, 1990) and P. Green *Alexander to Actium: The Historical Evolution of the Hellenistic Age* (Berkeley, 1990). On Rome's interaction with Etruscan culture see W. V. Harris *Rome in Etruria and Umbria* (Oxford, 1971) and *Etruscan Italy* (edited by J. F. Hall, Provo, Utah, 1996).

On the role of war in Roman culture see W. V. Harris *War and Imperialism in Republican Rome, 327–70 BC* (Oxford, 1979). On the Roman triumph and its significance see H. S. Versnel *Triumphus: an Inquiry into the Origin, Development and Meaning of the Roman Triumph* (Leiden, 1970) and S. Weinstock *Divus Julius* (Oxford, 1971) pages 60–79.

On the construction and inculcation of masculinity see Chapter 6 below and look out for Robert Kaster's forthcoming study of Roman identity. For an excellent discussion of Cleopatra see Maria Wyke 'Augustan Cleopatras: female power and poetic authority' in *Roman Poetry and Propaganda in the Age of Augustus* (edited by A. Powell, Bristol, 1992) pages 98–146.

A good starting point for understanding the Roman 'virtues', along with other terms central to Roman culture and ideology, is Appendix 3 in G.-B. Conte's *Latin Literature: A History* (translated by Joseph Solodow, revised by Don Fowler and Glen Most, Baltimore, 1994) pages 794–805. The Appendix on 'The Latin and Greek lexicon of honour' in J. E. Lendon *Empire of Honour: The Art of Government in the Roman World* (Oxford, 1997) pages 272–9, is a useful discussion of the Latin and Greek terminology. On the relationship between fathers and sons see E. Eyben 'Fathers and sons' and Richard Saller

'Corporal punishment, authority, and obedience in the Roman household', both in *Marriage, Divorce, and Children in Ancient Rome* (edited by Beryl Rawson, Oxford, 1991) pages 114–43 and 144–65 respectively. M. O. Lee *Fathers and Sons in Vergil's Aeneid* (Albany, 1979) offers a Jungian reading of the *Aeneid*, demonstrating a different approach to the topic from the one advocated here.

An understanding of the deeply militaristic and machismic nature of Roman culture is essential. To this end, study of any of the many battle scenes in Roman epic poetry is valuable, such as passages from Virgil *Aeneid* 9–12, from Lucan's *Civil War* and from Silius Italicus' *Punic War*. It is worth asking whether it is the case that (as is often alleged) the post-Virgilian writers privilege horrific effects.

Another project is to study the father–son relationship in Terence's play *The Brothers*, asking what were its possible implications for Terence's contemporary audience. Helpful here is the edition of the play by A. S. Gratwick (Cambridge, 1976) especially pages 16–26, and John Henderson's essay 'Entertaining arguments: Terence, *Adelphoe*' in *Writing Down Rome: Satire, Comedy, and Other Offences in Latin Poetry* (Oxford, 1999) pages 38–66.

Chapter 6

Performance and spectacle, life and death

6.1 This chapter will develop the ideas introduced in Chapter 5 about the importance of masculinity in Roman identity by concentrating on the fact that the life of the Roman elite was lived in public, with almost nothing that we would recognize as private time or private space. The result of this was that life was a performance – and so was death. Members of the Roman elite were continually aware of the need to perform their masculinity and of the fact that life and death could become a spectacle. At any moment, a member of Roman society might be a 'player' himself or part of an audience watching someone else's performance. This awareness is reflected in Latin literature in the importance attached to the concept of *dignitas*, which we can render as 'face' or 'appearance' or 'standing'. Putting on a good show (however 'good' is defined) in life and in death is crucial to understanding the mentality of the Roman aristocrat.

6.2 This chapter will look first at the performance of masculinity in the context of the public speeches made by orators, such as the statesman Cicero. Then we shall turn to the phenomenon of performing on stage and in the gladiatorial arena to discover that this kind of performance was viewed as a threat to the performer's masculinity and therefore outlawed for members of the elite. The spectacle of two gladiators fighting to the death in the arena takes us to the topic of death as performance. Gladiatorial combat is a central underlying theme of Lucan's epic on the civil war between Caesar and Pompey: we shall look at Lucan's narrative of the death of Pompey to demonstrate the importance of 'face' and we shall consider the phenomenon of the Stoic suicide, epitomized in the stories about Cato. Finally we shall study an episode from Tacitus' *Annals* which makes a funeral procession into a highly spectacular performance in which all the 'players' are acutely aware of the impression they are making.

6.3 One of the most important opportunities for the display of masculinity was in the practice of oratory, or public speaking. The entire education system was designed to prepare the young aristocrat for public speaking, as we can see from information that survives throughout the classical period, from the anonymous handbook we call the *Rhetorical Treatise to Herennius* written in the 80s BCE to Quintilian's *Training of the Orator*, a comprehensive educational theory, written nearly two centuries later. Under the Republic, this training in public speaking had a tangible result. Skilful oratory could and did advance a man's political career and enable him to carry out the duties involved in wielding power to maximum advantage. Under the Principate, the cut and thrust of political debate seems to have diminished, but the ability to debate matters with flair and originality was appreciated and consequently was fostered in schools of declamation, which we can get a glimpse of in the memoirs of the elder Seneca (*c.*50 BCE–40CE).

6.4 In a convention taken over wholesale from Greek education, oratory was divided into three types: (1) judicial or forensic: speeches delivered in the law courts which were located in the forum (hence 'forensic'); (2) deliberative: speeches delivered before an audience, for example the Senate or assemblies of the People, to persuade the adoption or rejection of a particular course of action; and (3) epideictic: speeches written for display purposes on a special occasion or at a ceremony, such as the arrival of an important person or the dedication of a public building. All three types of oratory demonstrate the importance of performance and 'face' in Roman culture. The first and second categories adopt a strongly adversarial mode in the assertion of masculinity and *Romanitas*, while the third category, which will be dealt with in the following chapter, becomes particularly important under the Principate as panegyric (praise) develops as a central element in public life.

6.5   Cicero's speeches provide ample material for understanding the workings of Roman public life in the late Republic. Cicero (106–43 BCE) was actually something of an outsider who broke into the Roman elite, chiefly through his oratorical skill. He was a 'new man' (*novus homo*), which is not a comment about his attitude to housework or women or babies, but a technical term meaning that he was the first of his family to reach the Senate and the consulship. As so often happens, the newest member of a group is the fiercest advocate of that group's standards. That is what makes the evidence of Cicero's speeches, which he wrote up for publication and of which fifty-eight survive either complete or in part, so valuable. Following the typical career pattern, he made his name by a spectacular prosecution, but after that he concentrated on defence cases. These brought fewer risks of making enemies and functioned to consolidate the complex web of relationships of *amicitia*, which literally means 'friendship' but actually denoted the network of mutual favours that involved all members of Roman society at some level (see Chapter 7).

6.6   Cicero's career is framed and punctuated by three series of attacking speeches. He made his name in 70 BCE with the successful prosecution of Verres for the corrupt administration of the province of Sicily where he had been governor. Then, when he was consul in 63 BCE, Cicero foiled a planned *coup d'état* by the aristocrat Catiline who had been unsuccessful in his own ambitions for the consulship. Cicero attacked Catiline in four speeches in the Senate and was granted extraordinary powers to deal with the crisis. Finally, after the death of Julius Caesar in 44 BCE, he wrote more than a dozen speeches called *Philippics* which articulated in no uncertain terms his opposition to Mark Antony. This led to his death: he was added to the proscription list and died in 43 BCE. Even this much information demonstrates the intersection of the judicial and political processes in Roman society.

6.7   But what strikes us most about these speeches is the unbridled vigour of the invective they contain. Cicero makes allegations about the sexual behaviour of the people he is attacking in a way that we would find shocking in a modern court of law or political debating chamber. Yet courtroom character assassination, even if it was Cicero's forte, was evidently standard. Familiar accusations included promiscuity or adultery by any women associated with the opposition and effeminacy by the men on the other side. Effeminacy includes not only style of dressing (as when Cicero's enemy Clodius invades the all-female rites of the Good Goddess in 62 BCE) but also the sexual practices of performing oral sex on men and women and taking the role of the passive (i.e. penetrated) partner in same-sex intercourse, both of which were regarded with contempt according to Roman ideology, which (as we saw in the previous chapter) was nothing if not macho.

6.8   It is important to realize that the Romans constructed their ideas of sexuality differently from modern times. It mattered much more whether you played the active or passive role in the sexual act than whether the sexual act was performed with a male or female partner. (One important corollary of this is that the word 'homosexual' has no exact equivalent in the ancient world.) Obviously, women were relegated to the passive role – and that meant that boys and men who also took the passive role in same-sex intercourse were socially diminished to the much lower status of women. Understanding this provides the necessary background to the insults that Cicero throws at Verres and Clodius, of being 'a woman among men and a man among women'. This kind of attack is clearly an assertion of masculinity which is achieved by a denigration and diminution of the opponent's masculinity.

6.9   Perhaps the classic case of this kind of attack is Cicero's invective against Mark Antony. Consider, for example, this passage from the *Second Philippic*, possibly Cicero's single most famous speech, which was not actually delivered but circulated privately:

> You assumed the toga of manhood, which you at once turned
> into a woman's toga. First you were a public whore and the price

of your shame was fixed – and it wasn't small. But soon Curio intervened, led you away from the prostitution business and, as if he had given you a bridal gown, established you in a steady and fixed marriage. No boy bought for lust was ever so much in the power of his master as you were in Curio's. How many times his father threw you out of his own house, how many times he posted guards to keep you from crossing the threshold! But you, with night assisting you, with your lust urging you on, with your payment compelling you, were let in through the rooftiles. These were outrages that that house could bear no longer. Don't you know I'm talking about things well known to me? . . . But now let us pass over your sex crimes and outrages. There are some matters which I cannot pronounce with decency. You, however, are that much freer, since you have allowed things to your discredit which you could not hear named by an enemy who had any sense of shame.

> (Cicero *Second Philippic* 44–5 and 47,
> adapted from Amy Richlin)

Cicero makes several shocking statements about Antony – that he wore a woman's toga (the dress of a female prostitute), that he prostituted himself and that Curio kept him as a wife – as well as further innuendoes. And he does this while maintaining a veneer of decency himself by refraining from actually describing sexual acts – thus remaining morally superior.

6.10 Another classic example of Cicero's invective occurs not in a prosecution speech but in a defence speech, where Cicero's method is to turn defence into attack. He is defending a young man called Caelius who was accused of organizing riots, beating up ambassadors, seizing property illegally and murder. Quite a catalogue of charges. A fifth charge was the attempted poisoning of Clodia Metella, with whom Caelius had had an affair. Although Caelius was probably guilty of the first four charges, Cicero deflected attention to the fifth charge and was cleverly able to depict the prosecution as a vengeful plot by Clodia, who was the sister of Clodius, a sworn enemy of Cicero's. Caelius was acquitted. An excerpt from the speech illustrates the kind of implication and innuendo that was evidently standard (or at least acceptable) in a Roman court of law:

> This whole case, gentlemen of the jury, revolves round Clodia. She is a woman of noble birth but also of notoriety. ... Since the elimination of this woman from the case will also mean the elimination of every single charge facing Caelius, we who act as his counsel are left with no alternative. If someone attacks Caelius we are obliged to show they are wrong. Indeed, my refutation would be framed much more forcibly if I did not feel inhibited by the fact that the woman's husband – sorry, I mean brother, I always make that slip – is my personal enemy. But since that is so, my language will be as moderate as I can make it, and I will go no further than my conscience and than the case itself oblige me. It is a fact that I never imagined I should have to engage in quarrels with women, much less with a woman who has always been regarded as everyone's friend rather than anyone's enemy.
>
> (Cicero *For Caelius* 31–2, adapted from Michael Grant)

6.11 So, in his first few sentences about Clodia, Cicero has already implied that she had an incestuous relationship with her brother Clodius and was widely promiscuous. He goes on to conjure up the speaking image of one of her ancestors from 250 years earlier to reprimand her for her outrageous behaviour:

> Woman, what business have you with Caelius, who is little more than a boy and a stranger? Why have you formed such a close friendship with him that you lend him gold, or such a deep enmity that you are afraid of poison? Did you not know, from what you have seen, that your uncle, your grandfather, your great-grandfather, your great-great-grandfather, and your great-great-great-grandfather were all consuls? And did you not recall that you had lately been married to Quintus Metellus, a most notable, courageous and patriotic man who only had to set foot out of doors to outshine almost all his fellow-citizens in quality,

glory and rank? When your marriage had transferred you from one illustrious family to another, why did you form so intimate a link with Caelius? Was he a blood-relative, or a marriage connexion, or a close friend of your husband? He was none of these things. What other reason, then, could there be except reckless lust?

(Cicero *For Caelius* 34)

This passage demonstrates the use of sexual innuendo to win a court case along with the power of appeals to ancestors and tradition in the culture and ideology of the Roman elite (as seen in Chapter 5.23–26). It also demonstrates very clearly that in the Roman world 'the personal is the political'.

6.12 Skill in public speaking in the context of court cases and political debate was respected and rewarded. By contrast, to use one's voice in public by acting on stage was viewed with horror and disgust. This is illustrated by the case of Laberius, a playwright of equestrian status (as a knight he was a member of the elite) who was humiliated by Julius Caesar by being compelled to appear in one of his own plays. A later source represents him as making a protest about this degradation in the prologue to his play:

He [Caesar], after all, is denied nothing by the gods themselves, so who could let a mere mortal like me say no to him? So, after living sixty years without blemish, I left my house a Roman Knight and I shall return home – an actor.

(Macrobius *Saturnalia* 2.7.3)

The degradation seems to have consisted of association with or assimilation to slaves and prostitutes. So it is not surprising that to be an actor was to incur *infamia*, literally a 'negative reputation', which deprived the individual of the legal privileges and protection that citizens enjoyed. For example, actors had no protection from corporal punishment, they were excluded from participation in politics and, significantly, their evidence was treated as less than reliable in legal contexts. They were seen as the essence of unreliability because they earned money by using their voices to pretend to be something which they were not. Even worse, they displayed their bodies as well as their voices on stage and they did so for the entertainment and delectation of the spectators. This rendered them like prostitutes and brought profound disgrace.

6.13 Yet, despite the degradation entailed, acting on stage clearly had its attractions for members of the elite. This is revealed clearly by the existence of legislation passed by Augustus and Tiberius, including the important fragmentary inscription known as the '*senatus consultum* from Larinum', which dates from 19 CE, forbidding members of the senatorial and equestrian orders from going on stage. This legislation would hardly have been necessary if aristocrats had refrained from acting. We can perhaps conclude that actors enjoyed the sex appeal and the power and freedom from normal constraint in what they said and did in the public eye. In short, in the case of actors, the Romans exhibit an ambivalence which is not apparent in the case of orators. Orators are engaged in a straightforward assertion of masculinity with a clear moral agenda before their audience, whereas the way that actors display themselves calls into question their morality. We can observe a similar ambivalence in our own culture, where actors and actresses are both revered and reviled, feted like royalty and faulted as riff-raff.

6.14 The same piece of legislation also prohibited members of the elite from appearing in the arena as gladiators. Here too we find the same mixed set of attitudes. Gladiators were of low social status, predominantly condemned criminals, prisoners of war and slaves. And yet gladiators, like actors, were also glamorous heart-throbs, as we see in Juvenal's sixth *Satire*, written in the early second century CE, where he attacks Roman wives for swooning over actors and gladiators. He uses as an extended example the senator's wife Eppia who abandons her husband, home and country to follow her gladiator lover across the sea (Juvenal *Satire* 6.82–113), which she does just because he's a gladiator.

6.15 Another passage from Juvenal's *Satires* takes us to the heart of the degradation for an aristocrat in entering the arena as a gladiator.

> And that's
> the disgrace of Rome: a Gracchus fighting, but not
> in a Murmillo's gear, and not with shield or curving blade.
> He rejects that sort of get-up, you see: look, he's brandishing
>> a trident.
> Once he has poised his right hand and cast the trailing net
> without success, he raises his bare face to the spectators
> and runs off, highly recognisable, all through the arena.
> There is no mistaking his tunic, stretched out golden
> from his throat, and the twisted cord bobbing from his tall hat.
> And so the Chaser told to fight against Gracchus
> suffered a loss of face more serious than any wound.
>> (Juvenal *Satires* 8.199–210)

As Juvenal represents it, for an aristocrat like Gracchus, who belonged to the illustrious Sempronian family and who had been a Salian priest (as indicated by his tunic and hat), to fight in the arena was itself degrading. Here the degradation is ultimate not just because Gracchus loses the fight and has to run away but, more importantly, because he appears in the arena not as a heavy-armed gladiator (a *Murmillo* or *secutor*, 'Chaser'), with body armour, shield and sword, but as the lowest type of gladiator, a net-thrower (*retiarius*), with only minimal gear: a tunic and a net, trident and dagger for weapons. It seems clear that the less the concealment, the lower the status of gladiators – and that is the satirical point that Juvenal makes at the end of the passage above. He claims that Gracchus' brazenness in appearing as a net-thrower and allowing his identity to be displayed to the spectators was more of a disgrace to his co-fighter than it was even to him.

6.16 Display of the body in acting and gladiatorial combat clearly provoked deep anxieties among the elite. The reaction to the obvious sex appeal of actors and gladiators was to label them as effeminate and over-sexed, two labels which for the Romans went hand-in-hand. As Catharine Edwards says in her excellent discussion of appearing as a spectacle in Roman society, 'to be excessively interested in sex was "unmanly" and "unRoman" . . . the inversion of the soldier-citizen, paradigmatically lacking in *virtus*.' And that is what Juvenal's

Gracchus is, as we see when we add to the passage above another description of him from *Satire* 2 (lines 117–48), where his appearance as a net-thrower in the gladiatorial arena is presented as even worse than his choice to get married to another man, with Gracchus himself taking the role of the bride.

6.17 Yet despite the strong tone of moral condemnation, there is no denying that Roman society was fascinated by these forms of entertainment, especially by gladiatorial combat. This form of fighting was originally a feature of Etruscan ritual performed at the funerals of warriors and it was allegedly introduced to Rome in the mid-third century BCE. This feature of indigenous Italian culture seems to have struck a deep chord with the Romans, since the image of two gladiators pitted against one another recurs in many different spheres in Roman culture. It turns up as an image for the contest between adversaries in the courtroom, for example in Horace *Satires* 1.7.19–20, where he describes two litigants as 'a pair as evenly matched as the fighters Bithus and Bacchius', where the word 'pair' is the technical term used of gladiators. But one of the most sustained usages of gladiatorial imagery is in Lucan's epic poem about the civil war fought between Julius Caesar and Pompey the Great. This takes us to the issue of the performance of death, which was a major concern in elite society, where life was lived (and death was died) essentially in public.

6.18 Lucan was a talented and prolific young poet, about the same age as his famous contemporary, Nero. He was favoured with high positions by the young emperor until their relationship cooled and Nero banned Lucan from public appearances as poet and orator. Whether this ban was connected with Lucan's poem about the civil war of a hundred years earlier, or whether it was for political reasons, remains a matter of hot debate. What is certain is that Lucan's poem is a stark condemnation of civil war in which he deglamorizes the heroism associated with the epic of Homer and Virgil to reveal the unpalatable aspect of Romans fighting Romans. To convey the horror of civil war, he employs as a recurring motif the imagery of two gladiators fighting to the death on the sand of the arena (which is the Latin word for 'sand'). The 'sand' in Lucan's poem is located in Spain, in

Greece and above all in Africa, all arenas of conflict in the civil war. He represents the blood shed in the sands of Africa as an appeasement of the ghost of Hannibal (see Chapter 1.7 on the role of Hannibal and Carthage in Roman history and ideology).

6.19 The image and idea of gladiatorial combat pervades the poem. It becomes explicit in the run-up to the battle between Caesar and Pompey at Pharsalus in Greece:

> The field of war contracts:
> here is held the blood which soon will flow over every land,
> here the casualties of both Thessaly and Libya are confined;
> civil warfare's madness seethes within a narrow arena.
>
> (Lucan *Civil War* 6.60–3)

Besides using explicit gladiatorial imagery, in the opening lines of *Civil War* 1 Lucan introduces his two protagonists by pitting them against one another like a pair of gladiators, using a striking pair of similes which graphically predicts the outcome of their conflict (1.120–58). First, Pompey the Great is described as a grand but decrepit oak tree, then Caesar is described as an irresistible and destructive thunderbolt. The implication is clear.

> He stands, the shadow of a great name;
> like in a fruitful field a lofty oak,
> bearing the people's spoils of old and generals'
> hallowed dedications; clinging with roots no longer strong,
> by its own weight it stands firm, and spreading naked
>> branches
> through the air, it makes shade with trunk, not foliage;
> and though it totters, ready to fall beneath the first East wind,
> though all around so many trees upraise themselves with sturdy
>> trunks,
> yet it alone is venerated . . .

and

> Just so flashes out the thunderbolt shot forth by the winds
> through clouds,
> accompanied by the crashing of the heavens and sound of
> shattered ether;
> it splits the sky and terrifies the panicked
> people, searing eyes with slanting flame;
> against its own precincts it rages, and, with nothing solid
> stopping
> its course, both as it falls and then returns great is the
> devastation
> dealt far and wide before it gathers again its scattered fires.
>
> (Lucan *Civil War* 1.135–43 and 151–7)

This pitting of Caesar against Pompey is a clever device by Lucan, because in reality the two never came face to face in single combat. But it is clear that the image of the duel evoked in this imagery was a potent one for the Roman audience. It is not enough, I think, to account for it by reference to the role of the duel in Homeric epic, although that is far from irrelevant: the single combat between Achilles and Hector in *Iliad* 22 and Virgil's reprise of it in the duel between Aeneas and Turnus in *Aeneid* 12 are inevitably important intertexts for Lucan. But I suggest that the foundation myth of Rome is more significant still. As Hardie in *The Epic Successors of Virgil* puts it:

> The epic power struggle constantly throws up doubles; the Latin epic greatly extends this innate tendency of the genre, because of the dualities that structure political power and its dissolution at Rome. The founding myth of the city, of the principate and of civil war is the Romulus and Remus story: Rome arises out of the violent replacement of a twosome by a unique founder.

This tension between monarchy and dyarchy is one that runs throughout Roman history from its earliest days to the emperor Diocletian's establishment of the so-called Tetrarchy in the late third century CE, in which he established the sharing of power with an equal.

6.20 I suggested earlier that the performance of death was a central concern in Roman culture. This is reflected in Latin literature in many different ways. Of the many available examples, I shall discuss Pompey and Cato; further striking cases of self-conscious death and suicide are found in the pages of Tacitus. We stay with Lucan's epic for his narrative of Pompey's death. Pompey has fled the battlefield of Pharsalus and is being pursued by Caesar through the Mediterranean. He has decided to take refuge at the court of Egypt, but as he is taken on board the Egyptian boat by Ptolemy's men he realizes that he has been betrayed and is about to be assassinated.

> Now the limit
> of his final hour had come and, carried off into the Egyptian
>   boat,
> he was not now his own master. Then the monsters of the king
> prepare to bare the weapon. When he saw the swords close by,
> he covered up his face and head, disdaining
> to present them bare to Fortune; then he closed his eyes
> and held his breath to stop himself from breaking
> into speech and marring his eternal fame with tears.
> But after murderous Achillas stabbed his side
> with sword-point, with not a groan did he acknowledge
> the blow and did not heed the crime, but keeps his body
>   motionless,
> and as he dies he tests himself, and in his breast he turns these
>   thoughts:
> 'Future ages which never will be silent about the toils of Rome
> are watching now, and time to come observes from all the world
> the boat and loyalty of Pharos: think now of your fame.
> For you the fates of lengthy life have flowed successful;
> the people cannot know, unless in death you prove it,
> whether you know how to endure adversity . . .'

> (Lucan *Civil War* 8.610–27)

Pompey's concern with the impression he is making on those around him and with his future reputation (*fama*) is a central element in his characterization by Lucan as a man obsessed with his own name.

At the same time, the self-control he exhibits in stopping himself from exclaiming or weeping also reflects an important feature of the Roman ideal of masculinity, which (as mentioned in Chapter 5.21) is reflected in the numerous 'virtues' in this category, such as Moderation, Restraint, Endurance, Tolerance, Calmness and so on.

6.21 But the self-control that Lucan's Pompey shows as he dies also represents an important point of intersection between Roman mentality and Stoic philosophy. The emphasis here upon taking control at the moment of death coincides with the doctrine of the Stoics, a philosophical sect which developed in Athens in the third century BCE and which came to exercise a significant influence on parts of the Roman elite, especially in the Principate, and on the development of Christianity too. The fullest articulation of Stoic views in Latin is found in the writings of Seneca the Younger (4 BCE–65CE), the tutor of the emperor Nero and the uncle of Lucan. In fact, it looks as if Seneca and Lucan shared the same outlook, as there is a strong Stoic strand running through Lucan's epic, *Civil War*. One of the central ideas of Stoic thought was that freedom was always available to the individual, no matter what their circumstances, through suicide, if necessary. In Roman thought, the archetypal case of Stoic suicide was that of Cato the Younger (95–46 BCE), who in the civil war became the figurehead of the Republican cause after Pompey's death. Lucan presents him as the Stoic wise man, stern, strict and austere, especially in Book 9 of the epic where the difficulties that Cato experiences in crossing the African desert represent in allegorical form the trials of the Stoic sage. It seems very likely that Lucan would have made the climax to his poem, which as it survives breaks off in Book 10, the victory of Caesar at the battle of Thapsus immediately followed by Cato's famous Stoic-style suicide.

6.22 His uncle Seneca provides a dramatization of Cato's suicide in his essay on providence, the idea that fate works to a plan, which was one of the central tenets of Stoic thought. This dramatization perhaps gives some idea of how Lucan might have handled the scene, with plenty of Stoic speeches and authorial commentary, which would have included philosophizing about freedom and slavery.

This is a spectacle fit for the regard of god as he contemplates his works. This is a pair fit for god – a brave man pitted against evil fortune, especially if the challenge came from the man. I do not see, I say, any finer sight on earth for Jupiter, if he wants to give it his attention, than the spectacle of Cato still standing upright among the ruins of the state, after his side has been smashed more than once. 'Although,' he said, 'all the world has fallen under one man's power, although Caesar's legions guard the land, his fleets the sea, and his troops attack the city-gates, Cato has a way out – with one hand he will make a wide path to freedom. This sword, unstained and innocent even in civil war, will at last do good and noble deeds: it will give to Cato that freedom which it could not give to his country. My soul, commence the task so long planned: rescue yourself from human existence. Already Petreius and Juba have fought and fallen, each killed by the other. That was a brave and noble agreement with fate, but it would not suit my greatness. It is as disgraceful for Cato to beg anyone for death as to beg for life.' It is clear to me that the gods watched with great delight as that hero, so ruthless in avenging himself, considered the safety of others and arranged the escape of his departing followers, as even on his last night he pursued his studies, as he drove the sword into his sacred breast, as he dispersed his vitals and with his own hand let out that most pure spirit, too wonderful to be defiled by the sword.

(Seneca *On Providence* 2.9–11)

Immediately obvious is Seneca's presentation of Cato's suicide in gladiatorial imagery, as a combat between 'a brave man pitted against evil fortune'. This is a novel kind of 'pair' (again we find the technical word for a pair of gladiators), with the gods as the spectators of this conflict. Equally obvious is Cato's self-consciousness of his own 'greatness' and of the fact that the manner of his death will be noticed by the watching world. This fact gives him the inner resources to live up to his austere reputation. Both Seneca's Cato and Lucan's Pompey are acutely aware that death is a public event and a spectacle that will be observed and talked about.

6.23 My final example of the performance of death in Roman culture is drawn from the pages of the historian of the early Principate, Tacitus. His description of the funeral of Germanicus, a prince of the imperial household, illustrates the awareness of spectacle and the importance of 'face' in Roman elite culture. It is also a classic example of this historian's exposure of the hypocrisy of which he accuses the emperor Tiberius. Here Tacitus, writing in the 110s and 120s CE, narrates events of 20 CE, when Agrippina brings back to Italy her husband Germanicus' ashes so they can be laid to rest. Germanicus, the nephew and adopted son and heir of the emperor Tiberius, had been very popular and had recently died in suspicious circumstances in the East.

> Without pausing in her winter voyage Agrippina arrived at the island of Corcyra, facing the shores of Calabria. There she spent a few days to compose her mind, for she was wild with grief and knew not how to endure. Meanwhile on hearing of her arrival, all her intimate friends and several officers, every one indeed who had served under Germanicus, many strangers too from the neighbouring towns, some thinking it respectful to the Emperor, and still more following their example, thronged eagerly to Brundisium, the nearest and safest landing place for a voyager. As soon as the fleet was seen on the horizon, not only the harbour and the adjacent shores, but the city walls too and the roofs, and every place which commanded the most distant prospect were filled with crowds of mourners, who incessantly asked one another, whether, when she landed, they were to receive her in silence or with some utterance of emotion. They were not agreed on what befitted the occasion when the fleet slowly approached, its crew, not joyous as is usual but wearing all a studied expression of grief. When Agrippina descended from the vessel with her two children, clasping the funeral urn, with eyes riveted to the earth, there was one universal groan. You could not distinguish kinsfolk from strangers, or the laments of men from those of women; only the attendants of Agrippina, worn out as they were by long sorrow, were surpassed by the mourners who now met them, fresh in their grief.

The Emperor had despatched two Praetorian cohorts with instructions that the magistrates of Calabria, Apulia and Campania were to pay the last honours to his son's memory. Accordingly tribunes and centurions bore Germanicus' ashes on their shoulders. They were preceded by the standards unadorned and the fasces reversed. As they passed colony after colony, the populace in black, the knights in their state-robes, burnt vestments and perfumes with other usual funeral adjuncts, in proportion to the wealth of the place. Even those whose towns were out of the route met the mourners, offered victims and built altars to the dead, testifying their grief by tears and wailings. Drusus went as far as Tarracina with Claudius, brother of Germanicus, and the children who had been at Rome. Marcus Valerius and Gaius Aurelius, the consuls, who had already entered on office, and a great number of the people thronged the road in scattered groups, every one weeping as he felt inclined. Flattery there was none, for all knew that Tiberius could scarcely dissemble his joy at the death of Germanicus.

Tiberius and Augusta refrained from showing themselves, thinking it below their dignity to shed tears in public, or else fearing that, if all eyes scrutinised their faces, their hypocrisy would be revealed. I do not find in any historian or in the daily register that Antonia, Germanicus' mother, rendered any conspicuous honour to the deceased, though besides Agrippina, Drusus, and Claudius, all his other kinsfolk are mentioned by name. She may either have been hindered by illness, or with a spirit overpowered by grief she may not have had the heart to endure the sight of so great an affliction. But I can more easily believe that Tiberius and Augusta, who did not leave the Palace, kept her within, that their sorrow might seem equal to hers, and that the grandmother and uncle might be thought to follow the mother's example in staying at home.

> (Tacitus *Annals* 3.1–3, translated by
> Church and Brodribb)

This entire passage (and its continuation too, in which an unfavourable comparison is made between Germanicus' funeral and the magnificent state funeral which his father Drusus received from the emperor Augustus) demonstrates the importance of display, first of all, in Agrippina's awareness of the effect that her arrival in the port of Brindisi might have on the spectators, second, in the emperor's awareness that the people will be scrutinizing his face and actions for signs of sincerity or otherwise, and third, in the historian Tacitus' delight in suggesting the hypocrisy of Tiberius and his mother by the use of innuendo.

6.24 In the first paragraph, Tacitus includes one tiny but significant detail that shows that Agrippina is stage-managing the scene of her arrival and disembarkation with Germanicus' ashes: 'the fleet slowly approached, its crew, not joyous as is usual but wearing all a *studied* expression of grief'. In general, Tacitus's presentation of this scene is like a crowd scene from cinema, with a camera roving above and among the crowds, so to speak. First we get the perspective of the crowd as they see the fleet come into sight on the horizon, then we get a universal overview of people swarming to fill every vantage point. The focus of the crowd upon Agrippina as she emerges from the ship determines our focus upon her too and the universal groan that goes up at the sight of her implies that this is the only possible reaction. That is, Tacitus' creation of an internal audience in his narrative directs the perspective of the external audience, that is, us, his readers. Although this narrative is heavily biased in favour of Germanicus and Agrippina, it gains an apparent objectivity from this technique.

6.25 In the second paragraph Tacitus builds on this picture of objectivity by describing the official element of the funeral procession through the south of Italy towards Rome but in a way that emphasizes the spontaneity of grief. We need to remember that the funeral procession of an aristocrat was invariably a noisy and spectacular event in Roman culture, but against that background Tacitus includes as significant details the fact that 'even those whose towns were out of the route met the mourners' and that the crowds at the roadside were 'every one weeping as he felt inclined', without the slightest thought of what impression this would make upon Tiberius. As Tacitus slyly adds here, 'all knew that Tiberius could scarcely dissemble his joy at the death of Germanicus'. The spontaneity and profundity of people's grief swamps the official marks of respect accorded to Germanicus by Tiberius at the start of the paragraph, so that when Tacitus now moves to the question of Tiberius' failure to appear in public he has already planted a negative impression of the emperor in his readers' minds.

6.26 In the third paragraph Tacitus suggests that the emperor Tiberius and his mother Livia (here called Augusta) were fully aware of public scrutiny of their reactions to Germanicus' death and that this awareness determined their decision to keep Germanicus' mother from appearing in public, in case a negative comparison between them and her might be drawn. In the sentence, 'thinking it below their dignity to shed tears in public, or else fearing that, if all eyes scrutinised their faces, their hypocrisy would be revealed', Tacitus typically presents speculations about motives, which is one of the hallmarks of his use of innuendo. Typically, it is the final speculation that lingers in the reader's mind and that carries the negative message. After all, given the importance of an aristocrat's dignity, to suggest that 'shed[ding] tears in public' might pose a problem is not in itself a criticism. But Tiberius and Livia's fear of being perceived (correctly) as insincere can only be construed in a negative light. The same applies to Tacitus' thoughts about Antonia's failure to appear: he makes his enquiry sound objective by reference to his research in the documents available and then proposes two possible reasons (ill-health and excessive grief) before offering a third opinion, 'I can more easily believe that . . .', which has damning implications for Tiberius and Livia.

6.27 This brief narrative, then, demonstrates clearly how Roman aristocratic life was a life of performance – even in the matter of death. In this chapter, we have seen how, in the courts of law, on stage, in the gladiatorial arena and in ceremonies like the funeral procession, the life of the Roman elite was lived in public, surrounded by an audience. The same was true of their deaths. They were clearly acutely aware of the performative aspect of life and death and this led to their setting a high premium upon the presentation of *Romanitas* and masculinity at all times.

Further reading and study

Many recent publications reflect the importance of 'face' in Roman public life. Of these J. E. Lendon *Empire of Honour: The Art of Government in the Roman World* (Oxford, 1997) is helpful on the importance of reputation, and Maud Gleason *Making Men: Sophists and Self-Presentation in Ancient Rome* (Princeton, 1994) is especially good on rhetoric as the display and performance of masculinity. Ellen Oliensis *Horace and the Rhetoric of Authority* (Cambridge, 1998) uses 'face' in her analysis of Horace's negotiations with power. Carlin Barton's *Roman Honor: The Fire in the Bones* (Berkeley, 2001) is also relevant.

On the phenomenon of the 'new man' see T. P. Wiseman *New Men in the Roman Senate 139 BC–AD 14* (Oxford, 1971) and Ernst Badian's entry 'novus homo' in the *Oxford Classical Dictionary*, 3rd edition.

On 'homosexuality' in Roman culture and thought see Craig Williams *Roman Homosexuality: Ideologies of Masculinity in Classical Antiquity* (New York and Oxford, 1999), including pages 4–8 on the inadequacy of the modern term. Important too is Jonathan Walters 'Invading the Roman body: manliness and impenetrability in Roman thought' in *Roman Sexualities* (edited by J. P. Hallett and M. B. Skinner, Princeton, 1997) pages 29–43.

On sexual insults in forensic speeches see Amy Richlin *The Garden of Priapus: Sexuality and Aggression in Roman Humor* (New York and Oxford, 1997 (revised edition)) pages 96–104, and A. Corbeill *Controlling Laughter: Political Humor in the Late Roman Republic* (Princeton, 1996) pages 99–173 on sexual insults and humour. Catharine Edwards *The Politics of Immorality in Ancient Rome* (Cambridge, 1993) has a discussion of the charge of effeminacy in Chapter 2 and Gleason (above) shows how Romans could achieve manhood through rhetoric.

On the prohibition against members of the elite appearing on stage see Barbara Levick 'The *senatus consultum* from Larinum' *JRS* 73 (1983) 97–115. On the implications of appearing as a spectacle in Roman society see Catharine Edwards (above) pages 98–136, quotation here from pages 130–1.

Important on gladiatorial combat in Roman experience is Carlin Barton *The Sorrows of the Ancient Romans: the Gladiator and the Monster* (Princeton, 1993). E. Gunderson 'The ideology of the arena' *Classical Antiquity* 15 (1996) 113–51 reads the arena as a way of reproducing Roman social relations. On gladiatorial imagery in Lucan see F. Ahl *Lucan: an Introduction* (Ithaca, 1976) chapter 3, especially 82–8, developed by M. Leigh *Lucan, Spectacle and Engagement* (Oxford, 1997). On the Roman penchant for thinking in terms of dualities in contexts of power see Philip Hardie *The Epic Successors of Virgil* (Cambridge, 1993), quotation from page 10.

On the 'theatricality' and 'social character' of Roman suicides see M. Griffin 'Philosophy, Cato, and Roman suicide' *Greece and Rome* 33 (1986) 64–77 and 192–202.

On the display component of Roman funerals see H. Flower *Ancestor Masks and Aristocratic Power in Roman Culture* (Oxford, 1996). On the visual aspect of Livy's history see A. Feldherr *Spectacle and Society in Livy's History* (Berkeley, 1998).

Rich topics for further study include (i) the dissection of virtually any speech of Cicero, including *Against Verres, For Caelius, Against Piso* and *Philippic* 2, with an eye for his exploitation of sexual insult and innuendo; (ii) analysis of the opposing speeches of Caesar and Cato that dominate Sallust's narrative of the debate in the Senate about the conspiracy of Catiline (*War with Catiline* 51–2); (iii) the performance of masculinity by Mucius Scaevola at Livy 2.12–13 and Valerius Maximus 3.3.1; (iv) the examination of other death scenes in Latin literature in terms of performance and spectacle, such as the death of Atticus at Nepos *Atticus* 21–2, the death of Seneca at Tacitus *Annals* 15.60–4 and the death of Petronius at *Annals* 16.18–19, along with the different reports of how Cicero met his end gathered in Seneca the Elder, *Persuasions* 6.14–27; and (v) trial scenes in Latin literature, for example in Seneca's *Pumpkinification* and the Festival of Laughter in Apuleius *Metamorphoses* 3. Finally, a modern analogy with the funeral of Germanicus is provided by the funeral of Princess Diana in September 1997: the event is ripe for a Tacitean-style narrative, full of insinuation and innuendo.

Chapter 7

Intersections of power: praise, politics and patrons

7.1 One of the most important things for a Roman aristocrat was the recognition by people around him of his public worth and standing – his *auctoritas* and his *dignitas*. Ideally this would be celebrated in panegyric – that is, praise written in prose or verse. In Chapter 6 I mentioned the three classic types of oratory current in Roman society. Of these, the third type is a standard vehicle for praise of an eminent man. This was epideictic oratory, which consisted of formal speeches for specific recurrent or unique occasions, especially the praise of individuals for their achievements. Often such speeches were intrinsically connected with politics. A classic case is the speech delivered by Cicero in 66 BCE to the assembly of the Roman people in which he argues that the position of commander-in-chief in the war against King Mithradates of Pontus (part of Asia Minor) should be transferred from Lucullus, who had just suffered some serious losses, to Pompey, who had just proved his mettle by clearing the Mediterranean of pirates. The speech, which is known as *On the Command of Gnaeus Pompeius* or *In Support of the Manilian Law*, includes fulsome praise of Pompey for his skills of military leadership:

> The ideal general, in my view, should possess these four qual-
> ities – military expertise, personal excellence, prestige and luck.

In knowledge of military affairs Pompey has never been sur-
passed. . . . Here is a man who moved straight from school and
the classroom into his father's army and the practical study of
war, in a terrible campaign against the fiercest enemies. When
Pompey was hardly more than a boy he served under a general
of outstanding distinction and as a teenager he commanded a
mighty army himself. . . . He has waged more wars than other
people have read about. . . . In his teenage years he gained military expertise not from the instructions of others but from commands he held himself, not from reverses in warfare but from
victories, not from campaigns but from triumphs. . . . Then again,
what words can be found to do justice to Pompey's personal
excellence? . . . He has all the qualities of leadership commonly
expected – application to duty, courage in danger, thoroughness
in operation, swiftness in action, wisdom in strategy – and on his
own he possesses these qualities to a greater extent than all other
generals that we have seen or heard of.

> (Cicero *On the Command of Gnaeus Pompeius*
> 28–9, adapted from Michael Grant)

Cicero's eloquent idealization of Pompey was successful and Pompey
was given the command against Mithradates. And one can argue that
Cicero's extravagant panegyric was justified, because Pompey defeated
Mithradates immediately.

7.2   A case from the end of Cicero's life and career gives a foretaste
of the role of panegyric in the imperial court. Cicero had supported
Pompey during the civil war against Julius Caesar but, after Pompey's
death in 48 BCE, Caesar pardoned Cicero and allowed him to return
to Rome. For some two years, Cicero, a great statesman and orator,
kept silent in the Senate as a kind of protest. But in 46 BCE he broke
his silence to offer a formal speech of thanks to Caesar for pardoning
another supporter of Pompey, Marcus Marcellus. A short extract will
give the flavour of Cicero's panegyric.

> Today brings to an end that long silence which has been my way
> in these recent times, not from fear but partly from pain and

literary patrons and circles throughout the late Republican era and early Principate. Later in the chapter I shall take a look at the inverse of panegyric – the satire directed at 'bad' patrons who abuse their powers. This will enable us to see that the models of 'good' and 'bad' patrons and emperors are closely interrelated.

7.5 I start with a brief discussion of literacy and the contexts of the production of poetry, because it is important to clear away any mis-apprehensions that arise from the very different circumstances of the modern western world. The level of literacy in Roman society is not known, but the best research suggests that, under the late Republic and the Principate, it was largely limited to the rich elite, particularly where 'literacy' goes beyond the practical applications of reading to include the ability to engage in literary pursuits. After all, it took time and education to acquire such skills – and both time and education were commodities based upon wealth. But at an earlier stage particularly, many of the finest poetic talents were people who did not enjoy wealth or status in their own right, but were educated individuals who attached themselves to a powerful man as part of his entourage, some of them slaves or former slaves with a Greek education. This reflects the circumstances of 'publication' in ancient Rome. Given that the book trade did not get under way until the first century BCE – and even then, authors paid rather than received money for publication – the circulation of poetry and literary prose generally took place through recitations organized by the elite and by having copies made privately. In other words, any study of the Roman literary scene is inextricably connected with the organization of Roman society on the basis of *amicitia* (as discussed in Chapter 6.5). A poet was in some sense the 'client' of his patron, like other clients, subject to similar duties (attendance at official and social events) and the recipient of similar rewards (protection, since 'patron' originally denoted your champion who defended you at law, presents, hospitality, positions of influence), yet he was also in a unique position, because he had the power to celebrate his patron's achievements and even to confer immortality upon him.

7.6 Our evidence for the earliest years of Latin literature provides a glimpse of the contexts which supported the production of literature. Livius Andronicus (see Chapter 3.10), reputedly the first to write Latin poetry, was a freedman belonging to the eminent family of the Livii which in 207 BCE provided Rome with one of her two consuls. Livius is said to have been a half-Greek from Tarentum in the south of Italy and, although the ancient biographers are far from reliable on such matters, this sounds plausible. In any case, Livius was clearly highly educated in both Greek and Latin and gave grammatical instruction to the children of aristocrats. He was clearly familiar with the traditions of heroic poetry from Greek culture as well as native Italian culture, since he uses the native Saturnian metre for his 'translation' of the *Odyssey*.

7.7   The poet Ennius (discussed in Chapters 1.8, 3.11–12, 5.8–13) was evidently of higher social status than Livius, but he too illustrates the combination of Greek and Italian culture in his skills. Like Livius, he received the support of powerful men among the Roman elite. He was brought to Rome in 204 BCE by Marcus Porcius Cato (consul in 195 and ancestor of the Cato discussed in Chapter 6.21–22) and there he was associated with some of the most important families, including the Cornelii, Sulpicii and Caecilii, teaching grammar to their children. In particular, he served on the military staff of the consul Marcus Fulvius Nobilior during the siege of Ambracia in 189 BCE and in 184 BCE he received Roman citizenship from Nobilior's son (consul in 153). The support he received from the Fulvii is reflected directly in his celebration of the elder Nobilior's exploits in his play *Ambracia* and in his epic poem, *Annals*. For example, in his *Annals*, Ennius invoked as his inspiration not the ancient Italian *Camenae* but the Greek *Musae* (Muses), whose cult had recently been established by Nobilior with a new temple on the Campus Martius. What is more, his *Annals* reached the climax of its narrative of the Roman people from the sack of Troy with Nobilior's triumphal return from the capture of Ambracia. From its earliest days, then, Latin literature reflects the circumstances of its production. It was poetry written with the support, that is, the patronage, of leading members of the elite and one of the chief consequences of that patronage was that it placed an obligation – which we should not assume was unwelcome – on the poets thus supported to celebrate the achievements of their patrons in panegyric.

More generally, poets like Livius and Ennius reflected glory upon their patrons by their cultural sophistication.

7.8 Perhaps the most significant name associated with Ennius was that of the great statesman and general, Publius Cornelius Scipio Africanus (236–183 BCE, consul 205 BCE). In a poem called *Scipio*, Ennius celebrated Scipio's campaigns in Africa which brought to an end the Second Punic War with the battle of Zama in 202 BCE and which earned Scipio the name 'Africanus'. Ennius also wrote an epitaph for Africanus which includes the lines '[here lies the man] whom no fellow-citizen or enemy can repay with the right reward of effort for his services' (*Epigrams* 5–6). What we see here is the poet's celebration of the individual aristocrat, but in terms which reflected the Roman ideals of patriotism and public service (as discussed in Chapter 5.23–27).

7.9 The same phenomenon recurs even more vividly in the case of Scipio Africanus' descendant, Cornelius Scipio Aemilianus, who was born the son of Lucius Aemilius Paullus and adopted by Scipio Africanus' son into the Cornelian family. (This is the Scipio whose dream is discussed at Chapter 5.26.) Adoption was a regular phenomenon among the Roman elite in cases of childlessness and functioned like dynastic marriages to forge alliances between powerful families. Scipio Aemilianus (185–129 BCE) was destined for high office and influence from the start by his family connections and he dominates our picture of the period. He was a renowned soldier and diplomat and held the position of consul in 147 and again in 134 BCE. He sacked Carthage in 146 and Numantia in 133 and was awarded a triumph on both occasions. But his importance for our understanding of Latin literature lies in his patronage of poets and philosophers.

7.10 Scipio evidently surrounded himself with a group of like-minded friends and associates who appear to have taken a remarkably welcoming attitude to Greek culture, against the natural conservatism and suspicion of things Greek which predominated in Rome. This attitude was especially associated at this period with 'Cato the Censor,' Marcus Porcius Cato (234–149 BCE, mentioned above), an eminent politician and orator who wrote the first historical work in Latin (*Origins* – it does not survive) and is seen as the founder of Latin prose literature. Names associated with Scipio include the comic playwright Terence, the satirist Lucilius, the Greek historian Polybius and the Stoic philosopher Panaetius, as well as a close friend called Laelius. A few details about these associates will indicate the interplay of literary patronage, culture and politics at this period.

7.11 Polybius was one of many eminent Greeks who were detained in Italy after Rome conquered Perseus, king of Macedon, in 168 BCE. He became part of Scipio's circle of associates and travelled extensively with him, being present at the sack of Carthage in 146, for example, and perhaps also at the siege of Numantia. His *Histories*, written in Greek, were designed to explain Rome's rapid rise to world domination in political and military terms and include a celebration of Scipio's virtues (31.23–30). Panaetius (*c.*185–109 BCE) was a philosopher from Rhodes who in 129 BCE became head of the Stoic school at Athens. He moved to Rome in 140 BCE and became part of Scipio's entourage and divided his time thereafter between Rome and Athens. The fact that these two important Greeks received Scipio's protection and support in Rome reflects his interest in bringing Greek culture to Rome.

7.12 Another foreigner who received patronage from Scipio was the playwright Terence. Terence (who died young in 159 BCE) is said to have been brought as a slave from Carthage to Rome, where he was given his freedom. Clearly he was highly educated in both Greek and Latin and in the 160s he wrote six comedies. Terence's link with Scipio is attested by the fact that his play *The Brothers* was commissioned by Scipio Aemilianus and his brother for the funeral games for their father Aemilius Paullus in 160 BCE. His association with this powerful grouping is mentioned obliquely in the prologue to the play:

> Then there are the spiteful accusations that eminent
> persons
> assist the author and collaborate closely with him.
> His accusers may think this a serious reproach,

> but he takes it as the highest compliment if he can win the
> approval
> of men who are universally approved of by you and the
> populace,
> men whose services in war, in leisure and in business
> each one of you has used as the need has arisen, without
> embarrassment.
>
> > (Terence *The Brothers*, prologue 15–21,
> > adapted from Betty Radice)

One of the most important things about Terence is that he was much more faithful to the Greek originals of his plays than was his predecessor Plautus (discussed in Chapter 3.8–9 and 3.12), whose comic inventiveness and exuberance led him to incorporate elements of the native Italian comic tradition. That is, Terence sets out to create a Latin equivalent to the simple and elegant Greek of Menander. We can assume that this was welcome to Scipio's philhellenism.

7.13 If Terence reflects an interest among Scipio and his friends in finding Latin equivalents to the classic achievements of Greek culture, then the satirist Lucilius (perhaps 180–102 BCE) demonstrates the importance of conforming to the standards of behaviour required by such a grouping. Lucilius' background contrasts sharply with that of Terence. He came from Campania and was a member of a senatorial family, although he did not hold political office but remained a knight (*eques*). He did however see military service with Scipio at the siege of Numantia. Although Lucilius' *Satires* survive only in brief fragments, it is clear from these, and from what later satirists say about him, that he utilized his poetry to attack his personal and political enemies – which included Scipio's enemies. The longest surviving fragment, just thirteen lines long, has often been regarded as an abstract disquisition on *virtus* ('virtue' or 'excellence' or, better, 'being a real man') but is now much more plausibly seen as highly engaged political poetry which reproaches a man called Albinus for some offence he has caused:

> Excellence, Albinus, is being ready to pay what is truly due
> in our business dealings and in life's affairs;

excellence is knowing what each matter involves for a person;
excellence is knowing what is right, useful, and honourable,
what things are good and what are bad, what is useless,
       shameful, and dishonourable;
excellence is knowing the end and limit of acquiring an object;
excellence is the ability to pay what is due to riches;
excellence is giving what is truly owed to honour,
being an enemy and no friend of bad people and conduct,
and on the other hand being a defender of good people and
       conduct,
valuing highly the latter, wishing them well, being a life-long
       friend to them;
and besides thinking first of the interests of our country,
then of our parents' interests, thirdly and lastly of our own.
                (Lucilius *Satires* 1196–1208)

7.14 Scholars of the nineteenth century went so far as to dub the group of poets and philosophers associated with Scipio the 'Scipionic circle', a term which enjoyed currency during the twentieth century. More recently, however, we have come to realize that to analyse Roman culture in terms of monolithic groups like this fails to do justice to the complexities of the organization of Roman society. All the same, it seems reasonable to suggest that Scipio's support of Latin poets offers a paradigm of literary patronage during the Republic and that his interest in Greek culture shifted perceptions. Our mistake would be to assume that Scipio was unique or that he had a monopoly on philhellenism. Rather, we might view him as the most visible case of a more widespread phenomenon – and a phenomenon that, in its essentials, remained constant throughout the period which concerns us.

7.15 One reason why Scipio dominates our awareness of this period is because Cicero makes him the central figure in two of his most influential works of philosophical prose, *On the Republic* and *On Friendship*. Cicero's *On the Republic* (which came up briefly in Chapter 5.26), written during the late 50s BCE, depicts a discussion set in 129 BCE between Scipio and his friends about different forms of government and about the Roman constitution, Roman imperialism and Roman education and leadership. In *On Friendship*, written in 44 BCE but set in 129 BCE, just after Scipio's death, Cicero represents his close friend Laelius praising him in idealized terms and lamenting the loss he feels at his death, for example:

> At the very beginning, when he was a young man, he showed incredible qualities of character, surpassing the highest hopes that his fellow-citizens had held for him when he was still a boy; he never stood for the consulate, but was made consul twice, the first time before the legal age, the second at the proper time for him, but for the Republic almost too late; and in destroying two cities that were most hostile to the Roman power, he put an end not only to present wars but also to any future wars. What should I say of his easy-going nature, his devotion to his mother, his generosity towards his sisters, his kindness to the members of his household and his fairness towards everyone? . . . I have the memory of our friendship to enjoy, and this makes me feel that my life has been happy, because I have shared it with Scipio. I used to consult him on public and private matters; I was associated with him both at home and on service abroad; and I experienced the essential strength of true friendship – the greatest possible community of interests, wishes and opinions.
>
> (Cicero *On Friendship* 11 and 15,
> adapted from Jonathan Powell)

What we see here is not only a depiction of 'friendship' as we understand it but an indication of the complexities of the concept in Roman culture. For the Romans *amicitia*, which we translate rather inadequately as 'friendship', denoted the entire network of social relations between superiors and inferiors, between 'patrons' and their 'clients'. *Amicitia* depended upon 'friends' (*amici*) helping each other in a whole range of ways in a never-ending sequence of services performed and obligations created. Literary patronage was just one way in which a great man could show himself a 'friend' and in return he expected to be glorified by the poets among his 'friends'.

7.16 Cicero's portrayal of Scipio through Laelius' eyes is, of course, an idealization. This kind of panegyric is reiterated in Horace's depiction of his satiric predecessor Lucilius relaxing, 'off-duty', with Scipio.

> When Lucilius first had the courage
> to write this kind of poetry and remove the glossy skin
> in which people were parading before the world and concealing
> their ugliness, was Laelius offended by his wit or the man who
> deservedly took his name from the Carthage that he conquered?
> Did they feel any pain when Metellus was wounded and Lupus
> was smothered in a shower of abusive verse? And yet Lucilius
> indicted the foremost citizens and the whole populace, tribe
> by tribe, showing indulgence only to Excellence and its friends.
> Why, when the worthy Scipio and the wise and gentle Laelius
> left the stage of public life for the privacy of home,
> they would let their hair down and fool around along with the
>   poet,
> while they waited for the greens to cook. Whatever I am, and
>   however
> inferior to Lucilius in rank and talent, Envy will have
> to admit, like it or not, that I've moved in important circles.
>   (Horace *Satires* 2.1.62–77,
>   adapted from Niall Rudd)

Horace clearly accepts the picture of intimacy between Scipio, Laelius and others ('Excellence and her friends', a phrase that probably echoes Lucilius' highly political definition of 'Excellence', quoted earlier) fostered by Lucilius. He claims that Lucilius used his satire to attack the foremost citizens, even naming some of his eminent victims, a claim that the surviving fragments certainly bear out. And – most importantly – he appropriates that entire scenario as part of his own credentials for acceptance as a satirist. In other words, he wants to imply that his relationship with his own patron Maecenas resembled that of the honest intimacy between his predecessor Lucilius and his patron Scipio.

7.17 Horace celebrated his relationship with Maecenas by dedicating to him most of his poetic output: *Satires* 1 (published around 35 BCE), *Epodes* (around 30), *Odes* 1–3 (published in 23) and *Epistles* 1 (around 20). As the son of a freedman Horace was much lower in status than Lucilius, but he turns this potentially negative factor into a compliment to Maecenas by praising him for accepting him into his clique, after an introduction by Virgil, on the basis of merit rather than birth (*Satires* 1.6). Later, after the gift of his Sabine estate, Horace praises him again but this time for allowing him a measure of independence (*Satires* 2.6 and *Epistles* 1.7). This demonstrates that patronage and panegyric go hand in hand, even in a genre like satire.

7.18 Maecenas is perhaps The Patron of all time. In Italian, his name has given rise to the word for patronage: 'mecenatismo'. He was a wealthy man of equestrian status and the most intimate friend of Octavian, the future Augustus, from early days. He was entrusted with vital political missions and responsibilities and he was clearly crucial to the flourishing of poetry around the time that Octavian came to power. He provides another illustration of the intersection of politics and poetry, although we will never know to what extent he actually intervened to influence the pro-Augustan element in the poetry of Horace, Virgil, Propertius and the other poets he supported. (The issue of Virgil's Augustanism was raised in Chapter 1.10–14.) We get a glimpse of Maecenas' 'circle' in another idealized passage at the close of Horace's first book of *Satires*:

> I'd like these poems to win the approval of Plotius and
>   Varius,
> Maecenas and Virgil, Valgius, Octavius, and the admirable
>   Fuscus;
> and I hope the Viscus brothers will enjoy them. I can also
>   mention
> you, Pollio, without incurring any suspicion
> of flattery, you, Messalla, and your brother, and also you,
> Bibulus and Servius, and you, my dear honest Furnius,
> and several other accomplished friends whose names I
>   purposely

omit. I should like them to find my work attractive,
such as it is, and I'd be sorry if they were disappointed in me.

(Horace *Satires* 1.10.81–90,
adapted from Niall Rudd)

Although this might look like a boring list of names, a few minutes'
work with a reference book reveals that this is an amazing roll-call of
the Great and the Good, men who wielded political power and poetic
influence in the last days of the Republic. For example, Asinius Pollio
(76 BCE–4 CE) was a supporter of first Caesar then Antony and after
his consulship in 40 BCE retired from political life and devoted himself
to literature. He founded the first public library in Rome and organized the first public recitations. He wrote history and poetry himself
and was the patron of Horace and Virgil. Valerius Messalla Corvinus
(64 BCE–8 CE) was a major public figure who saw military action in
the 40s and 30s BCE and who as consul with Octavian in 31 BCE took
part in the battle of Actium. He held various important offices during
the next two decades and was the patron of a literary circle that
included Tibullus and Ovid. Horace's ideal audience is by no coincidence a catalogue of some of the most influential men in public life.

7.19 This model of patronage persists throughout the Principate, but
with the leading role usually taken by the emperor. In essence there
is little change between Republic and Principate: the patrons of literature were always in a position to compel praise from their poets in
return for their gifts and favours. The only difference is that under the
Principate there was always one patron who was more powerful than
the rest. And, inevitably, the production of poetry became more and
more associated with the court. Two examples will illustrate the opera-
tions of panegyric in the imperial court.

7.20 The first comes from the pastoral poems modelled on Virgil's
Eclogues (discussed in Chapters 13 and 14) written by Calpurnius
Siculus early in Nero's reign (emperor 54–68 CE). This genre of poetry
uses herdsmen as its characters and incorporates panegyric indirectly,
mediated through a veneer of rustic life. In *Eclogue* 1, a herdsman
sees a prophecy written on the trunk of a tree and reads it out to his

companion. The prophecy clearly contains a panegyric of the new emperor Nero:

> The Golden Age is born again with carefree peace
> and kindly Themis at last returns to earth, shedding
> dirt and decay. Happy ages accompany the young man
> who won the case for his maternal Julii.
> While as god he rules the world, impious Bellona
> shall yield, her hands tied behind her back. . . .
> Full quiet will there be, a stranger to drawn steel,
> bringing a second reign of Saturn in Latium,
> a second reign of Numa . . .
> . . . a better god shall restore its old look
> and tradition to the forum, banishing bad times.
> (Calpurnius Siculus *Eclogues* 1.42–7, 63–5 and 72–3)

The detail about 'his maternal Julii' makes the reference to Nero (from the Julian family on his mother's side) unmistakable. This prophecy celebrates the new reign as a return of the Golden Age, an era of justice (Themis) and peace, and with the goddess of war, Bellona, completely overcome. Nero's reign is a reprise of the reign of Numa, the second king of Rome, who was associated with peace after war. Through this device of the prophecy, the poet is able to represent Nero as a god who restores Rome's traditions at the heart of the city, the Forum.

7.21 Divine imagery is a regular feature of imperial panegyric. Of the many examples available, here is a passage from the occasional poems written by Statius (*c.* 45–96 CE) called *Lumber*. (The Latin word *Silvae* denotes, roughly, 'raw material' or 'stuff', a modest title for some rather polished pieces; this case demonstrates the difficulty of rendering the conventional titles into English.) This is an excerpt from a thanksgiving to the emperor Domitian for a lavish banquet of thousands of guests held in his new palace on the Palatine Hill:

> I think I am reclining with Jupiter
> amid the stars and receiving the immortal draught proffered

by the hand of Ganymede! The barren years I have put
    behind me:
this is the first day of my allotted span, here the threshold
    of my life!
Is it you, ruler of the nations, great father of the subject world,
is it you, hope of mankind and concern of the gods, whom I
    behold
as I recline? Is it granted me to look upon this face beside mine
amid the drinking and feasting, and is it no sacrilege not to
    stand?
. . . Far above extends the vista: you could scarcely take in the
    roof
with your tired gaze and you would think it the ceiling of the
    gilded heaven.
Here when Caesar has commanded the leaders of the people and
    the columns
of robed knights to recline together at a thousand tables, . . .
    . . . I had no leisure for food . . .
in my desire to gaze at him, at him alone,
tranquil in his expression, with serene majesty
tempering his radiance, and modestly dipping
the standards of his eminence; yet the splendour that he tried
to hide shone in his countenance. Such a man even a
    foreign foe
and strange tribes could have recognized if they had seen him.
    (Statius *Lumber* 4.2.10–16, 29–33, 38, 40–5,
    adapted from Kathleen Coleman)

The emperor Domitian (here called Caesar) is represented as Jupiter,
the king of the gods, and his palace, which is described in some detail,
as heaven. The lavishness of Statius' panegyric, which seems so alien
to us, is far from unusual for court poetry of this and other periods
and cultures, including the English and French courts of monarchs
such as Elizabeth or James I and Louis XIV and court circles of recent
times such as those in Romania under Ceauşescu. I reproduce a short
excerpt from a poem published during the mid-1990s in the *Gulf Times*
in Qatar:

> Oh Your Highness the Halcyon Amir Sheikh Hamad Bin Khalifa
> Al-Thani – nothing is worth more than this happiest day of the
> first anniversary . . .
>> Last year, this day, the new Sun rose
>> for everyone in Qatar,
>> cherishing the inhabitants
>> with effulgent sunshine in their
>> hearts, their dreams come true.

The challenge for us in reading and interpreting panegyric is to resist
being blinded by the heaps of adulation and instead to discern the
differentiations made by different panegyrists, because in those details
and subtleties we can detect differences between emperors in their
handling of power and patronage.

7.22 Emperors are often criticized by modern scholars for abusing
their power by insisting upon panegyric from the poets they supported.
It is not clear that such criticisms are always justified. For example,
there was undeniably a flourishing of literature under Nero (emperor
54–68 CE) and again under Domitian (emperor 81–96 CE) and by no
means all of that literature was panegyrical. Under Augustus at least,
some poets felt able to resist the pressure to write panegyrical epic.
This is demonstrated by the 'refusals' (*recusationes*, almost a technical term) expressed by Propertius and Horace (for example,
Propertius 2.1, 2.34, 3.1, 3.3, 3.9, and Horace *Odes* 1.6, 2.12, *Satires*
2.1.10–20, and *Epistles* 2.1.250–70). And others were able to combine
panegyric with larger themes of patriotic, human, cosmic or metaphysical interest, as in the case of Virgil in his *Georgics* and *Aeneid*
(as suggested in Chapter 1) and in the case of Statius in his epic poem,
Thebaid. Such criticisms of emperors tend to ignore the structure of
reciprocal favours – *amicitia* – that was the basis of Roman society,
under Republic and Principate alike.

7.23 It is however true that the most memorable portrayals of bad
patrons, patrons who abuse their power, date from the Principate.
Perhaps the classic is Petronius' marvellous creation, Trimalchio, a
fantastically rich and vulgar ex-slave who lords it over a dinner party

in truly tyrannical fashion in the longest surviving episode from *Satyrica*, the novel written by Nero's 'arbiter of elegance' (sections 26–78). Incident after incident demonstrates how this patron stage-manages the banquet (e.g. 49, 54–5) and imposes his execrable tastes upon his guests (e.g. 35, 59), even to the extent of explaining his bowel movements to them (47) and finally saying 'Pretend I'm dead and say something nice' (78). Fellini achieves the same grotesque effect in his 1969 film of the novel and so does Greenaway in his 1989 film, *The Cook, The Thief, His Wife and Her Lover*.

7.24 Writing maybe sixty years later, the satirist Juvenal presents a similarly despotic dinner party host in *Satire* 5. Here the host has devised two completely separate menus – one for guests of his own status and another for his lowly clients whom he invites at the last minute to make sure there are no empty places:

> You might imagine that Virro is intent on saving money.
> No – he does it deliberately, to pain you. After all, what comedy
>   or farce
> is better than a whining gut? So, let me tell you,
> his entire intention is to make you vent your anger in tears
> and to keep you gnashing and grinding your teeth.
> In your own eyes you are a free man and my lord's guest.
> He reckons you're enslaved by the smell of his kitchen
> – and he's not far wrong. After all, how could anyone
> who in his childhood wore . . . the knotted leather thong of the
>   poor man
> be so hard-up as to put up with that patron more than once?
> It's the hope of dining well that ensnares you. 'Look, any
>   minute now
> he'll give us a half-eaten hare or a portion from the boar's
>   haunch.
> Any minute now we'll get a scrappy chicken.' So you all
> wait there in silence, brandishing your bread at the ready,
>   untouched.
> The man who treats you like this has good taste. If there is
>   nothing

you can't put up with, then you deserve it all. Sooner or later,
     you'll be offering
to have your head shaved and slapped and you won't flinch from
     a harsh
whipping. That's the kind of banquet you deserve, and that's the
     kind of friend.

(Juvenal *Satires* 5.156–73)

The choice of setting is significant: the dinner party was not only the
patron's reward to his inferiors but it was the climax to the Roman
day, which was lived in public and in company. That meant that the
way the patron treated his guests, ironically called his 'friends' here,
symbolized his attitude to them. This patron reveals himself to be a
tyrant.

7.25 *Satire* 5 is not the only poem in which Juvenal attacks an abusive
patron. In *Satire* 4 he attacks the emperor Domitian, who had died
maybe twenty years earlier, for abusing his power over his closest
advisers. He narrates an incident in which Domitian, here referred to
as King Atrides in a parody of Homer's depiction of Agamemnon,
summons his courtiers to an emergency meeting to discuss what he
should do with an outsize fish which has been presented to him.

The senators, shut out, watch as the food goes in,
right up to King Atrides. Then the fisherman from Picenum
     says,
'Receive a gift too big for a private kitchen. Let this be
a holiday. Hurry up and stretch your stomach by stuffing
     yourself.
Eat up a turbot preserved for your glorious epoch. It actually
wanted to be caught.' What could be more blatant? All the
     same,
the emperor's crest was rising. There's nothing
that godlike power can't believe of itself when it's praised.
But there was no plate that measured up to the fish. So his great
     advisers
are summoned to a meeting – people He hated,

people who showed on their faces the pallor of their awful,
mighty Friendship. The first to grab his cloak and hurry there,
while the Liburnian slave was still shouting, 'Get a move on, He
    is already seated,'
was Pegasus, the man recently appointed as slave-manager over
    an astonished Rome.

(Juvenal Satires 4.64–77)

Domitian is not the only object of satire here. Juvenal graphically
depicts the sycophancy of his courtiers, who fiercely compete with
one another to make the best recommendation. In short, the poem is
an attack on the complicity of all parties in the abusive relationship
between a bad emperor and his advisers.

7.26 Juvenal's *Satire* 4 demonstrates that it was possible to attack an
emperor – but only after he was dead, and especially once a new
dynasty had come to power. It is no accident that two of the most
reviled emperors of the early Principate are Nero and Domitian, who
were both the last in their dynasties to hold power. My final example
in this chapter shows how praise and attack can be combined. Early
in Trajan's reign (emperor 98–117 CE), the consul Pliny delivered his
Panegyric to the emperor. In this formal speech of gratitude, he praises
the new emperor for behaving like a citizen instead of a tyrant and
contrasts Trajan's behaviour with that of Domitian (emperor 81–96
CE), whom he depicts as a monster preying upon the Roman people.

> What's more, our visits to pay our respects to you are not
> followed by a quick exit and an empty hall. We stay behind and
> linger as if in a home we share, though this is the place where
> recently that terrible monster built his defences with countless
> horrors, where lurking in his den he licked up the blood of his
> murdered relatives or emerged to plot the massacre and destruc-
> tion of his most distinguished subjects. ... No one dared
> approach him, no one dared speak. Always he sought darkness
> and seclusion. ... Are not your meals always taken in public
> and your table open to everyone, with the pleasure of the feast
> there for us to share? Do you not encourage our conversation

and participate in it? . . . You do not arrive already gorged before midday on a solitary feast, to sit menacingly over your guests, watching and scrutinizing them, nor when they are fasting and hungry do you belch from a full stomach . . . and then take your-self back to secret gluttony and private excesses.

(Pliny *Panegyric* 48.3–49.6)

This text reveals two contrasting models of patron or emperor – and, after all, the emperor was just the most powerful patron in Rome. The good patron or emperor is marked by his openness, accessibility and friendly and tolerant attitude. The bad patron or emperor is marked by his tyrannical abuse of his powers to make life and death decisions about everyone around him, from the lowest slave to the most eminent senator. Celebration of the good model and condemnation of the bad model are found in the entire range of texts of Latin literature, including epic and pastoral poetry, lyric and elegiac poetry, satire and epigram, historiography, oratory and the novel. This can leave us in no doubt that how a powerful man behaved towards his peers and his subordinates was crucial to his social standing and to his political reputation.

Further reading and study

As in Chapter 6, J. E. Lendon's *Empire of Honour: The Art of Government in the Roman World* (Oxford, 1997) is important on the issue of public reputation.

On praise as a component of historiography see A. J. Woodman *Rhetoric in Classical Historiography* (London and Sydney, 1988) (index under 'praise').

On literacy, see *Ancient Literacy* (Cambridge, Mass., 1989) by W. V. Harris, who believes that its maximum, for literacy in any sense at all, was in the region of 15–20 per cent of the population.

On patronage in general see Richard Saller *Personal Patronage under the Early Empire* (Cambridge, 1982) and *Patronage in Ancient Society* (edited by A. Wallace-Hadrill, London and New York, 1989). David Konstan in 'Patron and friends' *Classical Philology* 90 (1995) 328–42 takes a different view, that in poetry *amicus* and 'client' cannot be identified. On literary patronage see *Literary and Artistic Patronage in Ancient Rome* (edited by B. Gold, Austin, 1982), B. Gold *Literary Patronage in Greece and Rome* (Chapel Hill, 1987), and P. White *Promised Verse: Poets in the Society of Augustan Rome* (Cambridge, 1993).

On Scipio Aemilianus see A. E. Astin *Scipio Aemilianus* (Oxford, 1967). For a political reading of Lucilius see Wendy Raschke '*Arma pro amico* – Lucilian satire at the crisis of the Roman Republic' *Hermes* 115 (1987) 299–318 and 'The virtue of Lucilius' *Latomus* 49 (1990) 352–69. On the relationship between Horace and Maecenas see I. M. Le M. DuQuesnay 'Horace and Maecenas: the propaganda value of *Sermones* 1' in *Poetry and Politics in the Age of Augustus* (edited by Tony Woodman and David West, Cambridge, 1984) 19–58.

On divine imagery used of emperors see S. Weinstock *Divus Iulius* (Oxford, 1971) pages 270–410. Discussions of panegryic include S. MacCormack 'Latin prose panegyrics' in *Empire and Aftermath: Silver Latin II* (edited by T. A. Dorey, London, 1975) pages 143–205 and the essays by Russell, Braund and Rees in *The Propaganda of Power: The Role of Panegyric in Late Antiquity* (edited by Mary Whitby, Leiden, 1998). For a contrasting view see Shadi Bartsch's discussion of Pliny in *Actors in the Audience* (Cambridge, Mass., 1994) Chapter 5.

Topics for further study include analysis of the literature for its panegyrical content, for example, the praise of Octavian in Virgil's *Eclogues* and *Georgics*, praise of Augustus in Horace's *Odes* and *Hymn for the Age*, praise of Nero at his accession in Calpurnius Siculus' *Eclogues* 1, 4 and 7, and in Seneca's *On Clemency*, and praise of Domitian and Nerva in the epigrams of Martial. The other side of the coin suggests the study of bad emperors. For this the biographies of Suetonius furnish plenty of material. For both sides of the coin turn to Seneca's short satirical skit *Pumpkinification* (instead of 'deification'), written in the early months of Nero's reign, in which he makes fun of the recently deceased emperor Claudius. Seneca includes fulsome praise of Nero in section 4 but chiefly attacks Claudius for his political policies and numerous executions and for his stutter and his limp, with no holds barred. On patrons more generally, Martial's epigrams alongside Juvenal's *Satires* are full of bad patrons. One starting point would be to discuss the quotation by Samuel Johnson: 'Is not a patron one who looks with unconcern on a man struggling for life in the water and, when he has reached ground, encumbers him with help?'

Another associated topic, which I do not have room to explore here, is the effect of patronage and the socio-political context on freedom of speech. This topic is central to Tacitus' *Dialogue on Oratory* (written in 100–105 CE), in which one of the speakers makes a connection between oratory and political circumstances, suggesting that skill in public speaking flourishes during periods of political turbulence and declines in periods of peace and stability. Tacitus' dialogue offers great opportunities to side with the different speakers in their opinions about the relationship between oratory and society.

Chapter 8

Annihilation and abjection: living death and living slavery

8.1   The texts we have studied so far have dealt with members of the Roman elite living their lives in public. For these individuals, most of them inevitably men, life was a performance, and so was death. In life, as in death, there were codes of masculinity and of *Romanitas* to conform to (see Chapters 5, 6 and 7, especially 5.1, 5.20–7, 6.7–9, 6.20–1, 7.1, 7.13). An awareness of these codes is essential to an appreciation of Latin literature. So too is an awareness of the ambitions of the Roman male elite to be recorded for posterity in panegyrical tones in literature as well as in three-dimensional forms of representation such as statuary, monuments and buildings. When Livy imagines his history of Rome as 'a conspicuous monument' displaying 'object-lessons of every type of model' (see Chapter 2, especially 2.2 and 2.19), he reflects a deep desire in the psyche of the Roman aristocrat.

8.2   For the next three chapters, we take a look at the other side of the coin, the representations of private life in Latin literature. The concept of 'private life' would probably have puzzled members of the elite, since their lives were conducted almost entirely in public. But there are aspects of life which fall under this rubric and here we find that the emphasis shifts from performance and visibility to invisibility and introspection, although even here we shall see that performance remains an issue (see my discussion of Seneca's *Medea* in Chapter 10.11–13). We also find that the texts that emerge as most central to this analysis focus upon the female almost as much as the male.

8.3 In this chapter I shall discuss two different forms of invisibility for the male member of the elite, the loss of status brought about by being sent into exile and by becoming a slave of love. Both conditions represent the antithesis of the Roman ideal of the active individual playing his part in society and both are expressed in terms drawn from public life, for example, in the 'campaign of love' (*militia amoris*) of the lover. Equally importantly, both conditions are articulated with a degree of subjectivity which we have not yet met in the 'public voice' used in the texts of epic poetry, historiography and oratory. This shift in presentation is mirrored by a shift in genre. The issue of what I have called invisibility is explored in the 'private voice' of love elegy, letters, essays and dialogues. The chapter will conclude with a brief glance at positive and negative depictions of withdrawal from public life and at the fear of the loss of public identity.

8.4 The poet Ovid (43 BCE–17 CE) is central to both sections of this chapter. Early on, Ovid chose poetry over conventional participation in public life and his exceptional skills won for him the support of the eminent patron Messalla (see Chapter 7.18). He is perhaps most famous for his love poems in the elegiac metre which he commenced in the mid-20s BCE, and for his unorthodox fifteen-book epic *Metamorphoses* which he completed in 8 CE. At this point he was the leading poet in Rome. But in this year Augustus suddenly exiled him to Tomis (modern Constanţa, in Romania) on the Black Sea. Ovid tells us that there were two reasons for his exile – 'a poem and an indiscretion' (*Sorrows* 2.207). The poem was clearly his *Art of Loving*, a playful didactic treatise on seduction, which perhaps offended Augustus since it ran counter to his programme of moral reforms which urged the elite to return to marriage and procreation. His 'indiscretion', which was surely the main cause for his exile, since the poem had been published several years earlier, is more mysterious. Scholars guess (and want to believe) that he was involved in a scandal in the imperial household. Whatever the cause, Augustus and his successor Tiberius remained implacable to all pleas to recall the poet – pleas made by Ovid himself in his exile poetry and by others on his behalf – and he never returned to Rome.

8.5 There can be no doubt that Ovid felt annihilated by his removal from Rome. He articulates his abjection in his nine books of exile poetry, his *Sorrows* and *Letters from the Black Sea*, all written in the elegiac genre, a genre traditionally associated with lamentation (Horace *Art of Poetry* 75–6). Ovid is typical of exiles in depicting himself as already dead when he composes his own epitaph:

> I who lie here, poet Ovid, played at tender passions
> > and fell victim to my own sharp wit.
> Passer-by, if you have ever been in love, don't grudge me
> > the traditional prayer: 'May Ovid's bones lie soft!'
> > > (Ovid *Sorrows* 3.3.73–6, adapted
> > > > from Peter Green)

His desperate longing for Rome is crystallized in the poem in which he imagines the triumphal procession celebrated by Augustus in 12 CE. *Sorrows* 4.2 provides the fullest surviving description of the Roman triumphal procession (as discussed in Chapter 5.17–19), a description which Ovid conjures from his memory. The closing passage articulates his sense of loss:

> All this, though exiled, I'll see in my mind's eye:
> > it's entitled to go where I cannot,
> can freewheel over enormous distances, reaches
> > heaven in its swift course, conveys my eyes
> to the heart of the City, will not ever let them
> > be deprived of so great a good: will find the means
> whereby in spirit I'll watch your ivory chariot –
> > a brief return, at last, to my native land!
> It's the lucky populace, though, that will enjoy the real
> > spectacle, the mob will be there to rejoice
> with their Leader, while I must visualize these pleasures

in fancy alone, hearken with distant ears,
and there'll be scarcely one soul dispatched here, so far from
Latium,
to tell me the story I long to hear. But even he
will bring stale news of a long-concluded triumph –
though however late I learn it, I shall rejoice,
and on that day I'll lay by my personal sorrows: the public
issue will far outstrip the merely private case.

(Ovid *Sorrows* 4.2.57–74)

Significantly, Ovid closes this passage by claiming to subordinate his personal tragedy to the joys of the Roman state, thus demonstrating the validity of the public/private dichotomy in Roman thought.

8.6 The loss that Ovid and other exiles experienced was indeed profound. Exile obviously entailed departure from Rome, which, as the passage from Ovid makes clear, was the scene of everything that mattered. But that was not all. In Roman law, exile was defined as loss of citizenship. This loss of rights amounted to a loss of identity, which makes it unsurprising that literary texts often depict exile as the equivalent of death, a living death. That helps to explain why exile was sometimes pre-empted by suicide. This was the case in criminal and in political contexts. A major difference between Roman society and modern western societies is that the Romans had no concept of imprisonment equivalent to ours. Major crimes were punished with either exile or death. An individual facing charges on a capital offence had the option of going into exile voluntarily. Exile was also a political tool. In the late Republic and especially under the Empire, the enforced exile of a political enemy or opponent was a frequent tactic in the struggle by powerful individuals to retain or gain power. This is illustrated by the cases of three other famous exiles, Cicero, Seneca and Boethius. After outlining the circumstances of their exiles, we shall briefly examine the different attitudes they show.

8.7 Of these we have the fullest information about the exile of Cicero, chiefly from his letters written to his friends and family at the time, which reveal his abject misery, and from speeches composed after his return to Rome, which rewrite his history in heroic terms. Cicero (106–43 BCE) went into exile in 58 BCE when Clodius, a tribune of the plebs who was a personal enemy of Cicero, invoked a law that punished with exile anyone who had executed a Roman citizen without a trial. This Cicero had done during his consulship of 63 BCE when he acted to forestall the conspiracy by Catiline to seize power (see Chapter 6.6). With the support of the Senate, which was swayed by the arguments of the hardliner Cato (the historian Sallust provides a graphic dramatization of the debate as a head-on conflict between Cato and Julius Caesar in his *War with Catiline* 51–2), Cicero had authorized the summary execution of five of the conspirators, all Roman citizens, one of whom held the high position of praetor. This was a risky act and it came back to haunt him before long. He soon made an enemy of Clodius by destroying his alibi for his intrusion, dressed as a female musician, into the all-female Bona Dea rites in 61 BCE and Clodius took his opportunity for revenge as soon as he had gained the influential position of tribune in 58 BCE. Cicero's return from exile, fifteen months later, was equally motivated by political machinations. Perhaps because Clodius was getting too powerful, Pompey engineered Cicero's recall, which seems to have been popular: Cicero (obviously not the most reliable informant in this case!) depicts his progress from Brindisi to Rome as a triumphal march.

8.8   We have much less secure information about the reasons for Seneca's exile, but again politics clearly played a major part. Seneca (perhaps 4 BCE–65 CE) was a wealthy man from an eminent Spanish family who is best known for his philosophical writings and tragedies and for the fact that he was tutor to the young emperor Nero. He was exiled, probably in 41 CE, for committing adultery with the emperor Claudius' niece, Julia Livilla. Messallina, wife of Claudius, may have been behind this and it is possible that the charge of adultery cloaked some political offence by Seneca. He spent seven or eight years on the island of Corsica and was recalled to Rome in 49 CE by Agrippina, who had married Claudius earlier that year, and appointed to a praetorship. Agrippina could therefore count upon Seneca's allegiance to her and he subsequently played an important role in the rise to power of her son, the future emperor Nero, who succeeded Claudius in 54 CE.

8.9   Another philosopher who was exiled for political reasons was Boethius (perhaps 480–524 CE), a Christian polymath and Roman statesman who held highest office under Theoderic, the Ostrogothic king of Italy, in the early sixth century CE. After being implicated in a senatorial conspiracy, he was accused of treason and sorcery and sent to Ticinum (modern Pavia). While he was imprisoned there, awaiting execution, he wrote his autobiographical *Consolation of Philosophy*, a dialogue between himself and Philosophy in the mixture of prose and poetry which we label Menippean satire.

8.10   Like Ovid, Cicero expresses his misery in extreme terms. His short notes to his friend, the Roman knight (*eques*) Atticus, as he travels away from Rome are marked by suicidal thoughts. In a letter to his family, written at Brindisi, the port of departure from Italy, on 29 April 58 he says to his wife:

> I send you letters less often than I could, because, miserable as every hour is for me, when I write to you or read your letters I am so overcome with tears that I cannot bear it. If only I had been less anxious to save my life! I certainly would have seen no sorrow in my days, or not much. But if fortune has spared me for some hope of one day recovering some measure of well-being, my error has not been so complete. But if these present evils are here to stay, then, yes, I want to see you, dear heart, as soon as I can, and to die in your arms, since neither the gods whom you have worshipped so piously nor the people to whose service I have always devoted myself have shown us any gratitude.
>
> (Cicero *Letters to his Friends* 14.4.1, adapted from D. R. Shackleton Bailey)

Clearly, life away from Rome is not worth living. Letters written late in 58 from Dyrrhachium (Durrës, in modern Albania), where he has chosen to stay because it was the nearest point to Italy, convey again and again Cicero's distress and self-blame and self-loathing. The abjectness of his position emerges when he reassures his wife:

Regarding my safety, you need not be concerned. That is no problem now, since even my enemies want me to stay alive in my present misery.

(Cicero *Letters to his Friends* 14.3.3)

8.11 In place of Cicero's self-pity, Seneca exhibits a more robust and philosophical acquiescence in his situation in the consolatory essays he writes from exile. It is fascinating to see how he adapts the ancient tradition of consolation from its usual context – condolence for bereavement – to his exilic situation. His prose essay to his mother, *Consolation to Helvia*, modulates from consoling a grandmother for the loss (death) of her grandson (Seneca's son) into consoling a mother for the loss, that is, the exile, of her son. In other words, Seneca plays on the idea of exile as death: he speaks as a voice from beyond the grave to comfort his 'bereaved' mother in Rome. At a time when he might be expected to need consolation himself, he consoles his mother with a picture of his own psychological strength and Stoic self-sufficiency. He depicts himself as happily absorbed in his philosophical studies and advocates that his mother occupy herself likewise. The closing passage of the essay is an exalted prose hymn in praise of the freedom of the mind.

This is how you are to think of me: I am as happy and cheerful as in my best times. And these are in fact my best times, because my mind is freed from all its occupations and has leisure for its own concerns. Sometimes it amuses itself with lighter studies, sometimes it rises to contemplation of its own nature and the nature of the universe. It investigates first the countries and their positions, then the character of the sea that flows around them and the ebb and flow of its tides. Then it examines the intervening space between earth and sky, full of terrors, disturbed by thunder, lightning, blasts of wind and falls of rain, snow and hail. Then, after traversing the lower realms, it bursts through to the heights and enjoys a most gorgeous sight of the divine, and remembering its own immortality it proceeds towards the entire past and future throughout all the ages.

(Seneca *Consolation to Helvia* 20)

This, then, marks a significant shift from preoccupation with the external world to inner concerns.

8.12 The same phenomenon recurs in the case of Boethius. Initially, in his *Consolation of Philosophy*, which is his dialogue with the female personification of Philosophy written in alternating verse and prose sections, he feels totally alienated from the life of the mind. The opening of the work finds him in his prison cell experiencing an inner exile, which takes the form of being deprived of his books. In the opening poem, the only poem in elegiac metre in all the five books, he laments his situation in terms strongly reminiscent of Ovid:

> Poems I once composed with flourishing enthusiasm,
> > but tearfully I now have to turn to mournful measures. . . .
> Blessed is Death when it does not interrupt our years of
> > > sweetness
> > and comes when summoned often by those who mourn.
> How deaf her ear as she turns away from people in misery
> > and cruelly refuses to close weeping eyes.
> While fickle Fortune favoured me with empty benefits
> > one bitter hour nearly drowned my life.
> Now that she has clouded her deceitful face
> > my cursed life prolongs its unwanted delays.
> My friends, why did you boast so often of my blessings?
> > A fallen man never stood on a firm footing.
> > > (Boethius *Consolation of Philosophy*
> > > 1.1.1–2 and 13–22)

In response to this, Philosophy tells him that he has been exiled not only from his home but from his true self and his true country, which consists of philosophical understanding:

> 'Earlier, when I observed your grief and tears, I at once real-
> ized that you were living unhappily in exile. But if you had not
> expounded it in your own words, I should never have grasped
> how distant was your place of banishment. But this distance you
> have travelled from your native land is the result not of expul-

sion, but of your going astray. If you wish to regard it as expulsion, such expulsion was self-induced, for no other person could rightfully have imposed such exile.'

(Boethius *Consolation of Philosophy* 1.5)

She proceeds to argue that philosophy, not poetry, holds the key to his consolation and his cure. Significantly, the poems that alternate with the prose sections are spoken by Boethius in Book 1, but after that by Philosophy, until Boethius shows that he is cured by breaking his silence with philosophical poetry in the final Book (5.3). Central to the work is Philosophy's poetic reworking at the end of Book 3 of the story told by Virgil and Ovid of how the singer Orpheus fails in his attempt to rescue his wife Eurydice from the Underworld (Virgil *Georgics* 4 and Ovid *Metamorphoses* 10.1–85). Orpheus' failure represents the failure of poetry to provide any comfort and clears the ground for 'the consolation of philosophy', which is here represented as a focus on things 'above':

Sadly, Orpheus his Eurydice
quitting Night's boundary
saw, lost and perished.
This tale is for you
who seek to steer your minds
up to the day above.
For he who, conquered, turns his eye
into hell's cave below,
loses such merit as he won,
by gazing on the dead.

(Boethius *Consolation of
Philosophy* 3.12.49–58)

Like Seneca, Boethius uses his own situation of loss to advocate a rejection of the externals of political and social life in favour of philosophical contemplation.

8.13 If exile is one form of annihilation, then slavery is another. Before we examine the use made by Roman elite writers of the image of slavery, we must consider briefly the role of slavery in Roman society. Rome, like Athens in antiquity and the slave states of the American South, the Caribbean and Brazil in more recent times, was a slave society with huge numbers of slaves. Roman slaves were supplied as captives of war and through trade and kidnapping by pirates and brigands, which were major hazards of travel in antiquity. Ancient slavery in its most extreme form entailed non-existence in legal and civic terms. The slave was not a human being but a thing or a chattel, who might be treated simply as a piece of property or tool of production and used or abused freely by the slave-owner. This was an attitude perpetuated by Christianity with its repeated tenet that slaves should obey their masters 'with fear and trembling' (e.g. *Letter to the Ephesians* 6.5). The fact that Seneca has to argue that slaves are human demonstrates the assumption in Roman society at large that they were not:

> I'm glad to hear from these people who've been visiting you that you live on friendly terms with your slaves. It is just what one expects of an enlightened, cultivated person like yourself. 'They're slaves,' people say. No. They're human beings. 'They're slaves.' But they share the same roof as ourselves. 'They're slaves.' No, they're friends, humble friends. 'They're slaves.' Strictly speaking, they're our fellow-slaves, if you just reflect that Fortune has as much power over us as over them.
>
> (Seneca *Moral Letters* 47.1,
> adapted from Robin Campbell)

Although this letter suggests an unusually humane attitude towards slavery, Seneca like other Stoic moralists was actually more interested in the moral well-being of the owners rather than the slaves. A central argument of Stoicism was that the emotions – such as anger and grief and envy and lust – are obstacles to the achievement of happiness and that the individual who wanted to become truly wise (*sapiens*) needed to eradicate the emotions by the exercise of reason. The dominance of the emotions is often described in terms of enslavement – to anger or grief or envy or lust – and that is what Seneca means by describing slave-owners, like himself and the addressee of his letter, as 'fellow-slaves'. In such contexts, then, slavery is a metaphor for the loss or absence of autonomy.

8.14 This metaphor is deployed in Latin literature nowhere more graphically than in love elegy, the genre of poetry which, inspired by Catullus (writing probably in the 50s BCE), flourished briefly in the late Republic and very early Principate in the hands of Gallus, Tibullus, Propertius and Ovid (making up the canon named by Ovid himself at *Sorrows* 4.10.53–4 and by Quintilian at *Training of the Orator* 10.1.93), along with one of our rare female poets, Sulpicia, discussed in Chapter 9.21. In the image of 'the slavery of love' (*servitium amoris*), the lover typically depicts himself as the utterly abject slave (*servus*) of his lover who he calls his *domina*, using a word that is borrowed from the realm of slave-owning (a male slave-owner was a *dominus*, 'master') to denote her absolute power over him. The openings of poems by Propertius and Tibullus offer a clear articulation of the lover's abjection and helplessness:

> Why press me, Bassus, by your praise of all those girls
> > to change my mind and leave my mistress?
> Why not let me spend whatever life is left to me
> > in the familiar slavery?
> > > > (Propertius *Elegies* 1.4.1–4,
> > > > adapted from Guy Lee)

> Slave to a mistress! Yes, in recognition of my fate
> > I bid farewell now to the freedom of my birthright.
> My slavery is harsh and I am held in chains
> > and never, to my sorrow, does Love relax the bonds.
> He burns me too, regardless of my guilt or innocence.
> > I'm burning now. Ai-ee, cruel girl, remove the torch!
> > > > (Tibullus *Elegies* 2.4.1–6,
> > > > adapted from Guy Lee)

This metaphor of the slavery of love expresses a loss of the autonomy and self-control which was so essential to the public image of a Roman aristocrat. Whether voluntarily or involuntarily, the lover has succumbed to an extraordinary self-annihilation on the psychological level which he articulates in terminology borrowed from socio-political life.

8.15 Ovid likewise borrows from the public life of the Roman elite when he describes his surrender and enslavement to love in the terms of the Roman triumphal procession:

> Look, Cupid, I confess – your latest prize –
>   I hold out abject hands, my heart complies.
> No need of war. Favour and peace are all;
>   no praise for you – unarmed to arms I'll fall. . . .
> Myself, a fresh prize, my wound still raw shall wear,
>   and in my captive heart new fetters bear.
> In the triumphal train Good Sense you'll see,
>   hands bound behind her back, and Modesty –
>   whatever stands against Love's armoury.
> All things fear you. In welcome loud and long
>   the cheering crowd will chant the triumph song.
> Endearments, Madness, wanderings of the brain,
>   shall be your escort in the happy train,
> constant supporters, following your cause.
>   With these fine troops you conquer in your wars
> both men and gods: their service lost, you'd be
>   all undefended in your nudity.
>
>   (Ovid *Loves* 1.2.19–22 and 29–38,
>   adapted from A. D. Melville)

8.16 Propertius again depicts himself as the slave of love when he fantasizes about his funeral, imagining his lover, Cynthia, lamenting him and memorializing him:

> Whenever therefore death shall close my eyelids
>   let this be the order of my funeral:
> no long procession bearing ancestral images,
>   no trumpet vainly wailing for my fate,
> no couch with ivory fittings to carry me,
>   spread for my death with cloth of gold,
> no line of incense-bearing platters, but the small-scale
>   rites of a plebeian funeral.
> Procession enough for me if I have three slim volumes

> to bring as my gift to Persephone.
> But you must follow, tearing your naked breasts,
> > tirelessly calling out my name,
> pressing final kisses on my frozen lips
> > and pouring Syrian unguent from full onyx.
> Then when the heat below has turned me into ashes
> > let a small clay pot receive my spirit,
> and above it plant a bay-tree on the tiny grave,
> > to shade the site of my burnt-out pyre,
> and write there these two lines: 'Who now lies horrid dust
> > was once the slave of just one love.'
>
> > > (Propertius *Elegies* 2.13.17–36,
> > > adapted from Guy Lee)

Significantly, Propertius rejects the trappings of the grand and showy funerals typical of the elite (see Chapter 6.23, 25), which were very much public occasions, and instead turns this into a private occasion.

8.17 This rejection of public life for private life is one of the central characteristics of the genre of love elegy. Another important manifestation of this is where the lover depicts himself as a soldier waging a 'campaign of love' (*militia amoris*). As when Propertius imagines his funeral, the lover–soldier of elegy appropriates the language of public life to the concerns of private life: 'By birth I am ill-equipped for glory or for arms; | Fate has drafted me for this campaigning' (Propertius *Elegies* 1.6.29–30). The use of military language in the context of success and failure in love affairs must have been an inversion shocking to conventional public morality. Perhaps the fullest and most playful expression of this idea is found in Ovid in a poem where he takes the metaphor and makes it literal:

> Lovers are soldiers, Atticus. Believe me,
> > lovers are soldiers, Cupid has his corps.
> The age that's right for fighting's fine for Venus;
> > old men are ridiculous in loving and in war.
> The spirit captains look for in a soldier
> > a pretty girl will look for in her man.

> Both keep night watches, resting on hard ground,
> > each for his girl or captain guardian.
> Long marches are a soldier's job: a lover
> > will go after his girl to the world's end. . . .
> Soldier or lover, who but they'd put up with
> > the rain, the sleet, the snow, the cold of night?
> One's sent to spy upon a dangerous enemy,
> > one keeps his rival, like a foe, in sight.
> Besieging cities, or a hard girl's threshold,
> > on barbicans – or doors – they spend their night.
> > > (Ovid *Loves* 1.9.1–10 and 15–20,
> > > adapted from A. D. Melville)

8.18 The love elegists' replacement of the life of the soldier with the life of love represented a challenge to conventional morality, such as advocated by the emperor Augustus, that was easily seen as subversive. It amounted to a rejection of the militaristic ethos of Roman life (as discussed above, Chapter 5.10–18) that can almost be labelled pacifist. Consider, for example, Tibullus' escapist fantasy about the life of seclusion he will lead if his lover Delia recovers from her illness:

> In my folly I had dreamed that the lucky life was mine
> > if you recovered, but the god willed otherwise.
> 'I'll farm' I thought 'and Delia will be there to guard the grain
> > while the sun-baked floor threshes harvest in the heat.
> Or she will watch the grapes for me in laden troughs
> > and the white new wine pressed by trampling feet.
> She'll learn to count the sheep and house-slaves' children
> > will learn to play and chatter on their loving mistress' lap.
> She will offer to the farmer-god grapes for the vines,
> > ears for the standing corn, a victim for the flock.
> She can rule us all, take charge of everything,
> > but I'll enjoy non-entity at home.
> > (Tibullus *Elegies* 1.5.19–30, adapted from Guy Lee)

8.19 This fantasy of leisure and of voluntary 'non-entity' is in flagrant contradiction to the elite ideal of active and energetic involvement in public life at Rome. While withdrawal from public life was advocated by the elegists in order to indulge the life of love, some of the philosophical schools which were gaining prominence at this period promoted quietism as a way of achieving the ultimate happiness. The classic advocates of quietism were the Epicureans, but at least some of the Stoics too argued that detachment from political life, along with other forms of mental disturbance, was the right goal for the sage. Epicureanism has consistently had a bad press from antiquity onwards because of a mistaken assimilation with hedonism. In fact, the Epicureans believed in avoiding or minimizing all sources of disruption – whether caused by love and lust, by grief and fear, by ambition and envy. That is why Lucretius, the Roman poet who encapsulated the philosophy of Epicurus in a six-book poem of epic hexameters, *On the Nature of the Universe*, depicts in strongly satirical terms people whose lives are dominated by fear or lust or political ambition or dissatisfaction. His poem, probably written in the early 50s BCE, is devoted to explaining the true workings of the universe as the route to happiness, for example:

> People feel plainly enough within their minds a heavy burden
> whose weight depresses them. If only they perceived
> with equal clearness the cause of this depression, the origin
> of this lump of evil within their breasts,
> they would not lead such a life as we now see all too often –
> no one knowing what they really want and everyone for ever
>   trying
> to change their situation, as though mere change could throw
>   away the load.
> Often the owner of some stately mansion, bored stiff
> by staying at home, takes his departure, only to return as
>   speedily
> when he feels himself no better out of doors.
> He races to his country seat, driving his ponies furiously,
> hurrying as if to save a house on fire.
> No sooner has he crossed its doorstep than he starts yawning
> or retires moodily to sleep and seeks oblivion,
> or else he rushes back to visit the city again.

> In doing this he's really running from himself, but since
> reluctantly
> he remains bonded to the self he just cannot escape, he grows to
> hate him,
> because he is a sick man ignorant of the cause of his malady.
> If he could only see this, he would cast other thoughts aside
> and devote himself first to studying the nature of the universe.
>
> (Lucretius *On the Nature of the Universe*
> 3.1053–72, adapted from R. E. Latham)

8.20 Lucretius argues for a quiet life of detachment from the demands of society, a life of devotion to philosophy. Another text written at around the same time provides perhaps the most terrifying depiction of the consequences of misplaced devotion. In a highly original and experimental poem (see Chapter 14.12), Catullus explores the loss of self which follows an act of religious devotion. A young Greek man called Attis travels east to Phrygia (in Asia Minor, modern Turkey) to dedicate himself to the goddess Cybele. This dedication takes the form of self-castration. The poem explores the consequences of this act, as Attis wakes from his religious frenzy to the chilling realization that he has lost everything:

> 'O country that gave me being, O country that gave me birth,
> abandoned by miserable me as runaway servants
> abandon their masters, I brought my feet to the forests of Ida,
> to be among snow and wild beasts' frosty lairs,
> and in my madness draw near their every lurking-place –
> where or in what place, my country, do I think you lie?
> My eyeballs of themselves long to turn their gaze on you,
> while my spirit for a while is free of fierce mania.
> Can I be rushed to these forests far distant from my home?
> Be away from my country, possessions, parents, friends?
> Away from the forum, palaestra, stadium and gymnasia?
> Ah wretched, wretched spirit, you must forever grieve.
> What kind of human figure have I not undergone?
> A woman I, a young man, an ephebe I, a child.
> I've been the flower of the gymnasium. I was glory of the oil.

For me the doors were crowded, for me the threshold warm.
For me the house was hung with flowery garlands
when it was time at sunrise for me to leave my bed.
Shall I now be called Gods' handmaid and Cybele's serving-
     girl?
Am I to be a Maenad, half me, a male unmanned?
Am I to haunt green Ida's cold, snow-mantled regions?
Shall I spend my life beneath the high summits of Phrygia,
with the woodland-haunting hind and forest-ranging boar?
Now what I've done appals me – I'm sorry for it now.'
              (Catullus 63.50–73, adapted from Guy Lee)

In other words, Catullus paints a horrific picture of the abjection and annihilation which results from a frenzy of devotion to a power from outside the sanctioned civic context. In this poem the eastern goddess Cybele is constructed as a threat to young men of the elite both in her femaleness and in her foreignness, a threat that is reiterated in many other texts of Latin literature which depict terrifying female power. The devotee of Cybele loses everything that matters about his identity – his homeland, his family, his civic status and his masculinity. This is the ultimate degradation – the figure of Attis combines the motifs of exile and slavery. No wonder that Catullus closes his poem with a prayer to Cybele (63.92–3): 'Far from my house be that frenzy of yours, O queen. | Drive others to ecstasy, drive others raving mad!'

Further reading and study

On public and private life see Michel Foucault *History of Sexuality* vol. 3 *The Care of the Self* (translated by R. Hurley, New York, 1986), Paul Veyne 'The Roman Empire' in *A History of Private Life* vol. 1 (edited by Paul Veyne, translated by A. Goldhammer, Cambridge, 1987) pages 5–234, Paul Veyne *Roman Erotic Elegy: Love, Poetry and the West* (translated by D. Pellauer, Chicago, 1988). (Foucault and Veyne were colleagues in Paris.) For a detailed study of this division see A. Riggsby '"Public" and "private" in Roman culture: the case of the *cubiculum*' *Journal of Roman Archaeology* 10 (1997) 36–56.

The experience of annihilation is discussed by Carlin Barton *The Sorrows of the Ancient Romans. The Gladiator and the Monster* (Princeton, 1993). For a full discussion of the Roman experience of exile see Jo-Marie Claassen *Displaced Persons. The Literature of Exile from Cicero to Boethius* (London, 1999); and Gareth Williams *Banished Voices: Readings in Ovid's Exile Poetry* (Cambridge, 1994) offers a literary analysis of Ovid's exile poetry.

On slavery in Roman society see K. R. Bradley *Slaves and Masters in the Roman Empire* (New York, 1987) and *Slavery and Society at Rome* (Cambridge, 1994). On slavery in literature see William Fitzgerald *Slavery and the Roman Literary Imagination* (Cambridge, 2000). R. O. A. M. Lyne *The Latin Love Poets from Catullus to Horace* (Oxford, 1980) discusses *servitium amoris* on pages 78–81 and *militia amoris* on pages 71–8. On how the mistresses of elegy hold power over their lovers see J. P. Hallett 'The role of women in Roman elegy: counter-cultural feminism' *Arethusa* 6 (1973) 103–24, also in J. Peradotto and J. P. Sullivan *Women in the Ancient World: the Arethusa Papers* (Albany, 1984) 241–62, and Ellen Greene *The Erotics of Domination: Male Desire and the Mistress in Latin Love Poetry* (Baltimore, 1998). Further reading on elegy, including Sulpicia, appears in Chapter 9.

W. R. Johnson demonstrates how Lucretius can still be relevant to our contemporary concerns in *Lucretius and the Modern World* (London, 2000).

An important discussion on gender in Catullus 63 is that of M. Skinner '*Ego mulier*: the construction of male sexuality in Catullus' *Helios* 20 (1993) 107–30, reprinted in *Roman Sexualities* 129–50.

This chapter invites study of the language of relationships between lovers used by Catullus, by the love elegists (Tibullus, Propertius and Ovid) and by the first century CE writer of epigrams, Martial. It also suggests further study of the depictions of terrifying female power in Latin literature. These are found in texts that focus upon notorious 'witches' such as Medea (in Ovid's *Metamorphoses* and Seneca's *Medea*), Canidia (in Horace's *Satires* and *Epodes*) and Erichtho (in Lucan's *Civil War* 6). Apuleius' novel *Metamorphoses* combines stories of witches (Books 2 and 3) and the Egyptian goddess Isis (Book 11) who has the power to restore to human form the narrator,

Lucius, whose curiosity about witchcraft has led to him being transformed into a donkey. And the term 'witch' itself demands interrogation and invites deconstruction.

Chapter 9

Writing 'real' lives

9.1 The texts studied in Chapter 8 depict aspects of private life in a framework which is taken over from public life, but in a negated or inverted form. This demonstrates the force of the ideal for a male member of the Roman elite – a life of active involvement in the running of the state, whether through military prowess or oratorical skills. Departure from this ideal, voluntary or involuntary, is perhaps inevitably articulated in terms of the ideal. This invites us to ask if there are any alternative frameworks for the depiction of private life in Latin literature. In particular, we might ask what kind of access, if any, Latin literature grants us to the lives of women who are almost never the authors of the texts we read. This chapter, then, will focus upon different types of evidence which seem to promise insights into 'real' lives, including epitaphs, funeral speeches and obituaries memorializing the dead, literature we might categorize as biography and autobiography, along with some texts that perhaps hardly qualify as 'literature' (see Chapter 3.3) such as curses and spells. But before we turn to this evidence, we will start by revisiting the genre that figured so prominently in the previous chapter – love elegy – to consider the difficulties involved in using such highly crafted and self-conscious texts as straightforward evidence for 'real life'.

9.2 The Roman love poets seem to invite their readers to envisage the women they are in love with as real women. Readers and critics from antiquity onwards have been happy to accept this invitation. For example, Apuleius, a renowned philosopher based at Carthage during the 160s CE, identifies the 'real' women behind the pseudonyms (*Apology* 10). According to Apuleius, Catullus' Lesbia was really an aristocratic woman called Clodia, Gallus' Lycoris was an actress called Cytheris, Propertius' Cynthia and Tibullus' Delia were women, perhaps married, called Hostia and Plania. Only Ovid's Corinna resists identification. This approach took off in the late eighteenth century and dominated scholarship in the nineteenth and early twentieth centuries, with critics of the post-Romantic sensibility attempting to reconstruct the chronology of love affairs on the basis of the poems.

9.3 The classic case is Propertius' Cynthia, who is centre stage with the first word of the first poem of the first book: 'Cynthia first, with her eyes, caught wretched me | Smitten before by no desires' (1.1.1–2). She dominates the book, which (to judge from Martial *Epigrams* 14.189) may have been called 'Cynthia', though some manuscripts give it the title 'Monobiblos' ('One Book'), a lead followed by scholars. For some readers, Propertius' description of her has made her really live:

> I was free and planning to live and sleep single,
> > but after the truce Love double-crossed me.
> How is it such human beauty lingers here on earth?
> > Jupiter, I can forgive your early lapses.
> Red-gold hair, long hands, big build – she moves like
> > Juno, fit sibling for Jupiter himself,
> like Pallas pacing by Ithacan altars,
> > breasts covered by the snake-haired Gorgon,
> or like Ischomache, the Lapith heroine,
> > sweet booty for Centaurs amid their wine,
> or virgin Brimo who lay with Mercury, they say,
> > by holy waters of Boebeis.
> Make way now, Goddesses, seen once, stripping
> > on Ida's peak by a shepherd.

> O may old age refuse to mar her beauty
>> though she live for the Sibyl's centuries!
>>>> (Propertius *Elegies* 2.2,
>>>> adapted from Guy Lee)

Certainly, there are physical features here which could easily belong to a real live woman. But this Cynthia is also constructed in exceptionally literary terms, as a collage of goddesses and heroines of mythology, in a series of more or less learned references which cast Propertius himself in the role of a god or a hero. Even her name speaks volumes, with its reference to one of the cult-titles of the god of poetry, 'Cynthian' Apollo (after Mount Cynthus on the island of Delos, which was Apollo's birthplace).

9.4   Another poem which seems to offer support for the biographical approach is Propertius 1.3, perhaps because here 'Cynthia' actually speaks. At the same time, the poem demonstrates its literariness time and time again, through the abundance of mythological images that frame Propertius' fantasies about his lover as she sleeps.

> As the girl from Knossos, while Theseus' keel receded,
>> lay fainting on a deserted beach,
> and as Cephean Andromeda in first sleep rested,
>> from hard rocks freed at last,
> and as a Maenad, no less tired by the ceaseless dance,
>> swoons on grassy Apidanus,
> so Cynthia seemed to me to breathe soft peace,
>> resting her head on relaxed hands,
> when I came dragging footsteps drunken with much Bacchus
>> and the boys were shaking torches in the small hours.
> Not yet bereft of all my senses I prepared
>> to approach her, gently, pressing the couch.
> But, though a prey to double passion, under orders
>> (from Love on this side, Bacchus on that, both ruthless
>> Gods)
> to edge an arm beneath her, reconnoitring,
>> and kiss, with hand at work, and stand to arms,

still I did not dare disturb my lady's peace,
    fearing the fierce abuse I knew so well;
but there I stuck, intently staring, like Argus
    at Io's unfamiliar horns.
And now I took the garland from my forehead
    and placed it, Cynthia, on your temples,
or pleased myself by re-arranging your stray hair,
    or to cupped hands gave stolen fruit.
But all my gifts were lavished on ungrateful sleep,
    gifts rolled from my pocket often as I leant.
Whenever, rarely moving, you drew a sigh,
    I froze in superstitious dread
that dreams were bringing you strange fears
    and some man forced you to be his –
until the moon, passing the window opposite,
    the busy moon with lingering light,
opened those calm closed eyes with weightless beams.
    'So!' (and she dug an elbow into the couch)
'At last, humiliation brings you back to our bed,
    thrown out from another woman's door!
Where have you wasted the long hours of my night,
    feeble now the stars are set?
Villain, O how I wish you could endure such nights
    as you always inflict on wretched me!
Sometimes I cheated sleep with crimson thread
    or with a tired tune on Orpheus' lyre,
or I whispered complaints to my forsaken self
    at unmarried love's long absences –
until I dropped off, stroked by Slumber's welcome wings.
    That thought, above all, made me weep.'

              (Propertius *Elegies* 1.3)

9.5 Although the dangers of the biographical fallacy have been perceived in recent years, this tendency still seems almost irresistible and critics sometimes end up in self-contradictory positions. The essential question turns on whether Elegiac Man is more a lover or a poet. Maria Wyke in a series of articles has performed a great service by demonstrating that Elegiac Woman is not only the beloved but also narrative material – a fiction that can be finished and discarded. She is the poet/lover's 'written girlfriend' (*scripta puella* – for a modern parallel think of the pop song 'My Legendary Girlfriend' by the Sheffield band Pulp). And this idea is further developed by Alison Sharrock in her article on 'Womanufacture'. The denial that there are real women in elegy may be disappointing, especially to the romantic souls among us, but, in compensation, an awareness that ways of reading apparently 'private' poetry have changed since antiquity is a huge asset in understanding Roman culture on its own terms and without anachronisms. It is an inescapable fact that, even when we feel that we are dealing with real personalities and real individuals, the literariness of Latin literature (aspects of which will be discussed later in Chapters 11, 12, 13 and 14) intervenes to complicate our quest for 'real lives'.

9.6   With that in mind, we now turn to the kinds of text which explicitly aim to describe the lives of individuals. The first category consists of memorializations of the dead in the form of epitaphs – the inscriptions carved on tombstones, speeches delivered at funerals and what we might call obituaries composed by historians. Let us start with a modest epitaph from Rome dating from the second half of the second century BCE for a woman called Claudia:

> Friend, I have not much to say – stop and read it.
> This is an unbeautiful tomb for a beautiful woman.
> Her parents gave her the name Claudia.
> She loved her husband in her heart.
> She bore two sons. One of them
> she left on earth, the other she put beneath it.
> She was pleasant to talk with and she walked with grace.
> She kept the house. She worked in wool. That is all.
>   You may go.
>
> (Epitaph of Claudia (CIL 6.15345),
adapted from E. Courtney)

The blandness and generality of this epitaph convey hardly any sense of Claudia as an individual – as is often the case in the memorials that we erect to our own dear departed, as a tour of any graveyard will prove. What it does reveal, though, is the Roman typology of the good woman: she should be a devoted wife, produce children, be easy to live with and run the household efficiently. This epitaph is typical of hundreds of similar inscriptions. For example, in his *Themes in Greek and Latin Epitaphs* Richmond Lattimore lists around 250 epitaphs which record marriages free from quarrelling (page 279 notes 107 and 108). Wives are often praised for their spinning and weaving, the paradigmatic occupation of the ideal wife (as we saw in Livy's narrative about Lucretia in Chapter 2.4–5), for their obedience and modesty, for their fertility and for their loyalty, which takes its highest form in the case of the 'one-man woman' (*univira*), a woman who was married to only one man in the course of her life. This last was something of an achievement in a society where marriages were often ended by death or divorce and where young girls were often married to much older men who were likely to predecease them (provided the woman herself did not die in childbirth, a major hazard until the late nineteenth century in many cultures). With this kind of evidence, it is the rare departures from the standard formulaic patterns that provide a glimpse of individuality.

9.7   Much the same applies to the epitaphs and funerary laudations for men, except that they naturally reflect the much greater range of achievements in public life available to men. One important early body of material consists of the so-called Scipionic *elogia*, epitaphs inscribed in verse found in the tombs of the Scipio family, composed during the third and second centuries BCE (see Chapter 7.2). In these and in later inscriptions, we find a set of formulae praising the virtues of the deceased and promising their survival through their own reputation and the devotion of their relatives, a pattern which persists, with modifications of course, into the Christian era. Even the 'obituary' of a famous individual such as Cicero is composed in generalities:

> Here is Livy's 'epitaph' – to use the Greek word – for Cicero:
> 'He lived sixty-three years, so his end could not be thought premature if it had happened without compulsion. His genius was blessed in its works and their rewards and he himself long

enjoyed good luck. But during the long flow of success he was from time to time afflicted with great wounds, exile, the collapse of his party, the death of his daughter and his own painful and bitter demise. Yet he faced none of these disasters as a man should, except his death – and even that, in the eyes of a truthful critic, could have seemed less undeserved because his victorious enemy behaved towards him no more cruelly than he would have behaved if he had had the opportunity. But weighing his qualities against his defects, he was a great and memorable man – and to sing his praises you would need a Cicero.'

(Livy quoted by Seneca the Elder
Persuasions 6.22)

It is instructive to observe that Roman 'obituaries', like epitaphs and funerary speeches, operate according to a set of conventions. For example, in the case of a male member of the elite, his manner of death and the attitude he displayed in the face of death were regarded as crucial statements about his worth. The emphasis was on the public face presented. At first sight, it might seem that the obituaries written in our newspapers (which also have their own set of conventions) share this focus upon the public role played by the subject. But there is an important difference: in modern obituaries the obliqueness and reticence about the day-to-day realities of private life reflects our sense of decorum, whereas for the Romans the public life of a man was the only thing that mattered.

9.8 In the case of Roman women, by contrast, the opposite is the case. The evidence of epitaphs for women confirms what other sources suggest – that Roman women were expected to be virtually invisible. As one scholar has put it, 'The intervention of women in [the] public, formal domain was usually felt to be a lamentable abuse of social spheres and, more precisely, as the intrusion of the dangerous and intangible force of feminine sexual power.' One exception is recorded in the extraordinary text known as the 'Praise of Turia' (although the name Turia does not occur in the inscription and may be a mistaken identification), a funerary inscription set up by the aristocratic husband of an exceptional woman, who clearly showed initiative and courage beyond what was expected of a wife. This text, the longest known private Roman inscription, takes the form of a funerary speech addressed by the husband to his wife. In effect he presents his wife's biography along with the story of their marriage: 'Rare are such long marriages, ended by death, not broken by divorce; for we were so fortunate that it lasted till its forty-first year without animosity.' In words borrowed from conventional epitaphs, he praises her 'domestic virtues', only to pass over them:

> Why should I mention your domestic virtues – your concern for your reputation, obedience, affability, reasonableness, industry in working wool, religious observance without superstition, modesty of dress, unadorned appearance? Why dwell on your love for your relatives, your devotion to your family . . . your countless other virtues in common with all Roman matrons who care for their good name?
>
> (Praise of Turia, adapted from E. Wistrand)

He is more concerned to record how they shared their duties out of a mutual regard and provides a fascinating document of how his wife acted to protect him and his property during the turbulent years of the proscriptions, executions and confiscations imposed by the triumvirs in 43–42 BCE. He includes an exciting narrative of her personal intervention with the triumvir Lepidus:

> But I must say that the bitterest event of my life was what happened to you. When thanks to the kindness and judgement of the absent Caesar Augustus I had returned home as a citizen, his colleague, Marcus Lepidus, who was present, was confronted with your request concerning my recall, and you threw yourself to the ground at his feet, and not only did he not raise you up but he had you dragged away and carried off brutally like a slave. Your body was covered with bruises, but your spirit was quite unbroken and you kept reminding him of Caesar's edict with its congratulations for my reinstatement. Although you had to listen to insults and suffer cruel injuries, you pronounced the words of the edict in a loud voice, to expose him as the cause

of my deadly perils. He soon suffered as a result of this affair. What could have been more effective than the virtue you displayed? You managed to give Caesar an opportunity to display his clemency and, while preserving my life, to brand Lepidus' outrageous cruelty by your admirable endurance.

(*Praise of Turia*)

Clearly 'Turia' had shrugged off the usual invisibility of Roman women to make a public intervention on behalf of her husband and this is expressed in masculine terms, for example, 'your spirit quite undaunted' and 'your outstanding endurance'.

9.9   Her husband then mentions their unfulfilled wish to have children, as a result of which his wife volunteered divorce, a suggestion he depicts himself as rejecting passionately:

You said that you would vacate the house and hand it over to another woman's fertility. Your intention was to personally seek out and provide a wife who was a fit and worthy match for me, relying on our known harmony. You declared that you would regard future children as joint and as if they were your own. ... I must admit that I so flared up that I almost went out of my mind – I was so horrified at your project that I found it difficult to retrieve control of myself. To think that separation should be considered between us before fate had decreed it! To think that your mind could conceive the idea that you might cease to be my wife while I was still alive, when you had remained utterly faithful when I was an exile and practically dead!

(*Praise of Turia*)

What emerges from this text is a remarkable portrait of a couple. The husband is prepared to give his wife her full meed of praise and is beside himself with grief at her death. His wife was an exceptionally strong woman who was not afraid to enter the male realm of public life to protect her family's interests. It is hard to think of 'Turia' as typical. But this text certainly records a 'real' life.

9.10 The Roman funeral laudation was an ancient Italian custom which reveals a deep interest in the recording of lives, itself related to the display of the masks of ancestors in the *atrium* of the house (see Chapter 2.2). This, combined with the influence of 'Lives' written in Greek, makes it no surprise that biography (which is Greek for 'the writing of a life') was a popular type of literature at Rome. Roman biography took a number of different forms. Besides the inscriptions mentioned above, biography appeared in prose texts in various forms and in poetry too. In addition to the short 'obituaries' incorporated into longer historiographical narratives (like Cicero's, above), we know of the *Likenesses* by the late Republican polymath Varro, in which brief descriptions were attached to the portraits of seven hundred individuals, and of several hundred short biographies *On Famous Men* by Nepos, the historian who is the dedicatee of Catullus' first poem. Only a few of these survive, including lives of Cato the Elder and of Atticus, Cicero's friend. A more substantial work which perhaps belongs in the category of biography is Tacitus' essay about his father-in-law, Agricola, who was governor of Britain for seven years, although the work embraces much larger issues of Roman politics and morality. It is harder to categorize Cicero's forays into biography and autobiography in poetry: his epic poem on Marius, a Roman general from the same town who changed the course of Roman history in the previous generation, and his poem on his own consulship of 63 BCE demonstrate the flexibility of the epic form and the difficulties of applying strict generic categories (on which see further Chapter 14.21).

9.11 But the name which is most closely associated with Latin biography has to be Suetonius, a contemporary of the historian Tacitus and the satirist Juvenal. He was a scholar who held important posts in the imperial administration under the emperors Trajan and Hadrian and who wrote 'Lives' of emperors, some of them lengthy, and shorter 'Lives' of poets, historians, orators, teachers of rhetoric and grammarians. Most significant was his *Caesars*, biographies of the twelve rulers of Rome from Julius Caesar to Domitian, which revolutionized the treatment of biography to such an extent that it more or less supplanted traditional forms of historiography thereafter (at least in Latin), with the so-called *Augustan History* adopting Suetonius' model

161

for biographies of the emperors from Hadrian to Carinus (117–284 CE). Only Plutarch's *Parallel Lives*, written in Greek around the same time or a little earlier, exceeded Suetonius' 'Lives' in their influence. And Suetonius' impact can still be felt today in the form of Robert Graves' novels on the emperor Claudius, *I, Claudius* (1934) and *Claudius the God* (1935), both reprinted often.

9.12 What distinguishes Suetonius' approach from the narrative, moralistic approach favoured by Plutarch and earlier Latin writers is his rejection of chronology as an organizing principle in favour of topics centred upon the personality of his subject. His standard pattern was to deal with his subject's ancestry and early life, then to apply a template of set headings, often called 'rubrics', discussed below, and to end with a standard sequence consisting of his subject's appearance, superstitious beliefs, death and last will and testament. Suetonius is explicit about his decision to organize his biographies like this, as we see from what he says early in his *Augustus*:

> Now that I have given a summary of his life, I shall now follow its elements one by one, not in chronological order but by headings, to make them more readable and intelligible.
>
> (Suetonius *Augustus* 9)

These headings can most easily be summarized as sets of corresponding virtues and vices. Suetonius homes in on four antitheses – clemency versus cruelty, civility versus arrogance, generosity versus avarice and self-restraint versus self-indulgence in extravagance and lust. So in his *Augustus* he catalogues his subject's generosity (41–3), clemency (51–6) and self-restraint in his simple life-style (72–8) and in his *Tiberius* he records his civility (26–32), extravagance and lust (42–5), avarice (46–9) and cruelty (50–62). He is able to draw conclusions from the material in these catalogues – that Augustus was adored (*Augustus* 57–60) because of his virtues and Tiberius feared (*Tiberius* 63–7) because of his vices. In the case of Domitian, he sees virtues and vices in balance initially before Domitian turns his virtues into vices (*Domitian* 3.2).

9.13 If this technique were conducted at a level of generality it might be hard to see the appeal. But Suetonius has a particular talent for inserting anecdotes that illustrate the virtue or vice in question, not least on the topic of sexual outrages, where he often supplies lavish detail. For example, of Nero he says:

> He exhibited his arrogance, lust, extravagance, avarice and cruelty gradually and covertly at first, as if in the waywardness of youth, but even then no one doubted that those were defects of character rather than of time of life. Straight after twilight he would grab a cap or a wig and head for the bars or roam about the streets fooling about, not without damage. He would beat men up on their way home from dinner and assault them if they fought back and dunk them in the sewers. . . . He castrated the boy Sporus and even tried to turn him into a woman, marrying him with the usual ceremonies, including the dowry and the veil, and conveying him to his house in a huge party and treating him as his wife. And that clever jibe that someone made is still current – what a good thing for the world if Nero's father Domitius had had a wife like that. This Sporus, wearing the finery of the empresses and riding in a litter Nero took with him around the tribunals and markets of Greece and later in Rome along the Street of the Images, kissing him from time to time. . . . He prostituted his own decency to such an extent that, after defiling almost every part of the body, he finally devised a kind of game in which he was covered in the skin of a wild animal and let loose from a cage and made an assault on the genitals of men and women who were tied to stakes.
>
> (Suetonius *Nero* 26.1, 28.1–2 and 29)

This kind of lurid anecdote displaces what we might expect to find in a regular work of historiography, such as lengthy accounts of the subject's handling of political affairs and military campaigns. To give an example, Augustus' conquests are presented in a brief list (*Augustus* 21–3) which takes the same amount of space as Suetonius' discussion of his attitude to military discipline (*Augustus* 24–5).

9.14 The question we should ask at this point is whether Suetonius' method of organization is an aid or an obstacle to understanding the lives of his subjects. Certainly, his approach has not appealed to everyone. For example, the great Jacobean thinker Francis Bacon said that because Suetonius' material is 'gathered into titles and bundles' it seems 'more monstrous and incredible'. But perhaps Bacon was missing the point. The repeated use of this template suggests that Suetonius saw this method as the best way to assess his subjects. For him and for his audience, the *Caesars* had to be judged against an ideal standard. This reveals something important in ancient mentality, which liked to construct a canon of virtues by which to assess the good ruler, although precisely which virtues belonged in the canon was disputed. For the Greek philosopher Plato, the four cardinal virtues of the ruler were Courage, Justice, Self-control and Wisdom, and his ideas had a strong influence on the ideas of the Stoics. In the early days of the Principate at Rome, the so-called Shield of Virtue (see Chapter 1.14) celebrated Augustus' Virtue, Clemency, Justice and Piety. Other virtues appear in panegyrical texts, such as those mentioned at Chapter 7.1–2, and on coins, where the virtues are often depicted as female personifications, a phenomenon which reached its peak at the time that Suetonius was writing, with Hadrian minting a series of 'virtue' coins depicting Justice, Clemency, Indulgence, Patience, Liberality and Tranquillity.

9.15 Even if Suetonius' analysis of an individual in terms of their virtues and vices does not seem to us the most obvious way of writing biography, there is one aspect of his construction of a 'Life' that is very modern. This is his distinction between public and private, not that he actually uses the term 'private'. So, for example, in his *Augustus* he makes the transition from one kind of material to another like this:

> This completes my account of how Augustus conducted himself in military and civil positions and in ruling the state throughout the world in peace and in war. I shall now give an account of his indoor and domestic life, his character and his fortune at home and among his household, from his youth until the last day of his life.

> (Suetonius *Augustus* 61)

At first sight, this distinction might seem to contradict my earlier assertion that the Roman elite had little conception of a 'private life', in
our sense. But the emperors of Rome were in a different category from
the rest of the elite and I believe that Suetonius understood this.
Relations between a man and his wife and slaves and other members
of his household were not the usual stuff of ancient biography, but in
the case of men who wielded absolute power, like Suetonius' *Caesars*,
anyone who had privileged access to them had the opportunity to influence policy. That helps to explain why Suetonius opens up a realm
usually consigned to invisibility. An emperor's conduct behind closed
doors could be made to speak volumes about the flavour of his autocratic rule. I complete my discussion of Suetonius with my favourite
image of an emperor behind closed doors, an eloquent image designed
to convey Domitian's cruelty:

> At the beginning of his reign he would spend hours on his own
> every day, doing nothing but catching flies and stabbing them
> with a specially sharpened pen. So, when someone once asked
> if there was anyone inside with Caesar, Vibius Crispus gave the
> clever reply: 'No, not even a fly.'
>
> (Suetonius *Domitian* 3.1)

9.16 It will be obvious that Suetonius is in the business of passing
judgements about his subjects. Analysis in terms of virtues and vices
amounts to an invitation to see the *Caesars* as heroes or villains. The
heroization or vilification of the subject in turn connects with one of
the central functions of ancient biography and autobiography – justification. Roman culture offers many examples of biographical texts
which have apologetic or propagandistic aims. Julius Caesar's war
commentaries (*Gallic War* and *Civil War*), in which he writes about
himself in the third person (making them in effect autobiography), are
a particularly sophisticated version, and so is Tacitus' essay on his
father-in-law Agricola in which he validates a policy of principled
collaboration with an autocrat, such as he himself pursued. More direct
are the biographies of Cato and other Stoics such as the members
of the elite who dramatically committed suicide under compulsion
from the emperor Nero and other 'mad' emperors. Works such as the

Deaths of Famous Men written during the first century CE constitute the beginnings of a literature of martyrs, a genre which comes into its own with the rise of Christianity and the persecutions and religious feuds that accompanied it. A classic case is the narrative of the martyrdom of Perpetua and her slave Felicitas in Carthage in 202 CE. Martyrology in turn is the beginning of hagiography, that is, the biographies of saints, a type of writing well represented in the Latin literature of late antiquity.

9.17 Above all, it is autobiography that has a clear political and ideological agenda. Cicero's poems on his consulship are a good example of this and so is the inscription which we call *Achievements of the Divine Augustus*. This is the autobiographical statement that Augustus left for posterity, inscribed upon bronze columns in Rome and elsewhere in the empire. The columns at Rome do not survive, but the text, which is preserved on the temple of Rome and Augustus at Ankara in Turkey, can now be seen incised on the side of the building that houses the Ara Pacis in Rome. Augustus constantly reworked the text of this monument until 2 BCE, when he was awarded the highest accolade of the title *Pater Patriae*, which forms the climax of the inscription:

> In my thirteenth consulship the Senate, the equestrian order and the whole people of Rome gave me the title of 'Father of the Country' and resolved that this should be inscribed in the porch of my house and in the Julian Senate-house and in the Forum of Augustus below the chariot which had been placed there in my honour by decree of the Senate.
>
> (*Achievements of the Divine Augustus* 35.1, adapted from P. A. Brunt and J. M. Moore)

The inscription presents a highly selective account of Augustus' rise to power which is designed to justify his early, blood-stained, years. Consider the moral loading of the very opening, in the words 'championed', 'liberty', 'oppressed', 'tyranny' and 'faction':

> At the age of nineteen on my own initiative and at my own expense I raised an army with which I successfully championed

the liberty of the republic when it was oppressed by the tyranny of a faction.

(*Achievements of the Divine Augustus* 1.1)

Augustus goes on to say:

I drove into exile the murderers of my father, avenging their crime through legally established tribunals. Afterwards, when they made war on the republic, I defeated them in battle twice.
(*Achievements of the Divine Augustus* 2)

This way of representing the assassination of Julius Caesar and the ensuing civil war is highly questionable, as Tacitus sees in his astute analysis of Augustus' motives at *Annals* 1.9–10. Autobiography by an emperor is bound to be political as much as personal. This would doubtless apply too to the memoirs that we know were written by emperors, including Augustus, Tiberius, Hadrian and Septimius Severus. We also know that Agrippina (15–59 CE), the wife of Claudius and mother of Nero, wrote memoirs. Unfortunately, they do not survive. If only they did. We would then have a unique view of the Principate by a woman of the imperial household.

9.18 The missing element in all this material in the voice of intimacy. One place where we find something like this is in Cicero's substantial correspondence with his family and friends, especially his friend Atticus, a Roman knight (*eques*) who preferred to live in Athens (in Attica, hence his name). These were letters written with no idea of future publication and, published posthumously, they inadvertently reveal facets of Cicero's personality that he might have preferred to remain unrecorded. One example shows how in 65 BCE Cicero was planning his candidacy for the consulship and considering taking on the defence case for Catiline, the man whom only two years later he demonized for his attempted *coup d'état* (see Chapter 6.6):

I have the honour to inform you that I have become the father of a little son, in the consulship of Julius Caesar and Marcius Figulus. Terentia [Cicero's wife] is well. It's a long time since I heard from you. I have already written to you in detail about my prospects. At the moment I am proposing to defend my fellow-candidate [for the consulship] Catiline. We have the jury we want, with full cooperation from the prosecution [Cicero's future enemy Clodius]. If he is acquitted I hope he will be more inclined to work with me in the campaign. But if it goes otherwise, I shall bear it philosophically. I need you home pretty soon. There is an emphatically strong belief that your noble friends are going to oppose my election. Clearly you will be invaluable to me in winning them over. So be sure you are in Rome by the beginning of January as you arranged.

> (Cicero *Letters to Atticus* 1.2, adapted
> from D. R. Shackleton Bailey's translation)

Here, and in letters with tones of pettiness, spitefulness and egotism that some readers have reacted against strongly, we certainly have the 'real' man, as we like to think.

9.19 Later collections of letters, such as Seneca's and Pliny the Younger's (which date from 62–5 CE and 97–111 CE respectively), are self-conscious documents clearly written with an eye on publication and self-promotion. It is in writings addressed to the self or to God that we first find the notion of self-exploration that we might expect from autobiography. The emperor Marcus Aurelius (who ruled 161–80 CE) was an innovator with his notebooks written in Greek, to which we give the title *Meditations* but which were probably called 'To himself'. These seem to have been personal documents, not known to his contemporaries. In Latin literature, then, it is not until Saint Augustine (354–430 CE) that we find autobiographical self-analysis.

9.20 Augustine was born and educated in the Roman province of Numidia (modern Algeria), became a teacher of rhetoric at Carthage and Rome and served as public orator at Milan, the capital of the emperor Valentinian II. He joined the Manichee sect in 373 but converted to Christianity in 386 CE and became first priest (391) then bishop (395) of Hippo in north Africa, where he stayed for the rest of his life. His *Confessions* (written perhaps 397–400) give an account

– highly selective – in thirteen books of his life up his return to Africa in 388. They document his childhood and adolescence, his education, including his hatred of studying Greek (1.14), and his successive 'conversions' – to philosophy (3.4, after reading Cicero's 'exhortation to philosophy', *Hortensius*, which does not survive), to Manicheism (a Gnostic sect) (3.6), to astrology (4.3) and, under the influence of Ambrose, bishop of Milan, to Catholicism, a Christianized version of Neoplatonism (Books 6–8, culminating in the climactic 8.12), which for Augustine was the 'Divine Philosophy' (*Letter* 2, written just before his baptism). For the first time in Latin literature, we seem to have access to an individual's authentic inner thoughts:

> As a boy I began to pray to you, 'my help and my refuge' [Psalms 93:22], and for my prayer to you I broke the bonds of my tongue. Though I was only a small child, there was great feeling when I pleaded with you that I might not be caned at school. And when you did not hear me, which was so as 'not to give me to foolishness' [Psalms 21:3], adult people, even my parents, who wished no evil to come upon me, used to laugh at my scars, which were at that time a great and painful evil to me.
>
> (Augustine *Confessions* 1.9, adapted
> from Henry Chadwick)

And, in adolescence:

> I came to Carthage and all around me seethed a cauldron of illicit loves. As yet I had never been in love and I longed to be in love; and from a subconscious poverty of mind I hated the thought of being less inwardly destitute. I sought an object for my love; I was in love with love, and I hated safety and a path free of snares [Wisdom 14:11; Psalms 90:3].
>
> (Augustine *Confessions* 3.1)

And in maturity:

> In this way I understood through my own experience what I had read, how 'the flesh lusts against the spirit and the spirit against

the flesh' [Galatians 5:17]. I was torn between them, but there was more of me in that which I approved in myself than in that which I disapproved.

(Augustine *Confessions* 8.5)

And, after the death of his mother:

My Lord, my God, inspire your servants, my brothers, your sons, my masters, to whose service I dedicate my heart, my voice, and my writings, that all who read this book may remember at your altar Monica your servant and Patrick her late husband, through whose physical bond you brought me into this life without my knowing how. May they remember with devout affection my parents in this transient light, my kith and kin under you, our Father, in our mother the Catholic Church, and my fellow citizens in the eternal Jerusalem.

(Augustine *Confessions* 9.13)

9.21 To close this chapter, I return briefly to the question of whether we have any access at all to the authentic voices of Roman women. With so few texts by women being written and still fewer surviving, the answer might seem to be a resounding 'No'. But if we probe a little, we can uncover a few items that at least begin this quest. There is Sulpicia, niece of the Messalla who was the patron of Tibullus and the young Ovid. Her six short love elegies to her lover Cerinthus (like the other elegists, she uses a Greek pseudonym) are preserved in the collection of Tibullus' poetry (printed in modern editions as 3.13–18 or 4.7–12). There is another Sulpicia, a poet who lived under Domitian, who according to the epigrammatist Martial wrote love poems to her husband Calenus (only one fragment survives) expressing a combination of fidelity and sensuality (Martial 10.35 and 38). There is Proba, an educated Christian woman living in Rome in the mid-fourth century CE who composed a really unusual poem, a Virgilian cento (that is, a poem stitched together – *cento* means a 'blanket' of lines and half-lines from Virgil's poems) on material from *Genesis* and the *New Testament*. And there is Egeria, who wrote an account of her pilgrimage to the Holy Land in the late fourth century CE, known as

Egeria's Travels. There are also letters, everyday letters, found at the military fort of Vindolanda near Hadrian's Wall in northern England (and called the Vindolanda Tablets). Among the letters on official and military subjects are letters written by the officers' wives to one another. And there are magic texts which survive from antiquity, some of which, even if not written by women personally, express women's wishes more or less directly, especially when they depart from the formulaic patterns that emerge. These texts take the form of curse tablets, many of which survive inscribed on thin sheets of lead, designed to invoke divine justice or retribution for a theft or a slander, and binding spells, designed to make a desired man fall in love with the woman or to win back the affections of an unfaithful lover or husband. One example is the inscription on a lead tablet found near Innsbruck, Austria, dating from perhaps around 100 CE, in which a female victim of theft appeals to Mercury and a Celtic deity called Moltinus, with help from Cacus, an ancient Roman monster:

> Secundina commands Mercury and Moltinus concerning whoever it was that stole two necklaces worth fourteen denarii, that deceiving Cacus remove him and his fortune, just as hers was taken. . . . She hands her things over to you so that you will track him down and detach him from his fortune, from his family and from his dear ones. She commands you on this – you must bring them to justice.

> (adapted from Gager no. 101)

In another example, a binding spell which does not reveal the sex of the curser, we find a fascinating feature typical of these texts, that the victim is identified not, as in elite culture, by his father's name but by his mother's. This reversal of normal public and civic practice seems to be typical of what we know of ancient magic. The spell was found in a mineral spring near Arezzo and is dated to the mid-second century CE:

> Quintus Letinius Lupus, also called Caucadio, who is the son of Sallustia Veneria or Veneriosa: he is the man whom I deliver, dedicate and sacrifice to your divine power, so that you, Aquae

> Ferventes, unless you prefer to be called Nymphs or by some
> other name, so that you kill him, cut his throat this very year.
>
> (adapted from Graf *Magic in the*
> *Ancient World* page 126)

Magic spells like these supply the virtually invisible backdrop to
literary texts such as Virgil's *Eclogue* 8, in which he has a herdsman
sing a song in the person of a woman trying to win back her lover:

> Bring water and around this altar wind soft wool. . . .
> As by these magic rituals I hope to turn
> my sweetheart's sanity – all I need now is spells.
> > Bring Daphnis back from town, my spells, bring
> > Daphnis home. . . .
> First with these triple threads in threefold different colours
> I bind you, then three times around this altar I take
> your puppet self – uneven numbers please the god.
> > Bring Daphnis back from town, my spells, bring
> > Daphnis home.
>
> (Virgil *Eclogue* 8.64, 66–8, 73–6,
> adapted from Guy Lee)

9.22 In conclusion, then, what chance do we ever have of accessing
'real' lives through Latin literature? Very little. Texts which purport
to depict the love affairs of 'real' men and women turn out to be
swathed in clouds of literariness which must make us distrust the
evidence of love elegy as in any way simply biographical or autobiographical. The categories of epitaphs, funeral speeches memorializing
the dead, and prose biography all turn out to be written according to
'rules' that in the same way make access to individually lived lives
rather remote. The category of autobiography also turns out to involve
particular difficulties, not because it has a set of 'rules' (on the contrary, it is unusually resistant to analysis) but because of its political
agenda. Even non-literary texts like curses and spells are often written
formulaically. We are left, then, with two unique documents in Latin
– Cicero's *Letters*, which he never intended for publication, and Augustine's *Confessions*, which create a model for modern soul-searching,

a model which was alien to the ancient world. I hope it is not an exaggeration to assert that Augustine paved the way for later and modern forms of autobiographical self-reflection, of which I can offer no more astonishing and moving example than *Love's Work* by Gillian Rose (1995).

Further reading and study

Suzanne Dixon provides a wonderful, state-of-the-art discussion of the difficulties of retrieving real women's lives from our ancient evidence in *Reading Roman Women. Sources, Genres and Real Life* (London, 2001). She is especially persuasive on the role of genre in generating particular stereotypes: 'How *do* we "read" the Roman women who appear as excellent mothers, pious daughters and faithful freed-women on tombstones, as wicked step-mothers in law and literature, as scheming trollops in history, biography and law court speeches, as desirable mistresses in elegiac poetry, as witches in satire, as prostitutes in comedy and graffiti and as mid-wives in tombstone reliefs, medical writings and epitaphs?' (page 16).

An important resource is the Diotima website, http://www. stoa.org/diotima, which includes texts, translations, images, bibliographies and essays on women and gender issues in antiquity. It is named after the priestess from whom Socrates in Plato's *Symposium* claims to have learned his theory of love.

For judicious accounts of the attempts to reconstruct elegiac love affairs see A. W. Allen 'Sunt qui Propertium malint' in *Critical Essays on Roman Literature: Elegy and Lyric* (edited by J. P. Sullivan, London, 1962) pages 107–48 and T. P. Wiseman *Catullus and His World* (Cambridge, 1985) pages 211–18.

On the fabrication of 'woman' in elegy see Maria Wyke 'Written women: Propertius' *Scripta puella*' *Journal of Roman Studies* 77 (1987) 47–61, 'The elegiac woman at Rome' *Proceedings of the Cambridge Philological Society* 33 (1987) 153–78, 'Mistress and metaphor in Augustan elegy' *Helios* 16 (1989) 25–47, published together as *The Roman Mistress: Gender, Politics, Love Poetry, Reception* (Oxford, 2002), and A. R. Sharrock 'Womanufacture' *Journal of Roman Studies* 81 (1991) 36–49. Recent booklength studies of love poetry include

William Fitzgerald *Catullan Provocations: Lyric Poetry and the Drama of Position* (Berkeley, 1995) and Micaela Janan's Lacanian readings of Catullus and Propertius, *When the Lamp is Shattered: Desire and Narrative in Catullus* (Carbondale and Edwardsville, 1994) and *The Politics of Desire: Propertius IV* (Berkeley, 2001).

For the evidence of epitaphs and inscriptions see Richmond Lattimore *Themes in Greek and Latin Epitaphs* (Urbana, 1962), G. Williams 'Some aspects of Roman marriage ceremonies and ideals' *Journal of Roman Studies* 48 (1958) 16–29, E. Forbis 'Women's public image in Italian inscriptions' *American Journal of Philology* 111 (1990) 493–512. E. Courtney *Musa Lapidaria: A Selection of Latin Verse Inscriptions* (Atlanta, 1995) is a sourcebook of these materials with translations.

On the rigid demarcation of male and female spheres see J. Blok 'Sexual asymmetry. A historiographical essay' in *Sexual Asymmetry. Studies in Ancient Society* (edited by J. Blok and P. Mason, Amsterdam, 1987) 1–57, quotation from page 36, and J. P. Hallett 'Women as *same* and *other* in Classical Roman Elite' *Helios* 16 (1989) 59–78. On the invisibility and inaudibility of ancient women see Barbara Gold '"But Ariadne was never there in the first place": finding the female in Roman poetry'in *Feminist Theory and the Classics* (edited by N. S. Rabinowitz and A. Richlin, London and New York, 1993) 75–101.

On ancient biography in general see the *Oxford Classical Dictionary*, 3rd edition, entries on biography, Greek and Roman, by C. Pelling, and on Suetonius in particular see Andrew Wallace-Hadrill *Suetonius* (London, 1983). Wallace-Hadrill discusses Suetonius' use of rubrics at page 13 and canons of virtues and vices at pages 142–74, especially 151–8.

On Cicero's letters, see G. O. Hutchinson *Cicero's Correspondence: A Literary Study* (Oxford, 1998), a close reading of selected letters grouped into categories such as consolation, exile and so on.

There is now a large bibliography on the love poet Sulpicia which makes it neatest to cite simply B. L. Flaschenriem 'Sulpicia and the rhetoric of disclosure' *Classical Philology* 94 (1999) 36–54 which mentions earlier studies on Sulpicia. On the other Sulpicia see the papers by Holt Parker, J. P. Hallett and Amy Richlin in *Classical World* 86 (1992) 89–140.

For the evidence of daily life in a military camp see A. K. Bowman and J. D. Thomas *The Vindolanda Writing-Tablets* (London, 1994).

An excellent starting point on curses and magic is J. G. Gager *Curse Tablets and Binding Spells from the Ancient World* (New York and Oxford, 1992) and F. Graf *Magic in the Ancient World* (translated by F. Philip, Cambridge, Mass. and London, 1997).

There are many projects for further study in the area of biography and autobiography. A fruitful question is to consider further the persistence of autobiographical readings of Horace: what is it in his poetry that leads so many readers (though not this one) to feel that they know the man? His *Satires* along with *Epistles* 1 will be the most central texts for this enquiry. Another topic is the examination of Sallust's representation of himself and of his decision to exchange politics for writing history in the prologues of his *War with Catiline* and his *War with Jugurtha*. Tacitus' biography of his father-in-law Agricola (*Agricola*) can be assessed in terms of its differences from what we consider as biography: which virtues does it aim to teach and how does it relate to literature that celebrates famous deaths, such as the deaths of the Stoic martyrs? Finally, one might study the epitaph of Allia Potestas as a record of a 'real life': see N. Horsfall '*CIL* 6.37965 = *CLE* 1988 (Epitaph of Allia Potestas): A commentary' *Zeitschrift für Papyrologie und Epigraphik* 61 (1985) 251–72.

Chapter 10

Introspection and
individual identity

10.1   Roman literature offers little in the way of the exploration of identity and psychoanalysis that we associate with modern novels and other kinds of fiction. Perhaps the closest is Augustine's *Confessions*, which we met in the previous chapter, which with its autobiographical soul-searching seems very modern. Perhaps we would choose a different audience for our guilt and our agonizing – a psychotherapist rather than God – but there is a self-awareness in Augustine which is familiar to us and which would have seemed alien at earlier periods. But saying that does not mean that authors of Roman antiquity were incapable of exploring the idea of the self. There are numerous texts which demonstrate an interest in introspection and identity, including philosophical essays in prose by Cicero and Seneca and passages in various genres of poetry. The essential difference is that Augustine bares his own soul. By contrast, the earlier prose texts tend to use an abstract framework, while the poetic texts locate the issues of introspection and identity in more or less mythical characters. One obvious example occurs in a text studied in Chapter 8.20: the monologue of the young man Attis who in Catullus 63 wakes from a religious frenzy to discover that he has lost everything. For Attis, self-awareness comes too late. Other texts use the themes of introspection and identity in other ways. In this chapter, I shall look at just two examples taken from Latin poetry. The first is Ovid's version of the story of the beautiful young man Narcissus in his mythical epic poem, *Metamorphoses*, a story which provided psychoanalysis with the term 'narcissistic', used of people who are excessively in love with themselves. The second is Seneca's exploration of the conflict of identity experienced by Medea in his tragedy of that title, which provides a fascinating opportunity to glimpse the way in which Seneca Romanizes well-known stories from Greek drama, a topic to which I shall return in Chapter 14.2–5.

10.2   Ovid's fifteen-book epic poem *Metamorphoses*, written just before his exile in 8 CE, is a remarkable work which resists simple definition. It breaks the rules. Ovid uses a chronological framework for the construction of 'one continuous song | from the beginning of the world to my own times' (1.3–4). His poem is a compendium of Graeco-Roman and Near Eastern myth linked by the shared motif of transformation. Accordingly, he starts by describing the creation of the world from chaos (this is the first metamorphosis – the Greek for 'change of form' – in the poem) and he concludes by describing the apotheosis (that is, metamorphosis into a god) of Augustus' adoptive father, Julius Caesar. His choice of end point can be seen as panegyrical, although the political dimension of the poem is hotly disputed. This plan makes a radical break from the heroic epic of Homer, Ennius and Virgil. Faced with the difficult question of how to compete with his predecessors in the epic genre, a question faced by all post-Virgilian epic poets, Ovid typically adopts a highly original strategy and simply reinvents epic. The theme of metamorphosis is flexible enough to allow him myriad opportunities for storytelling, which he clearly relishes. Sometimes the metamorphosis is central to the story and sometimes incidental. And the poem as a whole is itself a metamorphosis. Just as his character, the sculptor Pygmalion, finds his cold marble statue coming to life (see Chapter 12.6–9), so Ovid the poet breathes life into the dead material he has found.

10.3   Ovid's story of Narcissus in *Metamorphoses* 3 (lines 339–510) ends with the transformation of the young man into a narcissus flower.

In that respect, it is a variation on a theme. We might compare the story of Daphne's transformation into the laurel tree (*daphne* is Greek for laurel) as she tries to escape from Apollo's lust (Book 1.452–567) or the explanation of the marks on the petals of the hyacinth, commemorating the death of Apollo's beloved boy, Hyacinthus (Book 10.170–219). In the case of Narcissus, his transformation is hardly the central element in the narrative. It comes about because he breaks the condition for enjoying a long life. The condition is that he must not 'know himself' – a paradox in direct contradiction of the famous command 'Know Thyself' inscribed at the oracle at Delphi. Ovid uses the story to focus upon what it means, or might mean, to 'know oneself' and the story incorporates two of his favourite themes, desire and death. He also innovates by combining, apparently for the first time, the story of the nymph Echo with the story of Narcissus, a combination which has become canonical.

10.4   Ovid starts by telling us that the sixteen-year-old Narcissus is beautiful but feels affection for no one. We don't have to know much about patterns of storytelling to sense that Narcissus' lack of reciprocity bodes ill for him. The nymph Echo sees him and falls in love, but because she cannot initiate speech (a punishment from Juno for assisting Jupiter's love affairs), she has to wait for an opportunity to make her feelings known. This idea brings out the best in Ovid's playful ingenuity:

> It chanced Narcissus, separated from his friends,
> called 'Anyone here?' and Echo answered 'Here!'
> Amazed he looked all round and, raising his voice,
> called 'Come this way!' and Echo called 'This way!'
> He looked behind and, no one coming, shouted
> 'Why run away?' and heard his words again.
> He stopped and, cheated by the answering voice,
> called 'Join me here!' and she, never happier
> to make response, replied 'Join me here!'
> and graced her words and ran out from the wood
> to throw her longing arms around his neck.
> He bolted, shouting 'Keep your arms from me!

Away! I'll die before I yield to you.'
And all she answered was 'I yield to you.'

(Ovid Metamorphoses 3.379–92,
adapted from A. D. Melville)

Echo fades away from unrequited love until she is just a voice without a body – another transformation. Narcissus continues to reject the love of other nymphs and boys, until retribution arrives in the form of unrequited love – for himself. He sees his own reflection in a pool and falls in love:

The boy lay down, attracted by the quiet pool,
and, while he slaked his thirst, another thirst
sprang up. As he drank he saw before his eyes
a form, a face, and fell in love with an unsubstantial
hope and thought the shape had substance.
Spellbound, he saw himself, and motionless
lay like a marble statue staring down.
He gazes at his eyes, twin constellations,
his hair worthy of Bacchus or Apollo,
his face so fine, his ivory neck, the glory
of his face, the snowy pallor and the blush.
All he admires that all admire in him,
himself he longs for, longs unwittingly,
praising is praised, desiring is desired,
and love he kindles while with love he burns.

(Ovid Metamorphoses 3.413–26)

At first, he does not understand why he cannot kiss or embrace the gorgeous boy he sees in the water and, like Echo, he starts to pine away. Then comes his moment of realization – of the self-knowledge which will be fatal to him:

'Come out, whoever you are! Why, matchless boy,
elude me? Where retreat beyond my reach?
My looks, my age – it cannot be that you
should shun them – the nymphs have loved me too!

Some hope I cannot name is promised by your
friendly face, and when I stretch my arms to you,
you stretch your arms to me, and when I smile
you smile, and when I weep, I've often seen
you weeping too, and to my nod your nod replies,
and your lovely lips appear to move in speech
though your answer does not reach my ears.
Oh, I'm the one! Oh, now I know for sure
the image is my own – it's for myself
I burn with love. I fan the flames I feel.
What shall I do? Pursue or be pursued?
Why pursue at all? My love's myself –
my richness renders me a beggar.
If only I could leave my body! I could wish
(strange lover's wish) my love were not so near!
Now sorrow saps my strength and not long is left
of my life's span – I die before my prime.
But death is nothing sad since death will end my sorrow:
I wish the one I love could live a long tomorrow!
But now we two will die one death together.'

(Ovid *Metamorphoses* 3.454–72)

He finally wastes away, like Echo, and only a flower remains where
his body was. But we are also told that even in the Underworld he
continues to gaze at himself in the pool of the Styx. His situation is
eternal.

10.5 The story of Narcissus can be read in several different ways.
Ovid invites us to revel in the texture of his language as he offers a
reprise of the clichés of love poetry which are here, paradoxically,
self-reflexive. This intricate language also invites us to ponder the
sterility of self-love. The moral of Ovid's narrative is that human beings
are not self-sufficient but need reciprocal relationships with one
another in order to flourish and survive. It turns out that the pool in
which Narcissus sees his reflection mirrors him not just literally but
symbolically too. Like Narcissus, it is beautiful. But that beauty has
a sinister aspect. It is a sterile and remote place, set apart from society.

Ovid makes his landscape reflect his theme. The story seems to be about the need for real self-knowledge – not the sudden overwhelming and immature self-love that Narcissus conceives but reciprocal love oriented towards others, the kind of love that Narcissus rejects when he rejects the nymph Echo.

10.6   Ovid's interest in the theme of identity and self-knowledge was appreciated by the poet John Milton (1608–74), as is clear from the reminiscences of this passage in Eve's first speech in *Paradise Lost*, a speech from the time of innocence:

That day I oft remember, when from sleep
I first awaked and found myself reposed
Under a shade on flowers, much wond'ring where
And what I was, whence thither brought, and how.
Not distant far from thence a murmuring sound
Of waters issued from a cave and spread
Into a liquid plain, then stood unmoved
Pure as th'expanse of heaven; I thither went
With unexperienced thought, and laid me down
On the green bank, to look into the clear
Smooth lake, that to me seemed another sky.
As I bent down to look, just opposite
A shape within the wat'ry gleam appeared
Bending to look on me: I started back,
It started back; but pleased I soon returned,
Pleased it returned as soon with answering looks
Of sympathy and love; there had I fixed
Mine eyes till now, and pined with vain desire,
Had not a voice thus warned me: 'What thou seest,
What there thou seest, fair creature, is thyself . . .'.
                        (Milton *Paradise Lost* 4.449–468)

Milton clearly echoes the *Metamorphoses* when he frames his portrayal of Eve on the verge of the loss of innocence in terms of the awakening of self-awareness by Ovid's Narcissus (though it is curious to note that Eve starts out as a Narcissus figure but will end up as an

Echo). This shows that he read Ovid's text on this symbolic level. It is also an excellent example of intertextuality, a kind of self-conscious allusion to other texts, a phenomenon which I shall discuss in Chapter 11, and it demonstrates the central place that Ovid holds in European literature.

10.7   The story of Narcissus, his self-awareness and self-love, continues to feature in western culture in the guise of the 'narcissistic personality' diagnosed by popular and serious psychology. This is part of the legacy of the thought of Sigmund Freud (1856–1939), who (like his follower Carl Jung, 1875–1961) was so influenced by classical myth. Perhaps the most famous of Freud's ideas is the Oedipus complex, in which a boy subconsciously desires his mother and wishes for the death of his father. Freud met the story of Oedipus in Greek tragedy – and it is from Greek tragedy that the Roman philosopher Seneca (who we met in Chapter 8) drew the material for his tragedy, *Medea*. In Seneca's hands, the story of Medea is an opportunity for a portrayal of introspection in the exploration of identity.

10.8   The powerful figure of Medea, granddaughter of the Sun and skilled in the use of magic drugs, clearly fascinated the ancients, as the varied portrayals of her in Greek, Etruscan and Roman literature and art indicate. She has continued to exert a fascination through the centuries in many media besides drama, including opera, ballet and cinema, as demonstrated in a recent book devoted to the representations and receptions of Medea. Above all, she is associated with Jason, who came to her homeland of Colchis (modern Georgia, on the Black Sea) with the Argonauts (the heroes who rowed the *Argo*) to steal the golden fleece from her father. Medea fell in love with Jason and with her magic powers she assisted him in this task, then abandoned her family and country to run away with him, killing her younger brother as she left to help their escape. In folklore terms she is a classic, if extreme, example of 'the helpful princess', mirrored by Ariadne and Dido in other stories from antiquity.

10.9   Versions of what happened next abound, but the single most influential version was the tragedy by the Athenian dramatist Euripides writing in the fifth century BCE. In his play Jason and Medea have reached the city of Corinth where Jason is improving his fortunes by marrying the king's daughter. Medea is distraught to be cast aside, as she will be an exile without status or refuge (for the devastating significance of exile in antiquity see Chapter 8.3–13), and the chorus of Corinthian women express their solidarity with her. Medea's revenge is the focus of the play. First she uses her magic powers to contrive the deaths of Jason's new bride and the king and then she kills her own children, as anticipated by the nurse in the prologue. The play ends with Medea's escape in the chariot of the Sun.

10.10 Between Euripides and Seneca came several other influential rewritings of Medea's story – by Apollonius of Rhodes, a Greek poet writing in Alexandria in the third century BCE, whose mould-breaking epic *Journey of the Argonauts* provides an empathetic picture of Medea falling in love, a picture which later influenced Virgil in his picture of Dido falling in love with Aeneas; by Ennius, who composed a play *Medea*, probably the first in Latin, of which only fragments survive; and by Ovid, who returned to the story at least three times, once in his epic poem *Metamorphoses* (Book 7.1–424), once in his innovatory series of verse letters supposedly written by heroines abandoned by their lovers ('Medea to Jason' in *Letters of Heroines* 12), and once in his tragedy, *Medea*, which lamentably does not survive, but which must have influenced later poets. The relationship between Greek tragedy and Latin poetry will be discussed again in Chapter 14.2–8. For now, what is clear is that Seneca follows Euripides in setting his tragedy in Corinth and in treating the same events, but that his treatment of the story and especially of Medea introduces novel psychological elements. This is most evident in her lengthy soliloquy in the final Act (893–978), which though superficially similar to Euripides' scene is on further examination significantly different.

10.11 Medea has just heard from the messenger that Jason's new bride and the king have been killed and the city of Corinth burned. She is delighted, but wants to follow this up with vengeance that will hit Jason harder. At first we see her galvanizing herself to action:

> So put your back
> into your anger, wake up from your sleep,
> and suction from the bottom of your heart
> the violence and aggression. Let everything
> you've done till now be called an act of love.
> Act – and make them learn how trivial
> and like a petty criminal's have been
> the past crimes I devised. They were the preludes
> to my rage. What power had my untrained arms
> to dare great deeds? The bloodlust of a girl!
> Now I really am Medea.
>
> > (Seneca *Medea* 902–10,
> > adapted from Fred Ahl)

This bold statement implies that Seneca's Medea is familiar with her reputation in earlier literature. She is rousing herself to fulfil her legend and her self-myth – in this case by killing her children – in a way that verges upon the metapoetic (a concept I shall discuss in Chapter 12). Briefly, the self-consciousness of her statement that 'now she really is Medea' draws attention to the fact that 'Medea' exists outside of and prior to Seneca's text.

10.12 The soliloquy is a vivid portrayal of how someone who feels she has been slighted or wronged arouses her own anger, a topic that Seneca also treated in his three-book prose essay *On Anger*, but it is not only that. It also portrays Medea's total self-absorption as she wrestles with the idea of killing the children that she and Jason have produced. Medea is at one moment a wronged and vengeful wife and at the next a loving mother:

> My mind's made up to penalize him thus
> as he deserves. My mind's made up and now
> must be prepared for the ultimate in crime,
> I recognize this now. Children, once mine,
> you pay the penalty for your father's crimes.
> My heart has missed a beat, my limbs are cold.
> I feel a shiver in my breast. Anger's gone,

the wife in me has been expelled,
the mother has returned. How can I shed
the blood of my children, my own flesh?
Anger and madness must not come to this!
This is a hideous and unnatural act. . . .
                    Passion's fierce swell
holds me but cannot decide which way
to toss me. It is as if I were the sea:
violent winds wage war, conflicting waves
attack from either side, the waters seethe
in indecision, just like my heart. Anger drives out love,
then love drives anger out.

                    (Seneca *Medea* 922–32 and 939–44)

At one level, this speech closely resembles Euripides' representation of Medea as torn between the different roles she might play. But at another, it is very different. In contrast with Euripides, where Medea's focus is upon her children throughout and where we are constantly reminded of the presence of the children on stage, Seneca's Medea is involved in a self-absorbed soliloquy in which she responds to no one other than herself. Her focus is upon her own character, upon her past and her future. She is questioning what identity remains for her once the role of wife and then of mother are removed and in this speech forges a new powerful identity which consists of a Medea who equals her reputation. In other words, Seneca develops Medea's conflict from one between maternal and vengeful instincts into a debate about self-hood and identity. Significantly, she ends her speech by addressing words of encouragement and resolve to her own spirit (line 976).

10.13 Seneca's portrayal of the tragic character Medea as totally absorbed in her dialogue with herself paves the way for the soul-searching that Augustine three and a half centuries later articulates in his autobiographical *Confessions* (see Chapter 9.20). But whereas Augustine's introspection reads as an individual's authentic inner thoughts, Medea's introspection is itself a performance. Her awareness of the roles available to her and of her reputation produces the paradox that an apparently private moment of introspection is actually a moment of public performance, the self-conscious performance of the internal conflict of the self. And so we come full circle, back to the issue of performance in Roman life and literature which was discussed in Chapters 5–7 (see also the opening of Chapter 8).

10.14 At the same time, Medea's inner conflict can also be read in an especially twenty-first century way, as a fragmentation of the self which chimes with the intellectual movement called postmodernism, a theory which emphasizes 'the death of the author' and which correspondingly throws the responsibility for interpretation of works of art and literature on the recipient – the viewer or reader. It was the French theorist Roland Barthes who first articulated the consequences of 'the death of the author' in his 1977 essay of that title, in particular the birth of the reader. Barthes had already produced an important (and now classic) demonstration of the multiplicity of meanings available from a text and its interaction with its readers in *S/Z*, his 1970 explosively multi-layered literary–cultural commentary on a short story called *Sarrasine* by Balzac. The schisms in the self that Seneca creates in his tragic heroine readily lend themselves to a postmodern interpretation, though these schisms are differentiated relatively clearly, with Medea torn between the roles of wronged wife and protective mother. The reader's job is to find a balance between them. By contrast, in another text from the same period we find no such differentiation. As a coda to this discussion of introspection and individual identity, then, I present a passage from Persius, a young satirist who was admired by his contemporary Lucan, Seneca's nephew, and who, like Seneca and Lucan, expresses himself in what we might call a Stoic idiom. In his short book of *Satires*, Persius creates an impression of total isolation and self-absorption. This is reflected in his Latin, which is possibly the hardest of any Latin poet, mainly because his language is an intense collage of shifting imagery, but also because he often changes voice or character without any indication in the text. In other words, his introspection goes hand in hand with confusion of identity. And significantly, of all Latin poets Persius shows perhaps the least interest in the performative aspect of Roman life.

10.15 My example is the opening of *Satire* 3, which I have interpreted here by separating out two voices, A and B. These can be seen as two conflicting voices within a single personality or as belonging to Persius and a well-meaning but bossy friend – an issue which continues to be debated by scholars.

[A]   Of course it's like this all the time. Already the bright morning
          is coming
    through the shutters, enlarging the narrow cracks with light.
    We're snoring enough to make the untamed Falernian stop
    frothing, while the shadow reaches the fifth line.

[B]   'Hey, what are you doing? The mad Dog-star has been baking
          the crops dry
    for hours now and all the herd's beneath the spreading elm,'
    says one of my mates.   [A] Are you sure? *Really*? Quick,
          someone,
    come here. No one around? My glass-green bile is swelling:
    I'm bursting – you'd think the herds of Arcadia were braying.
    Now my book comes to hand, and the hairless two-tone
    parchment, the paper and a jointed reed-pen.
    Then we start moaning: the liquid hangs from the nib too
          thickly.
    But when water's added, the black cuttle-ink thins and we moan:
    the stalk keeps doubling the diluted drops.

[B]   'You idiot, more idiotic by the day, is this the state
    we've got to? Deary me, why don't you act like a young pigeon
    or a little prince instead, and demand your baby-food cut up
          into tiny pieces,
    and throw a tantrum and refuse to let your mummy sing you
          to sleep?'

[A]   How can I work with a pen like this?   [B] 'Who are you
          fooling? Why do you
    keep reciting those evasions? It's *your* move. You're dribbling
          away mindlessly,
    you'll be a laughing-stock.

                       (Persius *Satires* 3.1–21)

This is pretty difficult stuff, requiring many footnotes of explanation, even when it is separated into two voices. Now just imagine that as text without any interpretation at all – which is how Persius wrote it. The difficulties of this text will be a deterrent for some readers, but for others they are an enticement to figure out the workings of the self that they portray. That is why Persius has to figure in any discussion of introspection and identity in Latin literature.

Further reading and study

On the political dimension of Ovid's *Metamorphoses* see Leo Curran 'Transformation and anti-Augustanism in Ovid's *Metamorphoses*' *Arethusa* 5 (1972) 71–91, D. Feeney *The Gods in Epic* (Oxford, 1991) pages 10–24, S. Hinds 'Generalising about Ovid' *Ramus* 16 (1987) 4–31.

For analysis of the Narcissus episode with an emphasis upon wit and tone see N. Rudd 'Echo and Narcissus' *Echos du Monde Classique: Classical Views* 30 (1986) 43–8, G. K. Galinsky *Ovid's Metamorphoses: An Introduction to the Basic Aspects* (Oxford, 1975) pages 52–60 and P. Hardie 'Lucretius and the delusions of Narcissus' *Materiali e Discussioni per l'Analisi dei Testi Classici* 20–1 (1988) 71–89.

It is fun to study analysis of folk tales, such as Vladimir Propp's *Morphology of the Folktale* (translated by Laurence Scott, Austin, 1968) and Stith Thompson's *Motifs Index of Folk Literature: A Classification of Narrative Elements in Folk-Tales, Ballads, Myths, Fables, Medieval Romances, Exempla, Fabliaux, Jest-Books, and Local Legends* (Bloomington, 1932–6, 6 volumes), in search of analogies with classical mythology. For a lively and very contemporary study of 'the helpful princess' as manifested in Ariadne, Medea and Dido see Judith de Luce 'Reading and re-reading the helpful princess' in *Compromising Traditions: The Personal Voice in Classical Scholarship* (edited by T. Van Nortwick and J. P. Hallett, London and New York, 1997) 25–37.

Medea has always attracted attention. See now *Medea: Essays on Medea in Myth, Literature, Philosopy, and Art* (edited by James J. Clauss and Sarah Iles Johnson, Princeton, 1997), especially the papers by Carole Newlands and Martha Nussbaum; on Medea's 'self-myth' see Helen Fyfe in *Seneca Tragicus: Ramus Essays on Senecan Drama* (edited by A. J. Boyle, Bentleigh, Australia, 1983) 77–93 at page 84, and on the nature of her conflict see Christopher Gill 'Two monologues of self-division: Euripides, *Medea* 1021–80 and Seneca, *Medea* 893–977' in *Homo Viator: Classical Essays for John Bramble* (edited by M. Whitby, P. Hardie and M. Whitby, Bristol, 1987) 25–37 (whose emphasis differs slightly from mine).

The classic essay 'The death of the author' by Roland Barthes is found in his book *The Rustle of Language* (translated by R. Howard, Oxford, 1986), pages 49–55, as well as in anthologies of his essays. Curiously, the phrase is now widely used as a slogan, as if to prove Barthes' point by its multiple appropriations. Barthes' classic interpretive study is *S/Z* (Paris, 1970 and reprinted often). This is well worth reading: be sure to read the Balzac short story, included in the volume, first.

A rich topic for further study is to investigate the use of 'narcissism'. You could start from its earliest use in English, in 1898 by Havelock Ellis*,* and trace it through the twentieth century. You could also investigate the influence of Ovid's formulation of the story of Echo and Narcissus on later European literature: see Louise Vinge *The Narcissus Theme in Western European Literature up to the Early 19th Century* (Lund, 1967) and K. J. Knoespel *Narcissus and the Invention of Personal History* (New York, 1985). Ovid also presents rich material for further enquiry into individual identity. A wonderful episode is his story of Salmacis and Hermaphroditus at *Metamorphoses* 4.285–388, which can be read with the analysis by Georgia Nugent 'This sex which is not one: de-constructing Ovid's hermaphrodite' in *Sexuality in Greek and Roman Society*, a special issue of *differences* (edited by D. Konstan and M. Nussbaum) 2.1 (1990) 160–85.

Chapter 11

Literary texture and intertextuality

11.1   So far we have studied a range of approaches to Latin literature along with its themes and the ways in which it reflects central concerns of Roman society, at least the concerns of the literate male elite. Now it is time to focus upon the qualities of the literature in its own right. In this chapter and the following two I shall discuss different aspects of the surface of Latin texts and the self-consciousness with which Latin texts were written. Chapter 11 will deal with some of the ways in which literary texture is created, not least through intertextuality, that is, the relationships between texts. Chapter 12 will consider what happens when the surface of the text is disrupted by self-referentiality, which happens in both narrative and dramatic genres when the text draws attention to its own functioning in a process we often call metapoetics. Chapter 13 will discuss allegory in Latin literature, a phenomenon which involves multiple 'messages' operating on different levels simultaneously, without necessarily disrupting the surface of the text but invariably adding layers of interpretation. These chapters will all draw substantially upon the work of other scholars who have dealt with the issues in detail and so will include a greater degree of reference to secondary literature than the earlier chapters. These chapters will also illustrate incidentally the enormous debt of Latin literature to Greek literature, a topic which will be tackled directly in the penultimate chapter, with discussions of the Romans' inferiority complex and of the generic hierarchy inherited from Greek literature (Chapter 14).

11.2   One element that can get lost in the study of Latin literature through the medium of English translation is a sense of the playfulness and sheer exuberance it is capable of in the hands of a clever wordsmith. It is my aim in this chapter to convey some sense of the ludic qualities of Latin. The chapter falls into three parts. In the first part I shall examine first a prose text, *Metamorphoses* by Apuleius, which is richly self-conscious of its own 'poetic' effects, and then some of the games played by scholars to emphasize this aspect of poetry written in Latin. In the second part I shall offer an introduction to the concept of intertextuality which is a crucial element in the understanding of Latin literature. Here I shall draw upon the essential work of Stephen Hinds and offer two brief case studies, the relationship between the satirists Horace and Persius and the multiple layers of allusion present at the close of the *Thebaid*, the epic poem by Statius. In the final part of the chapter I shall demonstrate how both literary texture and intertextuality pose problems for the translator – and for any of us reading the literature in translation. After all, an awareness of what can be lost or distorted in the process of translation is essential.

11.3   I start with Apuleius, an author who falls at the end of the classic canon of texts read in the British and American education systems. Apuleius was a peripatetic professor from Madaura in north Africa who spoke Punic and Greek and Latin and who wrote a range of philosophical, declamatory and poetic works during the second half of the second century CE. He is best known to us as the author of the first fully fledged Roman novel, the *Metamorphoses*, or, as Augustine called it, *The Golden Ass*. This tells the story of Lucius who is accidentally turned into a donkey because of his insatiable curiosity about magic. The novel, in eleven short books, describes his adventures during his quest to be turned back into a man and culminates in his conversion to the religion of the Egyptian goddess Isis, who assists his metamorphosis. It incorporates all kinds of entertaining and lurid stories drawn from Egyptian, Milesian, Greek and Latin sources about witches and magic and adultery, as well as the lengthy folk tale of Cupid and Psyche. Though I could draw an example from anywhere in the text to illustrate Apuleius' love of language, I have chosen an excerpt from the folk tale, because folk tale should be an archetypally simple kind of form, but in Apuleius' hands it becomes self-conscious and highly crafted in its sound effects.

11.4   The passage is Apuleius' luscious description of how Psyche falls in love with her husband Cupid on seeing him for the first time at *Metamorphoses* 5.22–3, a passage which has seemed to many readers to evoke a work of art. Psyche's first sight of Cupid is expressed with an abundance of linguistic features which serve to intensify the texture. In the sentence 'she sees of all wild creatures the softest and sweetest of beasts, none other than Cupid, *the beautiful god beautifully sleeping*' the adjective and adverb (*formonsum deum formonse cubantem*) form a jingle which, though a Homeric technique, is virtually unparalleled in Latin. Later, after feasting her eyes on his beautiful body, Psyche falls in love with Cupid, in the first of two puns that Apuleius makes on Cupid's names: 'So unknowingly Psyche through her own act *fell in love with Love*', *in Amoris incidit amorem*. In his second pun he intensifies Psyche's passionate reaction to the sight of her husband by describing her as 'ever more on fire with desire for Desire', *tunc magis magisque cupidine fraglans Cupidinis*.

11.5   These puns on their own bear witness to Apuleius' concern with literary texture, but they fade into insignificance when compared with the intricately swooning language of the single sentence with which he conveys Psyche's ravishment by Cupid's beauty.

She sees the glorious hair of his golden head dripping with ambrosia, a milky-white neck, and rosy cheeks over which strayed curls of hair becomingly arranged, some suspended in front, some suspended behind, shining with such extreme brilliance that the lamplight itself flickered uncertainly. On the shoulders of the flying god wings sparkle dewy-white with

glistening bloom, and though they are at rest the soft delicate
down at their edges quivers and ripples in incessant play.

> (Apuleius *Metamorphoses* 5.22, adapted
> from E. J. Kenney's translation)

A glance at the Latin text should reveal some of the sound effects
here by which Apuleius encourages us to read slowly and savour the
sensuousness of his description. There are many repeated sounds here
in alliteration and assonance, especially with the letters *u* and *l*:

> videt capitis aurei genialem caesariem ambrosia temulentam,
> cervices lacteasque genasque purpureas pererrantes crinium glo-
> bos decoriter impeditos, alios antependulos, alios retropendulos,
> quorum splendore nimio fulgurante iam et ipsum lumen lucer-
> nae vacillabat; per umeros volatilis dei pinnae roscidae micanti
> flore candicant et quamvis alis quiescentibus extimae plumulae
> tenellae ac delicatae tremule resultantes inquieta lasciviunt.

That is not all. When Apuleius describes the 'curls' of Cupid's hair,
using the onomatopoeic word *globos* (say it aloud), he invents two
remarkable words to describe how they stray across his cheeks and
neck, *antependulos* ('suspended in front') and *retropendulos* ('suspended behind'). And when he introduces into this static tableau the
merest hint of movement in the phrase 'quivers and ripples in incessant play', the tongue is made to participate in this movement with the
repetition of sounds in *tremule resultantes inquieta lasciviunt*. These
are just a few examples of the ways in which Apuleius exploits to the
full the resources of the Latin language to create his sophisticated, self-
conscious and playful version of folk tale, designed, like regular folk
tale, to be listened to, but with enjoyment of the surface of the story as
well as of the story itself. In Apuleius' hands, prose becomes poetic.

11.6   The playfulness, or ludic quality, so clearly shown by Apuleius
throughout his novel is a feature which has been detected by scholars
in many other Latin authors too, sometimes plausibly, but sometimes
straining belief. It may not be accidental that this interest in the shape
or form of the words themselves is so strongly in evidence in texts

that also narrate changes in shape or form – not just in Apuleius' prose novel *Metamorphoses* but in Ovid's epic poem *Metamorphoses* too, as we shall see in a moment. Literary texture – that is, its 'woven' quality (to bring out the etymology) – invites us to examine the component parts of a sentence, a line or even a word. This was something understood and exploited by the poet Lucretius (introduced at Chapter 8.19) in his exposition of the Epicurean version of atomism. To make comprehensible the workings of invisible atoms, he describes the phenomenon of spontaneous combustion in forests – the generation of fire from wood. He then connects this with the words themselves:

> Now do you see the point I made before,
> that it often makes an almighty difference
> how these same atoms combine, in what positions
> they are held, what motions they give and take,
> and that these same atoms by tiny mutual changes
> can make both fires and firs? As the words themselves
> consist of elements a little changed
> when we say fires or firs with different sounds?
>
> (Lucretius *On the Nature of the Universe*
> 1.907–14, adapted from A. D. Melville)

The Latin actually uses *lignum* ('wood') and *ignis* ('fire') as the key words in this passage. Their similarity (which has to be rendered with some sleight of hand; other translators have 'forests' and 'fires', or 'beams' and 'flames') makes it possible for Lucretius to explain the workings of the world by an analogy with the workings of language.

11.7   This kind of awareness of the linguistic level of Latin is put to playful use by other writers including Apuleius, as I have shown earlier, and above all Ovid, who is a very strong candidate for the title of champion of Latin wordplay. This is widely recognized by scholars who write about Ovid. Take John Henderson's discussion of the *Metamorphoses*, a discussion written for *Omnibus*, a UK magazine aimed at high school and university students:

The poem's title and first verse already introduce the idea that every word is bound to be a transformation of another – perhaps every other – word. [Ovid] shows that the Greek word *Metamorphoses* is itself a metamorphosis of its Latin translation *mutatas . . . formas*, a metamorphosis in which the two versions 'uncannily' stir each other's ingredients so that we can't miss them in either manifestation. *Meta-* and *muta-ta-* must have been 'meant' to 'mean' each other! *Morph-ê* and *form-a* derange each other. What the Poet does *with* language here is cue it in so readers can see that it's going to be his privileged theme.

Once you see the poem's work *upon* its language in these opening verses, you'll see what the whole shooting-match is 'about'. *Metamorphosis*. What happens when you write *verse-s* or *vers-ions*. (Both from *uerto*, to 'turn', transform, metamorphose.) What happens, then, when you write letters, re-write letters in a different order. (*Letters* 'make up' *tellers*: A *forma*, for example, is a linguistic 'form'. And do you know what *morphology* is? Let's just say that Ovid shows you that '*Metamorphosis*' is another name for *Language*, the poetry of language.)

(Henderson from *Omnibus* 19 (1990) 20)

11.8   You will notice that John Henderson's prose style is difficult and idiosyncratic. This is how he generally writes, making few concessions to the reader, as a deliberate provocation to us to look again at the texts and issues that he discusses. His focus upon Ovid's language is shared by Fred Ahl in his book *Metaformations*, published in 1985. In his preface, Ahl writes:

My hypothesis, then, is that Ovid accompanies his descriptions of changes in physical shape with changes in the shape of the words used to tell the tale. Soundplay and wordplay do not simply *occur* in the *Metamorphoses*: they are the basis of its structure. The rearrangement of material elements needed to transform men into animals or plants is reflected in language itself as the letters and syllables in words are shuffled.

(Ahl *Metaformations* page 10)

The argument that this approach works for Ovid's *Metamorphoses* is very persuasive and Ahl rightly concentrates upon Ovid for much of the book. But he provokes scepticism (from me, at any rate) when he tries to apply this approach to other texts. Consider, for example, his discussion of the role of Anna, Dido's sister, at the opening of Book 4 of Virgil's *Aeneid*:

> ANNA is introduced into the *Aeneid* in a burst of wordplay the morning after Aeneas has told his tale of suffering at Troy (4.1–4):
>
> > postera Phoebea lustrabat terras
> > UM*entem*que AURORa polo dimoverat UMbram,
> > cum sic unANimam adloquitur male sANA sORORem:
> > 'AN[N]A sOROR . . .'.
>
> The following day was shining on the lands with its light from Phoebus; the dawn [*AURORa*] had disMISSED the DAnK [*UMentem*] DArKNess [*UMbras*] when she spoke to the one whose thoughts were never ANy different from her own. In this mad mANNer her sISTER she addressed: 'ANNA, my sISTER.'
>
> We have already seen the plays on *OR* and *AUR* and on *UMor* (dampness) and *UMbra* (shadow) in Varro and Ovid. Now we find them in a Vergilian context, as Dido confesses her *AMOR* (love) for AENEAs, the destined founder of the ROMAn people. Her love, of course, has been inspired by Venus' substitution of AENEAs' brother, *AMOR*, for his son Iulus. ANNA's appearance is linked with the dawn both in the narrative and in the wordplay between *sOROR* and *AURORa*. And solar imagery subtly accumulates about her when she appears and as she speaks (4.31–32): *ANNA refert: 'O luce magis dilecta sORORi | SOLAne . . .?'* ('ANNA, in return: "You are loved more than light itself by your sister. Are you to be the SOLE . . .?"'). ANNA's advice to Dido that she indulge her love for Aeneas has its effect (4.54): *his dictis incensum ANimum inflAM[M]Avit AMore* ('With these words she stirred ANy breath left in her soul, already smouldering, from ASHES to pASSION').
>
> (Ahl *Metaformations* 310)

What is Ahl trying to do here? He is drawing attention to the texture of the text, even if his project as a whole tends towards over-interpretation. He brings out some of the effects which are undeniably present in the Latin and courageously attempts to render them into English – which is not an easy task, an issue I shall return to at the end of this chapter. What seems to me dubious is his labelling these sound effects 'wordplay' or seeing these patterns as self-conscious games by the poet. How far to go down this route of interpretation must be a decision for each individual. What is valuable, though, is the essential idea – that language is *poetic*, in the fullest sense of the term, that is, from the Greek *poiein*, 'made' or 'created'.

11.9   Another manifestation of poetic self-consciousness is the inter-textuality which is an indelible element in Latin literature. Intertextuality is a term developed during the late twentieth century to denote the inter-connections, deliberate or otherwise, between texts. It is wider than the term allusion, which attributes to the author a specific intention to refer to an earlier text. With 'the death of the author' in postmodern thought (see Chapter 10.14), it was perhaps inevitable that the term 'allusion' would become unsatisfactory. In its place, 'intertextuality' makes no claims about intention but simply asserts that one text is reacting to another or, better, interacting with another. The concept greatly enriches our appreciation of Latin literature by pointing to the sophistication of the culture of the Roman literary elite. This was a culture so deeply immersed in earlier literature, both Greek and Latin, thanks to the stable and conservative canon used in education, that authors and audiences could operate at a very high level of complexity.

11.10   The concepts of allusion and intertextuality have recently been given a superb treatment by Stephen Hinds in a brilliant book on Latin literature and there is no point at all in my trying to cover the same ground. His *Allusion and Intertext: Dynamics of Appropriation in Roman Poetry* (1998) is a book essential to anyone interested in under-standing Latin literature. One reason it is so important is that he rejects the stark choice between a view of allusion as privileging 'the inter-ventions in literary discourse of one intention-bearing subject, the alluding poet' and what he calls 'an intertextualist fundamentalism

. . . which privileges readerly reception so single-mindedly as to wish the alluding author out of existence altogether' (pages 47–8; all of Chapter 2 is crucial). Instead he applies the ideas of Umberto Eco about the ideal interaction between the 'model reader' and the 'model author' to argue for an 'enlarged version of "allusion" . . . which is good to think with' because it can accommodate the philological rigour traditionally associated with the tracking of allusions alongside a 'fuzzy logic' (Hinds here borrows a term from computer modelling) of allusive inexactitude (pages 49–51).

11.11 What I shall do instead is to present one brief case study of an intertextuality not discussed by Hinds, that between the satirical poetry of Horace and Persius, and to add a few comments to Hinds' discussion of the 'secondariness' of the closure of Statius' epic poem, *Thebaid*. Persius (who was introduced in Chapter 10.14–15) was a young satirist writing under the emperor Nero. His single book, probably unfinished, was highly praised by contemporaries and later by Quintilian, the professor of rhetoric (*Training of the Orator* 10.1.94). Persius' Latin is perhaps more difficult than that of any other author who features on student reading lists, mainly because of the strain he puts upon the language by creating startling mixed metaphors and compressed collages of meaning. But there is more to it than that. He is also totally immersed in the satirical poetry of his predecessor, Horace, as Niall Rudd has demonstrated in a brilliant exposition of imitation in Persius (Chapter 3 of his book, *Lines of Enquiry*). Virtually every sentence or phrase in Persius reworks a phrase or association of ideas found in Horace. To take just one example, early in his fifth *Satire*, Persius puts into the mouth of his Stoic tutor, Cornutus, a description of his own satirical style and method:

> 'You pursue words of the toga, skilled at the pointed combination, rounded with moderate utterance, clever at scratching sick morals and at nailing fault with well-bred wit.'

> > "verba togae sequeris *iunctura callidus acri*,
> > ore teres modico, pallentis radere mores
> > doctus et ingenuo culpam defigere ludo."
> >
> > > (Persius *Satires* 5.14–16)

This strikes me as an excellent description of how Persius overturns and rejuvenates literary and philosophical clichés and commonplaces, especially 'skilled at the pointed combination'. This phrase itself demonstrates his method. The passage as a whole is inspired by lines from Horace's *Art of Poetry*, where Horace is giving advice on a poet's choice of diction:

> When a skilful collocation makes a familiar word new, that is distinguished writing.

> > dixeris egregie notum si *callida* verbum
> > reddiderit *iunctura* novum.

> > > (Horace *Art of Poetry* 47–8)

Horace's Latin is elegant but not exactly exciting. Persius takes the same topic – choice of diction – and two of the same words – the noun *iunctura* ('combination' or 'collocation') and the adjective *callidus/a* ('skilled' or 'skilful') – and produces something strikingly original, the idea of the 'pointed' or 'harsh' or 'rough' (*acri*) combination. And this passage contains examples of just this technique – in the strange phrase 'words of the toga' (which means, in effect, common speech, since the toga was the regular dress of Roman citizens) and the odd mixture of physical and ethical ideas in 'scratching sick morals' (as if morals were itches) and 'nailing fault with well-bred wit' (as if fault were a tack). Leaving on one side Persius' use of 'pointed combinations', what concerns me here is the relationship between Persius and Horace. Persius is involved in the process of allusion. His reworkings of Horace combine imitation with original twists that make the borrowed material distinctively his own – a classic combination of *imitatio* and *aemulatio*, to use the Latin terms, 'imitation' and 'emulation'.

11.12 Almost any passage of Persius can be quarried for Horace's phrases and ideas, always in a new guise. For example, in the following passage from Persius *Satire* 5 all the phrases marked in italics rework material drawn from Horace's satirical writings:

> > Has training given you the capacity to live
> *with a straight ankle* and do you have the skill to distinguish
> > appearance from truths,

> so that there is no faulty jangle from *gold with copper
>   underneath*?
> *What should be pursued and what be avoided* in turn,
> *have you marked the first category with chalk and the other with
>   charcoal*?
> Are your desires moderate, your household frugal, *are you kind
>   to your friends*?
> Can you now close your granaries and now open them up,
> and *can you step over a coin stuck in the mud*
> and not suck in *Mercury's* saliva with a gulp?
>
>   (Persius *Satires* 5.104–12)

Space does not permit me to go into greater detail here but anyone interested can check Persius' Latin against these passages in Horace: 104 *recto . . . talo*: cf. Horace *Epistles* 2.1.176; 106 *subaerato mendosum . . . auro*: cf. Horace *Epistles* 1.7.22–3; 107 *quaeque sequenda forent quaeque evitanda*: cf. Horace *Satires* 1.2.75, 1.3.114, 1.4.115–16; 108 *illa prius creta, mox haec carbone notasti?*: cf. Horace *Satires* 2.3.246; 109 *dulcis amicis*: cf. Horace *Satires* 1.4.135, also *Epistles* 2.2.210; 111 *in . . . luto fixum possis transcendere nummum*: cf. Horace *Epistles* 1.16.63–5; 112 *Mercurialem*: cf. Horace *Satires* 2.3.25. Niall Rudd's essay, mentioned above, starts with a full discussion of Persius 5.111 and provides an extensive series of other examples, which complement my own above. By the way, I do not apologize for including Latin quotations or detailed analysis like this here, because only by careful study of the alluding and alluded-to texts can we understand the degree of imitation and therefore the degree of originality.

11.13 While the relationship between Persius and his satiric predecessor Horace may be particularly intense, it does demonstrate the kind of level of allusion possible in Latin texts. Persius knows the writings of Horace intimately and I suspect that he thinks at least some of his readers will recognize his allusions to Horace and enjoy their reworked presentation. This entire process is highly intellectual and it is crucial to appreciate this self-conscious dimension for a full understanding of Latin literature.

11.14 Self-consciousness is at the centre of Stephen Hinds' argu-ments about Latin literature and in his book *Allusion and Intertext* he demonstrates its many manifestations in Latin poetry. Particularly striking is his discussion of so-called 'secondary' epic on pages 91–8. Here he takes a term that is conventionally used to describe Virgil in relation to Homer, the 'original' and the champion in the epic genre, and uses it to explore the relationship between Statius' *Thebaid* and Virgil's *Aeneid*. His focus is the closing coda where Statius addresses his poem:

> My *Thebaid*, on which for twelve long years
> I burnt my midnight oil, will you endure
> in distant time to come, will you survive
> your author and be read? Already now
> your present fame has surely paved for you
> a kindly path and at your outset makes
> your mark for future times. Already now
> our great-hearted Caesar deigns to know you.
> Already too the youth of Italy
> learn and recite you. Live! That is my prayer,
> nor try to match the heavenly *Aeneid*
> but follow from afar and evermore
> venerate its steps. Soon, if envy still
> clouds you, it will die, and when I have passed away
> all due honours will be offered up.
>
> (Statius *Thebaid* 12.810–19, adapted
> from A. D. Melville)

Hinds suggests that the explicitly deferential and highly self-conscious claim to secondariness in lines 816–17 has played a large part in 'keep[ing] all post-Augustan epic out of the modern academic canon', a situation that is finally, gradually, changing now. He challenges the attention given to these lines in two ways. First he juxtaposes another programmatic statement made by Statius about his *Thebaid*, this time in his *Lumber*, where he actually asserts his ambition to rival the *Aeneid*:

> It is a fact that with you [my patron] as my loyal adviser
> my *Thebaid*, tormented by frequent use of the file,
> attempts with daring lyre the joys
> > of Virgilian fame.
>
> > > (Statius *Lumber* 4.7.25–8)

Though this passage is often neglected by scholars, Hinds rightly suggests that this at least reframes Statius' self-depreciation at the end of the *Thebaid*. Second, he points to Statius' use of the classic image of incapacity a few lines earlier:

> I could not, even if some god were to open out my breast
> with one hundred voices, match in worthy attempts so many
> > funerals
> of leaders and commoners alike, so many lamentations shared.
>
> > > (Statius *Thebaid* 12.797–9)

Hinds reminds us that epic poets from Homer onwards, including Ennius and Virgil, have used this *topos* (pages 34–47), so that it can hardly be taken as a novel statement of inferiority by Statius. Incidentally, Persius opens his fifth *Satire* with a satiric version of this poetic cliché:

> This is the way of bards, to demand one hundred voices,
> to pray for one hundred mouths and one hundred tongues for
> > their songs,
> whether serving up a tale to be uttered wide-mouthed by the
> > grieving tragic actor
> or the wounds of a Parthian pulling the weapon from his groin.
>
> > > (Persius *Satires* 5.1–4)

Through this study of allusion and intertextuality, then, Hinds demonstrates that Statius is acutely aware of his belated position in the history of epic and suggests that the way that he rises to this challenge might invite us to rethink the concept of 'secondariness'.

11.15   To close this discussion of intertextuality, I shall briefly offer a supplement to Hinds' analysis of the close of Statius' *Thebaid* which complements his view of the poet's epic ambition. Two further epic intertexts seem to me to assert Statius' self-confidence, although there is also an undercurrent of anxiety as the poet sends his poem out into the world, an anxiety deftly explored by Horace in *Epistles* 1.20. My first epic intertext is the coda with which the Alexandrian Greek poet Apollonius ends his *Journey of the Argonauts*:

> Race of blessed leaders, be gracious! And may these songs
> year on year be sweeter for people
> to sing. Now I have reached the glorious end point
> of your labours . . .
> joyfully you disembarked on to the beach of Pagasae.
> (Apollonius *Argonautica* 4.1773–6 and 1781)

Like Apollonius, Statius predicts an appreciation for his poetry that will grow and grow through the ages. The second epic intertext is the coda of Ovid's *Metamorphoses* where he prophesies immortal fame for his poem (*Metamorphoses* 15.871–9: the passage is quoted at Chapter 15.8). Ovid's language is itself laden with Horatian intertexts, one of which (*Odes* 3.30, quoted at Chapter 15.3) may in turn rework the end of Ennius' epic poem *Annals* – and so it goes on, or, rather, back. If I am right to see allusions to these epic predecessors here, it is Statius' way of asserting the merit of his own poem, indirectly and obliquely rather than boldly and directly. This is a far cry from the reading of the coda of the *Thebaid* as a blunt statement of inferiority.

11.16   An awareness of intertextuality and of literary texture is crucial to an understanding of Latin literature, yet this is often the first casualty when we read Latin literature through the medium of English translation. Unfortunately, a lot can be lost or distorted in the process of translation – and that is why the job of translation is so difficult. The translator ideally needs to be the kind of scholar who appreciates the self-consciousness of Latin literature as manifested in its linguistic play and in its use of allusion and at the same time a wordsmith with the

English language. There are few who meet that description. I conclude this chapter with a quotation from one translator who arguably combined these qualities as brilliantly as anyone else, Ted Hughes. The excerpt I have chosen comes from 'Echo and Narcissus' in his *Tales from Ovid* (London, 1997). The reason I chose this is not just because this passage was discussed in my previous chapter (Chapter 10.3–7) but because Ovid is one of the most self-conscious of poets. This incident, in which Echo echoes the end of Narcissus' phrases, is exceptionally demanding of the translator. Hughes responded to this challenge by departing from strict word-by-word translation of the Latin original with the multiple repetitions that he puts into Echo's mouth. This is not what *Ovid* does in the original Latin, but it excellently evokes our idea of an echo fading away.

> It so happened, Narcissus
> Had strayed apart
> From his companions.
> He hallooed them: 'Where are you?
> I'm here.' And Echo
> Caught at the syllables as if they were precious:
> 'I'm here,' she cried, 'I'm here' and 'I'm here' and 'I'm here.'
> Narcissus looked around wildly.
> 'I'll stay here,' he shouted.
> 'You come to me.' And 'Come to me,'
> Shouted Echo. 'Come to me,
> To me to me to me.'
> Narcissus stood baffled,
> Whether to stay or go. He began to run,
> Calling as he ran: 'Stay there.' But Echo
> Cried back, weeping to utter it, 'Stay there,
> Stay there, stay there, stay there.'
> Narcissus stopped and listened. Then, more quietly,
> 'Let's meet halfway. Come.' And Echo
> Eagerly repeated it: 'Come.'
> But when she emerged from the undergrowth
> Her expression pleading,
> Her arms raised to embrace him,

Narcissus turned and ran.
'No,' he cried, 'no, I would sooner be dead
Than let you touch me.' Echo collapsed in sobs,
As her voice lurched among the mountains:
'Touch me, touch me, touch me, touch me.
(Ted Hughes Tales from Ovid pages 76–7)

Further reading and study

In the early part of this chapter I refer to John Henderson 'A turn up for the books: yes, it's . . . Ovid's *Metamorphoses*' from *Omnibus* 19 (1990) 15–20 at page 20 and Fred Ahl *Metaformations* (Ithaca, 1985). An important study of etymological wordplay is J. J. O'Hara *True Names: Vergil and the Alexandrian Tradition of Etymological Wordplay* (Ann Arbor, 1996).

Intertextuality is explained superbly by Stephen Hinds *Allusion and Intertext: Dynamics of Appropriation in Roman Poetry* (Cambridge, 1998) with debts to G.-B. Conte *The Rhetoric of Imitation: Genre and Poetic Memory in Virgil and other Latin Poets* (translated by C. Segal, Ithaca, 1986). Other discussions of allusion and intertextuality include J. Farrell *Vergil's Georgics and the Traditions of Ancient Epic. The Art of Allusion in Literary History* (New York, 1990), R. F. Thomas *Reading Virgil and His Texts: Studies in Intertextuality* (Ann Arbor, 1999), Lowell Edmunds *Intertextuality and the Reading of Roman Poetry* (Baltimore, 2001) and Alessandro Barchiesi *Speaking Volumes: Papers on Ovid and Roman Intertextuality* (London, 2001), a collection of his superb papers on issues of contexts and intertexts, poetics and metapoetics.

The essay on Horace and Persius by Niall Rudd is found in his *Lines of Enquiry* (Cambridge, 1976) chapter 3. Hinds discusses Statius' *Thebaid* on pages 91–5 of *Allusion and Intertext*.

On the language of Apuleius see my essay 'Moments of love' in *amor : roma. Love and Latin Literature* (edited by Susanna Morton Braund and Roland Mayer, Cambridge, 1999 = *Cambridge Philological Society* Supplementary Volume 22) pages 180–5.

Ted Hughes' *Tales from Ovid* (London, 1997) offers exciting takes on many passages from Ovid's *Metamorphoses*.

One idea for further study of intertextuality is to examine the literary treatment of plagues. This topic can be tracked from the Greek historian Thucydides in Book 2 of his *History of the Peloponnesian War*, through Lucretius *On the Nature of the Universe* 6 and Virgil *Georgics* 3, to Seneca's tragedy *Oedipus*. Descriptions of the Underworld in Virgil *Aeneid* 6, the tragedies of Seneca, the epic of Lucan and (perhaps surprisingly) *Satire* 3 of Juvenal are all interwoven in an intertextual relationship. A more intriguing and complex tracery is provoked by seeing what happens to Homer's Cyclops after *Odyssey* 9. We have treatments of the story from the point of view of the survivor Achaemenides in Virgil *Aeneid* 3 and Ovid *Metamorphoses* 14: for one thing, this is the only retelling by Virgil of an episode in Homer; for another, it is fascinating to see how, in his narrative of Aeneas, Ovid interacts with Virgil's epic. The Cyclops Polyphemus also appears as a forlorn lover in Theocritus *Idyll* 11, which is an important inspiration for Virgil *Eclogue* 2. From there we can trace the intertextuality through the song of the Cyclops in Ovid *Metamorphoses* 13, Colin Cloute in Edmund Spenser's *January* of *The Shepheardes Calendar* (1579) and T. S. Eliot's 'The Love Song of J. Alfred Prufrock' (1915).

Chapter 12

Metapoetics

12.1   In the previous chapter I demonstrated the self-consciousness of Latin literature as manifested in its rich textures and intertextualities. Here we shall look at a different kind of self-consciousness, which occurs when the texts refer to their own processes of creation. This phenomenon, which occurs in narrative and dramatic genres, we can call 'metapoetics'. In this chapter I shall take my first example from drama, specifically from a comedy by Plautus in which the character Pseudolus in the play of the same title self-consciously takes on the role of director to produce a play within the play – a case of metatheatre. My second example is drawn from epic narrative, specifically the incident in which the sculptor Pygmalion in Ovid's *Metamorphoses* experiences his work of art coming to life. The metapoetics here, I shall argue, make Pygmalion a metaphor for Ovid's own process of creation. My third example is again taken from drama, this time tragedy. Here I shall consider the awareness shown by Seneca's character Medea that she has a literary history and analyse the pros and cons of interpreting an episode in his *Oedipus* as a case of '*mise en abyme*' – a critical term used to denote a particular form of metapoetical self-reflexivity. I complete my discussion of metapoetics with a discussion of the self-consciousness and self-referentiality found in a famously intricate piece of prose narrative – the short prologue to

Apuleius' *Metamorphoses*. In all four cases I am indebted to the work of other critics and my readers will find a greater level of reference to discussions in the secondary literature than in earlier chapters, which will accordingly allow them to pursue the debates in greater depth. I have chosen these four examples to offer an introduction to the role of metapoetics in Latin literature, all the time aware that it is impossible to argue categorically for a metapoetic interpretation of any text, as I shall make clear. But I hope that the levels of self-consciousness manifested in these texts make a good case for the possibility of metapoetic readings of Latin literature.

12.2 I shall start with metatheatre as an introduction to the broader concept of metapoetics. Metatheatre is a particular form of metapoetics which readily occurs in the genre of comedy, because comedy likes to have fun by drawing attention to its own processes and conventions. In one helpful definition, that of Calderwood, metadrama involves two things simultaneously, 'making-an-*illusion* and *making*-an-illusion'. That is, we are invited to alter our passive acceptance of the dramatic illusion into an active awareness of how the dramatic illusion is created. This is especially true of Plautus' plays (see Chapter 3.8–9) many of which have metatheatrical moments, such as when a character breaks the dramatic illusion to refer to the presence of the audience, in so doing drawing attention to the artifice of the situation – the actors on stage playing their parts and the audience accepting the dramatic illusion created by the actors. Plautus' supreme metatheatrical creation is one of his latest plays, *Pseudolus*, first staged in 191 BCE and so popular that it was still being performed more than a hundred years later, in Cicero's time. The play itself has a plot typical of Roman comedy, in which boy wants girl but cannot get her until some obstacle has been overcome. Here the plot is in minimal form, as the play seems to be more than anything else a vehicle for the creation of Plautus' most spectacular comic villain and his most ingenious slave, Pseudolus. The characters are all hilariously overwritten – Calidorus the infatuated young man, wallowing in his emotions and absolutely no help in practical terms; Ballio the unscrupulous, hard-nosed pimp, owner of the girl with whom Calidorus is in love and interested only in getting his money; and Pseudolus the clever slave, who rashly promises Calidorus that he will get him the money he needs to buy his girl from the pimp and then has to devise a scheme to fulfil his extravagant promise. Since this is a comedy, we can feel confident that Pseudolus will achieve this aim, even though for the first half of the play neither we nor he has the faintest idea how. But it is precisely that 'how' that opens the way for metatheatricality.

12.3   Plautus has planted a big clue to his dramatic intentions in the name he has chosen for his clever slave. 'Pseudolus' contains the Greek word for 'falsehood' or 'lie'. Pseudolus perhaps alludes to this when he stands alone on the stage wondering how he is going to help his young master:

> Now he's gone, that leaves you on your own, Pseudolus.
> What're you going to do, now you've entertained your young
>   master
> with a feast of fine talk? Where's it coming from?
> Here you are without the tiniest taste of a definite plan.
> You haven't a clue where to start weaving or where to finish off.
> But just think: when a poet sits down to write, he has to search
>   out
> something that exists nowhere on this earth – and he finds it
> and makes fiction look very much like fact. That's what I'll do:
> I'll be a poet and invent two thousand bucks
> which don't exist anywhere on this earth – and I'll find them.
>   (Plautus *Pseudolus* lines 395–408)

When he talks of turning himself into a poet, by which he means that he needs to write his own script, Pseudolus is clearly aware that he needs to invent a solution to Calidorus' problems. But what is that solution to be? After a scene in which we realize that Calidorus' father is determined not to be cheated out of any money which his son could use to buy the girl, Pseudolus is making no progress at all, as he admits to the audience directly in another metatheatrical moment:

> I suspect that you folks now suspect me
> of not doing what I said I would do

and of promising these impressive deeds
just to keep you amused as long as the play lasts.
Well, you're wrong. And as for knowing how I'll do it,
well I'm certain that I have no idea at all –
except that it'll be done. After all, what's an actor for,
if not to bring on stage some new-fangled surprise?
If he can't do that, he'd better make way for someone who can.
Now I'd like to go inside for a little while
to hold a mental muster of my ingeniosity.
But I'll soon be back – shan't keep you long.
In the meantime our fluteplayer will entertain you.

(Plautus *Pseudolus* 562–74)

12.4   When he reappears after the musical interlude, he sounds much
more confident as he casts himself in the role of the attacking general,
taking on both Ballio the pimp and Calidorus' father (575–91), yet
we are still in the dark about his plans. At this point, his luck changes
with the arrival of a messenger who is bringing a letter to Ballio to
authorize the release of the girl. The role-playing that Pseudolus had
flirted with earlier (he has had moments as a general 384–6, a tragic
actor 453–5, the Delphic oracle 480 and a free citizen 520) now brings
real results as he abandons his (alleged) plans and pretends to be
Ballio's slave so that he can trick a messenger out of the letter
(601–66). But he of course cannot perform the deception on Ballio
himself, because Ballio would recognize him, so he obtains another
clever slave to play the part of the messenger and trick Ballio into
handing over the girl. Significantly, this slave is called Simia, literally
'Ape', a name chosen to emphasize that he is playing a part by 'aping'
the messenger. Metatheatricality reaches its height as Pseudolus pre-
pares Simia for his part, scripting and directing him, costuming him
and providing him with the necessary props (in strongly militaristic
language):

That clears any doubts and uncertainties I had
and cleanses my mind completely. Now we can advance.
I'll lead my legions onwards now, in line beneath their
        standards,

with the bird on my left, the auspices favourable and to my
   liking.
I'm confident I can destroy my adversaries.
So now I'll go the forum and lay my instructions on Simia,
so he won't bungle the job, so he'll perform the con like an
   expert.
I'm going to make sure that we'll take this town of pimpery
   by storm!

(Plautus *Pseudolus* 759–66)

Later, Pseudolus watches from the sidelines as Simia perpetrates the
trick, commenting on his performance of his role (956–1023).

12.5   Pseudolus is, in effect, the author and director of a play within
a play. And that suggests that Pseudolus can be seen as a representation of the playwright Plautus at work on scripting his comedy,
transforming Greek comic drama ('New Comedy') into something that
will go down well with his Italian audiences. This view of Pseudolus-
as-Plautus is argued by John Wright in an important article called 'The
transformations of Pseudolus'. We can go still further. Niall Slater
argues that with the combination of 'script' and opportunistic improvization which Pseudolus uses to achieve his goals, Plautus reflects
the combination of those two elements in his own comic writing
(*Plautus in Performance*) – taking over the 'scripts' from his Greek
'originals' and the element of improvization from native Italian forms
of farce. Hence Slater's conclusion that 'Theatre celebrates itself in
the *Pseudolus* as it does nowhere else in Roman comedy'.

12.6   Plautus' comic drama is not the only place in Latin literature
where we find a poet using a character in his text to represent the
creative process in this metapoetic way. In Ovid's epic poem *Metamorphoses* we find the same phenomenon in his narrative of the story
of the sculptor Pygmalion (10.243–97). The outline can be told briefly:
in disgust at the behaviour of whorish women, Pygmalion turns away
from female company and sculpts the ideal woman in ivory. He falls
in love with his creation, kissing her, caressing her, bringing her gifts
and laying her on his couch. On the feast day of Venus his secret

prayer is for Venus to give him as his wife his ivory virgin. In the version of John Dryden (1631–1700) who towards the end of his life composed superb translations of all of Virgil and of substantial passages of other classical authors, the story concludes like this:

> The Youth, returning to his Mistress, hies,
> And impudent in Hope, with ardent Eyes,
> And beating Breast, by the dear Statue lies.
> He kisses her white Lips, renews the Bliss,
> And looks, and thinks they redden at the Kiss;
> He thought them warm before: Nor longer stays,
> But next his Hand on her hard Bosom lays:
> Hard as it was, beginning to relent,
> It seem'd, the Breast beneath his Fingers bent;
> He felt again, his Fingers made a Print,
> 'Twas Flesh, but Flesh so firm, it rose against the Dint:
> The pleasing Task he fails not to renew;
> Soft, and more soft and ev'ry Touch it grew;
> Like pliant Wax, when chafing Hands reduce
> The former Mass to Form, and frame for Use.
> He would believe, but yet is still in Pain,
> And tries his Argument of Sense again,
> Presses the Pulse, and feels the leaping Vein.
> Convinc'd, o'erjoy'd, his studied Thanks and Praise,
> To her who made the Miracle, he pays:
> Then Lips to Lips he join'd; now freed from Fear,
> He found the Savour of the Kiss sincere:
> At this the waken'd Image op'd her Eyes,
> And view'd at once the Light and Lover, with surprize.
>
> (Dryden *Fables Ancient and Modern*)

12.7 Since the Renaissance, Ovid's Pygmalion has been read as the myth of the artist, a myth which exalts the capacity of the artist to create a perfection beyond that found in nature. This is illustrated by the four-painting series by the pre-Raphaelite Edward Burne-Jones, *Pygmalion and The Image* (1875–78), entitled 'The Heart Desires, The Hand Refrains, The Godhead Fires, The Soul Attains', of which the second and fourth are reproduced here as Figures 6 and 7. It is no accident that the art critic Ernst Gombrich entitled the third chapter of his *Art and Illusion* 'Pygmalion's power'. He says of Ovid's version that he 'turned it into an erotic novelette, but even in his perfumed version we can feel something of the thrill which the artist's mysterious powers once gave to man'. On a metapoetical reading, then, Pygmalion represents Ovid at work on his lifeless material, the hackneyed myths of antiquity, succeeding through his passion in bringing them to life in the innovative shape of his fifteen book epic poem which embraces the history of the world from the creation to the deification of Julius Caesar in the year of Ovid's birth. The creation of living woman from lifeless ivory is paralleled in the creation of living poetry from lifeless myths.

12.8 It is important to realize that there are ways of reading the Pygmalion story other than as the success story of the artist. It can be seen as a story about artistic failure or the disappointment of the reader's desire or the exposure of how love poetry manufactures 'woman' or of Pygmalion's misogyny. For example, Eleanor Leach argues that, in becoming a lover, Pygmalion sacrifices his claim to being an artist. John (aka Jas) Elsner argues that the impossibility of the reader achieving Pygmalion's fantasy turns the reader into a mere voyeur, with consequences for the tone of the narrative: 'the miracle puts an irreparable distance between us and Pygmalion . . . the miracle (unachievable except in a myth of wish-fulfilment) is Ovid's reminder of the limits of fantasy and the unfulfillability of desire'. Alison Sharrock coins the word 'Womanufacture' for what Pygmalion is up to and reads the Pygmalion narrative as a key to the way that love-elegy operates by constructing its women as works of art: 'modelling wax, sculpting ivory, writing elegy – all manufacture woman' (see above, Chapter 9.5). In another article she argues that Pygmalion represents the fulfilment of the fantasy of reproducing without another's agency and that the result is a misogynistic composite of a wife who is a goddess and a whore. The reception of Ovid's story also opens up a variety of interpretations (some of which are discussed by Jane Miller in *Ovid Renewed*). Its most famous progeny is probably George Bernard Shaw's play *Pygmalion* (1913), which was turned into a

FIGURE 6 Edward Burne-Jones *Pygmalion and The Image*, ii 'The Hand Refrains'

Courtesy of Birmingham Museums and Art Gallery

FIGURE 7 Edward Burne-Jones *Pygmalion and The Image*, iv 'The Soul Attains'

Courtesy of Birmingham Museums and Art Gallery

musical called *My Fair Lady* in 1957 and which (with some up-to-date twists in the plot) inspired the 1983 movie *Educating Rita*. Shaw's plot portrays the transformation of a Cockney flower-seller, Eliza Doolittle, into an upper-class lady by the phonetician Professor Henry Higgins. Eliza rebels against this manipulation and by the end of the play achieves her independence, thus giving this a very different outcome from Ovid's version. The movie, too, turns the tables on the creator figure, a Professor of English literature, as Rita finds her own voice.

12.9   But despite the wealth of interpretive possibilities, critics are agreed that the significance of the Pygmalion story goes beyond its surface. And once we notice that the idea of 'the artist as hero' is a theme running through the *Metamorphoses* (as explored in the article by Leach mentioned above) and once we put this together with the fact that the narrator of Pygmalion's story in *Metamorphoses* 10 is not 'Ovid' but his character Orpheus, the quintessential artist of antiquity, it seems legitimate to read the story metapoetically, as a story not just by Ovid but also about Ovid.

12.10   The same kind of argument can be, and is, brought to bear on many other texts in Latin literature, with different degrees of plausibility. For my next example I shall consider the case made for reading passages in Seneca's tragedies as commentaries on the process of poetic creation. This case, which he acknowledges as ambitious, is made by Alessandro Schiesaro in his essay 'Passion, reason and knowledge in Seneca's tragedies'. His starting point is to argue that characters such as Medea and Atreus are prime movers and protagonists in their plays (*Medea* and *Thyestes* respectively) and that as they 'act within the plots they have constructed, while remaining unchallenged masters of their plans' they take on an 'authorial function' (page 97) which resembles that of the playwright. On this argument, these characters play the same kind of role as Pseudolus in Plautus' play. The difference, however, is that, where Plautus explicitly invites us to see Pseudolus as an author/director of a play within a play, Seneca inserts no such cues in his *Medea* or *Thyestes*. Medea and Atreus are indeed the prime movers of their plots and the plans they lay are indeed fulfilled, but this on its own is not enough to convince me that this amounts to metatheatricality.

12.11 Schiesaro is on stronger ground when he draws attention to Medea's own awareness of her literariness. He is thinking partly of her declaration in her long soliloquy in the final act (discussed in Chapter 10.10–13),

> Now I really am Medea,

which, as the eminent German critic Wilamowitz (1848–1931) famously observed, suggests that she must have read Euripides' tragedy about her, and partly of her explicit hopes for future recognition in literature of her deeds in the soliloquy which opens the play:

> I am wasting time.
> I did all that in virgin innocence. A deeper rage
> should rise within me – now I've given birth.
> Serious crimes can be expected. Bare your anger
> for fighting and prepare yourself for killing
> with full frenzy. When tales of your life
> are told, I hope that people will pair your divorce
> with your wedding in well-matched rivalry.
>   (Seneca *Medea* 48–53, adapted from Fred Ahl)

As Schiesaro says, 'the tragedy we are watching fulfils this wish' (page 93). The character's awareness that 'Medea' exists outside of (prior to, subsequent to) Seneca's text is a clear example of metapoetics.

12.12 But it seems to me harder to make the argument that the passage in Seneca's *Oedipus* in which Oedipus finally learns the truth about himself functions metatheatrically. The scene in question forms the horrifically atmospheric centrepiece of the play. It consists of Creon's account to his brother-in-law Oedipus of his consultation with Tiresias, a seer-priest who conducts a necromancy (prophecy through the dead) which culminates in the ghost of Laius, the father that Oedipus unwittingly killed, insisting that Oedipus be driven from the land of

Thebes (lines 530–658). To open up the Underworld and compel the truth from the ghosts Tiresias performs ghastly rites which invert standard ritual practice, for example:

> The seer himself gestures
> with his wand then dresses in a black cloak,
> a flowing funeral-robe that reaches to his feet.
> In these forbidding vestments, a wreath of poison yew
> in his silver hair, the old man steps forward, with gloomy face.
> Black-fleeced sheep and bulls, black too, are dragged in,
> backwards. The flames gulp in their rich food
> while the beasts, still alive, writhe in the killing fire.
> Now he summons the ghosts and Dis their king,
> repeating over and over a magic incantation, and fiercely,
> in a frenzy, chants a spell to the shimmering phantoms,
> now coaxing, now compelling them. . . .
> Suddenly Earth gaped, yawning in a bottomless
> abyss. With my own eyes I glimpsed through the shadows
> the stagnant water, the pale spirits, essential night. My frozen
> blood halted and blocked my veins. A wild army
> leaped out, snaked up, stood armed, the whole tribe,
> the horde of earth brothers sown from dragon-teeth.
> Then the ogre Erinys screamed, blind fury,
> horror, and every ghastly creature eternal darkness
> breeds and hides. Grief tearing its hair, sickness, old-age,
> fear, and the curse of our people, the wolf of Thebes, Plague.
> > (Seneca *Oedipus* 551–63 and 582–94,
> > adapted from David Anthony Turner)

12.13 Schiesaro's argument goes as follows (pages 95–6):

This scene powerfully re-enacts what poetry and poets do. The traditional connection between the magic and prophetic power of poets and of seers, crystallised in the use of *uates* ['prophet' and 'bard'] itself, here finds a new contextual motivation. The *uates* who through his song can bring to life the frightening creatures buried in the Underworld is like the poet who, on the strength of his inspiration, gives life to the characters of tragedy.

The regenerative powers of the *uates* and the poet actually intersect in the parade of characters described at 611–18: both can reach a domain open only to a non-rational and frightening form of inspiration.

He goes on to label this scene a '*mise en abyme*', utilizing a term from critical theory to designate an embedded or inset scene which is a microcosm of its larger framework. First formulated by André Gide in 1893 as a comparison with the practice in heraldry of putting a second representation of the original shield '*en abyme*' within it, this is a structure 'which makes reflection perceptible', hence Lucien Dällenbach's classic definition of *mise en abyme* as 'any aspect enclosed within a work that shows a similarity with the work that contains it'.

12.14   The idea that Seneca is somehow talking about his own creative process when he presents a seer-priest repeating incantations and chanting spells is clearly attractive and exciting – and not, at first sight, much different from the idea that Ovid is talking about himself through the story of Pygmalion. Some will be convinced that here we have another case of metapoetics. Not me, though, not yet. Whereas Ovid's *Metamorphoses* is preoccupied frequently, if not throughout, with the relationship between poets/narrators/artists and their material and so gives plausibility to a metaphorical reading of the Pygmalion story, I find no such preoccupation in Seneca's drama. The core of the argument for this case of metatheatricality in Seneca is the multivalency of the Latin word *uates*, which undoubtedly means both 'seer/prophet' and 'poet/bard'. But Seneca does not draw attention to the word. He introduces his seer-priest not as *uates* but as *sacerdos* (the standard word for 'priest': 548), then modifies this with the words *uates* and *senex* ('old man') in the next few lines (552 and 554), using *uates* just once more in the entire passage (571). And yet the fact that at least one critic of Seneca has read this episode metapoetically, taking it as an invitation to reflect on Seneca's dramaturgy and creativity, perhaps undermines resistance to this argument. Ultimately, it all depends on each person's criteria for proof. And in the activity of literary criticism it is undoubtedly a good thing that we are constantly questioning our criteria for proof.

12.15 I close my discussion of metapoetics in Latin literature with the case of a short, intriguing text which seems to revel in its self-consciousness and in the puzzles it poses for readers and critics alike – the prologue to Apuleius' novel, his *Metamorphoses* (see Chapter 11.3). First, the text:

> But let me join together different stories in that Milesian style, and let me soothe your kindly ears with an agreeable whispering, if only you do not scorn to glance at an Egyptian papyrus inscribed with the sharpness of a reed from the Nile. I begin a tale of men's shapes and fortunes transformed into different appearances and back again into themselves by mutual connection, that you may wonder at it. 'Who is this?' Hear in brief. Attic Hymettus and the Corinthian Isthmus and Spartan Taenarus are my origin of old, ever fertile regions recorded in even more fertile books. There it was that I acquired the Attic tongue in the first campaigns of boyhood; thereafter in the Latin city as a foreigner to the studies of Rome I took on and developed the local language with laborious effort and without the lead of a master. Look then, I ask your pardon at the beginning if I commit any offence, being an inexperienced speaker of the language of the forum which is foreign to me. Indeed, this very change of language corresponds to the style of switch-back lore which I have approached: I begin a story of Greek origin. Reader, pay attention: you will be pleased.
>
> (Apuleius *Metamorphoses* prologue, adapted from S. J. Harrison and M. Winterbottom)

12.16 The complexities of this playful text are many, as is reflected by the quantity of scholarship devoted to it, most recently the entire volume resulting from a conference held in Oxford in 1996 devoted to interpretation of the prologue alone, edited by Ahuvia Kahane and Andrew Laird and now published by Oxford University Press as *A Companion to the Prologue of Apuleius' Metamorphoses*. Apuleius was a sophisticated reader and writer, immersed in the classics of Greek and Latin literature produced during the preceding centuries. His 'belatedness' in the literary tradition, to adopt a central idea from the work of the American literary critic Harold Bloom, seems not to have been a burden but instead a delight. That is signalled by his emphasis in the prologue on pleasure. Two manifestations of his delight in literariness match the topics of this chapter and the previous one – intertextuality and metapoetics. This is not the moment to discuss the intertextuality of Apuleius' prologue, but let me just mention some of the intertexts proposed by scholars in the above volume and elsewhere: with passages from the Greek historians Hecateus (late sixth century BCE) and Xenophon (fifth and fourth centuries BCE); with the openings of the dialogues of Plato, including the *Phaedrus* and the *Symposium*; with prologues of plays by Plautus; with works, lost and surviving, of Roman satire; with the prose of the Greek philosopher Plutarch; and with Greek novels. This is not an exhaustive list, even though it may at first beggar belief to see such a brief text as this laden with so much intertextuality. When each argument is considered on its merits, it is hard to resist the conclusion that Apuleius is a profoundly literary author.

12.17 To turn now to metapoetics, it should perhaps be no surprise to find self-consciousness in a prologue. There are plenty of cases in comic drama, for example, where the character delivering the prologue confides in the audience and refers to the comedy that will follow as an artistic creation. This degree of detachment and self-referentiality is the essence of metapoetics. Here we are dealing not with a drama but with a narrative, a novel, yet a narrative that is constructed as a dialogue from the very start, with its 'you' and 'me' in the opening sentences. Jack Winkler in his ground-breaking book, *Auctor & Actor: A Narratological Reading of Apuleius' The Golden Ass* (1985), prints the prologue as a dialogue, and another narratologist, Irene de Jong, writing in the volume mentioned above, draws attention to the presence of not two but three participants in this opening conversation, an 'I', a 'you' and an anonymous third person to whom the question 'Who is this?' is addressed. It is this issue – who is addressed in the question 'Who is this?' – which has preoccupied readers and critics. Answers have included the book, personified; Lucius, the character who narrates the novel; and Apuleius the author. There is not enough information here to decide definitively. Apuleius has created an elaborate tease.

12.18 And what kind of story is this? Again, the details supplied seem to offer information, but they create certain tensions too. 'Milesian' tales are racy Greek stories, while studies in Rome refer to forensic eloquence, and the reference to 'an Egyptian papyrus' promises secret religious lore. In the same way, the emphasis in the prologue shifts between references to oral and written discourse, as Ahuvia Kahane shows in another deployment of narratology which illuminates this text (see 12.16). Kahane finds three basic levels of what he calls 'context' in the *Metamorphoses*: (1) the actual context, in which we as readers hold or read a physical book; (2) the primary fictional context, belonging to the time and place in which the speaker of the prologue introduces his tale; and (3) the embedded fictional context, belonging to the time and place in which the speaker narrates his adventures. And though this may sound to some overly complex, I believe that this is a useful way of getting straight about the self-conscious complexities deliberately created by Apuleius in his prologue. The 'Chinese Box' effect thus created finds analogues in novels from nearer our own time, like Laurence Sterne's *The Life and Opinions of Tristram Shandy* (1759–67), Italo Calvino's *If on a Winter's Night a Traveller . . .* (1981) and Umberto Eco's *The Island of the Day Before* (1994). That is perhaps one reason why Apuleius' novel strikes us as so 'modern'. The destabilization of the narrative framework and the regression from one frame to another, which make Sterne, Calvino and Eco such delightful frustrations and frustrating delights to read are highly self-conscious and metapoetic. And the same applies to Apuleius. In Kahane's neat formulation, 'I Write, Therefore I Efface Myself'.

12.19 The key phrase in Apuleius' prologue is perhaps its most obscure. He describes his shifting language as done in 'the style of switch-back lore', making a metaphor from switch-back riding of horses as performed by circus athletes for entertainment. This metaphorical and metapoetic phrase seems to indicate that, for Apuleius, switching between the different horses of his story – or stories – is the essence of his project. Metamorphosis is not only his subject matter, as he tells us in the prologue, but also his technique. In other words, the metapoetics of the prologue to the *Metamorphoses* give us a clue that Apuleius is determined to resist the categories and definitions that we as readers and critics impose on his text. As he says, 'Reader, pay attention: you will be pleased.'

Further reading and study

For a definition of metadrama see J. L. Calderwood *Shakespearian Metadrama* (Minneapolis, 1971) page 11. On metatheatre in Plautus see John Wright 'The transformations of Pseudolus' *Transactions of the American Philological Association* 105 (1975) 403–16 and Niall Slater *Plautus in Performance* (Princeton, 1985), quotation from page 146.

Gombrich's quotation about Pygmalion is from page 80 of Ernst Gombrich *Art and Illusion* (5th edition, Oxford, 1977). Illuminating discussions of Pygmalion are those of E. W. Leach 'Ekphrasis and the theme of artistic failure in Ovid's *Metamorphoses*' *Ramus* 3 (1974) 102–47, especially 124–5; John Elsner and Alison Sharrock 'Re-Viewing Pygmalion' *Ramus* 20 (1991) 154–80, quotation from 165–6; A. R. Sharrock 'Womanufacture' *Journal of Roman Studies* 81 (1991) 36–49, quotation from 48; Jane Miller 'Some versions of Pygmalion' in *Ovid Renewed* (edited by C. Martindale, Cambridge, 1988) 205–14. We can also study Pygmalion in art; for example, besides the Burne-Jones series, there is the painting by Gérôme; and in music we have the opera *Pygmalion* by the philosopher Jean-Jacques Rousseau (1775), not to mention W. S. Gilbert's *Pygmalion and Galatea: an entirely original mythological comedy in three acts* (1870).

For the reading of Seneca's tragedies as *mise en abyme* see Alessandro Schiesaro 'Passion, reason and knowledge in Seneca's tragedies' in *The Passions in Roman Thought and Literature* (edited by Susanna Morton Braund and Christopher Gill, Cambridge, 1997) pages 89–111, using the definition of Lucien Dällenbach in *The Mirror in the Text* (translated by J. Whitely and E. Hughes, Cambridge, 1989) page 8. A. J. Boyle *Tragic Seneca: an Essay in the Theatrical Tradition* (London and New York, 1997) chapter 6 'The theatricalised wor(l)d' also has extensive discussion of metatheatre in Seneca.

On Apuleius' prologue see *A Companion to the Prologue of Apuleius' Metamorphoses* (edited by Ahuvia Kahane and Andrew Laird, Oxford, 2001). A central book on Apuleius is J. J. Winkler

Auctor & Actor: A Narratological Reading of Apuleius' The Golden Ass (Berkeley and Los Angeles, 1985).

Harold Bloom's influential writings include *The Anxiety of Influence* (New York, 1973) and *A Map of Misreading* (New York, 1975), especially chapter 4 where he discusses 'The belatedness of strong poetry', for example, 'The affliction of belatedness, as I have begun to recognize, is a recurrent malaise in Western consciousness' (page 77).

Many other Latin texts provide rich material for metapoetic readings, especially in the genres of reflective poetry such as love elegy, pastoral and satire. You could explore the links between the character Cynthia and Propertius' literary project in poems such as 2.10–13 (on which see Maria Wyke's article, 'Written women: Propertius' *scripta puella*' *Journal of Roman Studies* 77 (1987) 47–61). A different kind of metapoetics may be operating in Ovid *Loves* 2.6, a lament for a dead pet parrot, which should be read with Stephen Hinds' 'Generalising about Ovid' *Ramus* 16 (1987) 4–31. Another good topic for discussion is furnished by Emily Gowers' discussion of Horace *Satires* 1.5, 'Horace, *Satires* 1.5: an inconsequential journey' *Proceedings of the Cambridge Philological Society* 39 (1993) 48–66: a class could debate whether or not they are convinced by this kind of reading. And a study of Silenus' song in Virgil *Eclogue* 6 and of the depiction of Gallus in *Eclogues* 6 and 10 has rich metapoetic potential.

Chapter 13

Allegory

13.1   For my third chapter devoted to the self-consciousness shown by Latin literature I turn to the trope, or figure of speech, called allegory. Allegory is a term of literary criticism which derives from the Greek word *allegoria*, 'saying one thing and meaning another'. The term itself dates from the first century BCE and seems to have replaced an earlier term, *hyponoia*, which we can readily translate as 'under-sense'. A modern definition describes allegory as 'a trope in which a second meaning is to be read beneath and concurrent with the surface story'. It goes on to distinguish allegory from metaphor and from parable through the extent of its story, which may connect with the surface narrative, citing as examples *The Faerie Queene* by Edmund Spenser (1590–6) and *The Pilgrim's Progress* by John Bunyan (1678–84). For the Latin professor Quintilian in the first century CE, the relationship between allegory and metaphor seems to be closer, and he also regards allegory and irony as interconnected:

> 'Allegory', which is translated in Latin as 'inversion', either presents one thing in words and another in meaning or else something at the same time opposite.
>
> (Quintilian *Training of the Orator* 8.6.44)

13.2 Straight away he gives an example, using Horace *Odes* 1.14.1–3:

> The first type is generally produced by a sequence of metaphors, as in:
>
>> O ship, you will be driven seaward again by fresh
>> Waves. O what are you doing? Bravely make haste to
>>> reach
>> Harbour,
>
> and the rest of the ode, in which Horace uses a ship in place of the state and storms in place of the civil wars as tempests and the harbour in place of peace and cooperation.

This allegory of 'the ship of state' was not an invention by Horace. He models this ode, like many others, on the poems of Alcaeus, a Greek lyric poet from Lesbos writing in the sixth century BCE. We know that Alcaeus' poems were read allegorically in antiquity and we can be confident that Horace and his well-educated readership were familiar with this interpretation and able to read the deeper political 'message'. And by the way, the image at the heart of this allegory persists in the English language to this day: the Latin word *gubernator*, from which we derive 'governor', literally denotes the 'helmsman' of a ship.

13.3 In a case like this, allegory clearly refers to a method of creation and a method of interpretation. But in some older cases of ancient allegorical readings, allegory seems to operate at the point of critical reception rather than authorial intention. This is particularly so in the case of Homer's *Iliad*, a text which was the centrepiece of education throughout antiquity, the close equivalent of the Bible in later, Christian, times, as a reading of the opening of Horace *Epistles* 1.2 will show. But some people were disturbed by Homer's stories of immoral behaviour by the gods, such as their stealing, committing adultery, deceiving one another and fighting. So they devised allegorical interpretations to defend Homer from attack on moral grounds, trying to make him into a proto-philosopher. Denis Feeney provides a full and lucid account of the history of allegorical interpretations of Homer in the opening chapter of *The Gods in Epic* (1991). Here we need only note that these allegorical readings took two forms – physical and ethical. The gods were read either as physical elements – Apollo as fire, Poseidon as water, Artemis as the moon and Hera as air – or as abstract ethical qualities – Athena as wisdom, Ares as battle-lust, Aphrodite as passion, Hermes as reason – with allegory here shading into personification and rationalization. Similar interpretations were also applied to the Bible in antiquity, for example, the reading which sees God's creation of Adam and Eve as an allegory of the creation of 'mind' and 'sense perception' and the serpent in the garden as an allegory of 'pleasure'. The importance of all this for our study of Latin literature is that this kind of sophisticated textual interpretation was part of the intellectual environment of writers and their audiences. To give just one illustration, the Stoic philosopher Cornutus, who was the teacher of Persius the satirist and Lucan the epic poet, not only wrote commentaries on Virgil but also an allegorical interpretation of Greek mythology (his one extant work).

13.4   Most of this chapter will draw examples of allegory in Latin texts from poetry written in hexameters – Lucretius' *On the Nature of the Universe*, Virgil's *Eclogues* and *Aeneid*, Statius' *Thebaid* and Prudentius' *Soul-Battle*. This introduction to allegorical interpretations of these texts will complement the material in the previous two chapters to demonstrate again the sophistication of these highly educated poets and of their audiences. Of course, in the case of allegory, it is possible to belong to the audience that reads only on the surface level. I hope to show the benefits in appreciating these literary artefacts that come from a fuller understanding of the multiple levels of meaning.

13.5   Let's go straight to the opening scene of Virgil's *Aeneid* and see how allegory can inform our reading of this text. The epic starts with Juno. Juno is a complex figure: she is the Homeric Hera, sister and wife of the king of the gods and enemy of the Trojan nation; she is the Carthaginian goddess Tanit, championing her city against its future Roman rivals; and she is the allegorical representation of air (in Latin *aer*), the lower air which was the realm of storms. In accordance with her (multiple) nature, then, Juno's first act in the poem is to provoke the storm that wrecks Aeneas' fleet on the coast of Carthage by persuading Aeolus, king of the winds, to let them loose (*Aeneid* 1.50–80). Philip Hardie has demonstrated how the storm episode is saturated with allegory inspired by interpretations of another revered and ancient Greek poem, Hesiod's *Theogony*. Hesiod's picture of the rebel Titans imprisoned after their defeat by Zeus was interpreted as an allegory of storm-winds held in check by divine providence. Hardie argues that Virgil evokes these interpretations by representing the storm-winds as confined beneath a mountain by Jupiter (*Aeneid* 1.60–3) and unleashed by Juno's intervention with Aeolus. This is a useful reminder that apparently simple narratives can operate on multiple levels of meaning.

13.6   Another example which demonstrates awareness of the potential of allegorical readings is found in the finale to Book 3 of Lucretius' *On the Nature of the Universe* (lines 978–1023). As mentioned in Chapter 8.19, Lucretius had set himself the task of expounding the philosophy of Epicurus to promote human happiness. One of his central concerns is to destroy the fear of death widely experienced by human beings. To make his case that 'all those torments that are said to take place in the depths of Hell | are actually present here and now' (3.978–9), Lucretius interprets the horrendous stories of mythology that people tell one another as allegories, allegories which actually relate to life before death, not to the afterlife. On his reading, Tantalus with his terror of a rock hanging over him is the equivalent of the superstitious coward, Tityos with his liver pecked non-stop by birds is the equivalent of the jealous and obsessive lover, Sisyphus rolling his stone up the mountain is the equivalent of the ambitious but failing politician, and the Danaids trying to fill leaky vessels with water are the equivalent of anyone 'for ever feeding a malcontent mind, filling it with good things but never satisfying it'. In this case, Lucretius is not so much creating an allegorical text but providing an allegorical interpretation of traditional stories.

13.7   Another kind of allegorical reading is invoked in the case of Virgil's *Eclogues*. Virgil developed the genre of pastoral from the experimental form associated with the Greek poet Theocritus writing in Alexandria in the third century BCE (to be discussed further in

Chapter 14.13–14). As its name suggests, this type of poetry typically had a rustic setting and was peopled by herdsmen singing songs. In Virgil's hands the genre becomes a vehicle of moral and political messages, some of which seem to feature Virgil and his contemporaries, not directly, but through allegory. Ancient readers of Virgil along with the commentators were in no doubt about the allegorical level of these poems. Quintilian, for example, cites *Eclogues* 9.7–10 (here in Guy Lee's translation) like this:

> On the other hand, in the Eclogues Virgil introduces allegory without any metaphor:
>
>> Surely I'd heard that everything, from where the hills
>> Begin to drop down, sloping gently from the ridge,
>> Right to the water and the old beeches' broken crowns –
>> That all this your Menalcas salvaged with his songs?
>
> That is, in this passage, with the exception of the proper name, the words bear no more than their literal meaning. But Menalcas is to be understood as referring to not the shepherd but Virgil himself.
>
> (Quintilian *Training of the Orator* 8.6.46–7)

Apuleius (*Apology* 10) tells us that through the masks of the herdsman Corydon and the young city boy Alexis in *Eclogue* 2 Virgil is expressing his feelings for a slave boy who belonged to his patron Pollio. The commentary written by the schoolteacher Servius in the fourth century propounds an allegorical reading of the *Eclogues* and his source, the grammarian Donatus, took the view that allegory could be found 'neither nowhere nor everywhere'.

13.8   Clearly it is possible to take different views of where allegory begins and ends. Some allegorical readings of the *Eclogues* – or of any text – will seem more persuasive than others. But what is fascinating is that some modern scholars have resisted absolutely this kind of interpretation, especially where an allegorical reading would politicize the text of Virgil. Perhaps the clearest example of this occurs in *Eclogue* 5. The poem contains two balancing 'songs' sung to one another in a spirit of friendly rivalry by a younger man, Mopsus, and an older man, Menalcas. Mopsus' song, which is indebted to the lament for Daphnis in Theocritus *Idyll* 1, is a lament about the death of Daphnis, who was clearly the revered leader and Master Shepherd of the rustic community. Menalcas' song celebrates Daphnis' deification and promises ritual worship by the rustic community for the future. Nothing disrupts the pastoral framework. And yet an allegorical reading gives the poem a telling political dimension. To see this we need to set the poem in its historical context. In the late 40s BCE, the most significant political event in the Roman world was surely the assassination of Julius Caesar (March 44 BCE) – and his subsequent deification on 1 January 42 BCE. The telling passage that supports an allegorical reading of Daphnis as Julius Caesar comes in the middle of Menalcas' song:

> Daphnis in white admires Olympus' unfamiliar threshold,
> and sees the planets and the clouds beneath his feet.
> Therefore keen pleasure grips forest and countryside,
> Pan too and the shepherds and the Dryad maidens.
> The wolf plans no ambush for the flock, the nets
> no snare for the deer: Daphnis the good loves peace.
> In joy even the unshorn mountains fling their voices
> toward the stars; now even the orchards, even the rocks
> echo the song: 'A god, a god is he, Menalcas!'
> O bless your folk and make them prosper! Here are four altars:
> look, Daphnis, two for you and two high ones for Phoebus.
> Two goblets each, frothing with fresh milk, every year
> and two large bowls of olive oil I'll set for you,
> and, best of all, making the feast merry with plentiful Bacchus
> (in winter, by the hearth; at harvest, in the shade),
> I'll pour Ariusian wine, fresh nectar, from big stoups.
>   (Virgil *Eclogues* 5.56–71, adapted from Guy Lee)

The Games for Apollo (*Ludi Apollinares*) were celebrated on 6–13 July, with the final day, which was also Caesar's birthday, the principal day of celebration. In 42 BCE a Sibylline oracle recommended that Caesar's birthday be celebrated on 12 July to avoid this clash (Dio *Roman History* 47.18.6). Virgil's association in a single line of verse of the altars to Daphnis and to Phoebus Apollo seems an unmistakable invitation to connect with contemporary events. In the words of Robert Coleman in his commentary on the *Eclogues*: 'It is incredible that anyone in the late 40s could have read a pastoral poem on this theme without thinking of Caesar.'

13.9   While the allegorical, political dimension of *Eclogue* 5 seems to me beyond doubt, that does not mean that we have to press every detail about Daphnis to make it fit Julius Caesar in some kind of mechanical way. As Charles Martindale appositely says in his discussion of the political dimension of the *Eclogues* in his essay 'Green politics', 'allegory is precisely a figure of disjunction'. The same goes for the other poems in Virgil's pastoral book susceptible of an allegorical reading, poems in which he expresses views about politics and about poetry (*Eclogues* 1, 4, 6, 9 and 10). The point about allegory is that it creates two levels of text, a surface level and a submerged level.

13.10   Later writers followed Virgil's lead in deploying pastoral as a vehicle for political and poetic allegory, with more or less subtlety. The Neronian poet, Calpurnius Siculus, incorporates panegyric of his patron and the emperor into his *Eclogues*. In the revival of pastoral during the Renaissance, Petrarch (1304–74) and others composed *Eclogues* in Latin and in their vernacular languages rich in references to other poets and their contemporaries. Spenser's *Shepheardes Calendar* (1579) includes panegyric and church allegory alongside the standard singing competitions of pastoral. This takes us readily to another important manifestation of allegory in Latin texts – religious allegory. I shall conclude this discussion of allegory by considering briefly three different cases of religious allegory in Latin texts: Apuleius' *Metamorphoses*, Statius' *Thebaid*, and Prudentius' *Soul-Battle*.

13.11   In a nutshell, Apuleius' *Metamorphoses* tells the story of the narrator Lucius' fascination with magic, his transformation into an ass when a magic spell goes wrong (Books 1–3), and the adventures he has while trying to get changed back into human form (Books 4–10). It culminates with his metamorphosis from ass to man through the intervention of the goddess Isis (Book 11). The story is apparently based on an original in Greek which has survived from antiquity and so allows us to set the two texts side by side. What this reveals is that, in the Greek version, there was nothing resembling Lucius' religious conversion to Isis in Book 11 of Apuleius. It seems very likely, though certainty is impossible, that the religious conversion is Apuleius' original contribution to the story. Does this make any difference to how we read the rest of the novel? I think it does, or can. I think it offers an invitation, at the least, to go back and reconsider the earlier parts of the novel in the light of how it ends. When we discover that the ass was an animal seen as demonic by the devotees of Isis and her divine consort Osiris, as Plutarch tells us, then we can start to see that Lucius' metamorphosis into an ass might have an allegorical significance, alongside the fact that it makes for a hilarious story in its own right. The theme of religious conversion and salvation can also affect our reading of the long folktale of Cupid and Psyche which dominates the central books of the novel. And we might also recall the reference to 'Egyptian papyrus' in the prologue (discussed in Chapter 12.15–19) and feel that Apuleius has planted a clue right at the start telling us to look a little deeper at the religious dimension of the narrative.

13.12 Backtracking from the mid-second to the late first century CE, we find a different kind of religious allegory in the *Thebaid* of Statius, his twelve-book epic version of the story treated in Greek epic and drama, for example, by Aeschylus in his play *Seven Against Thebes*. In a rich and under-appreciated poem, Statius depicts the feud between the two sons of Oedipus, Eteocles and Polynices, in which Eteocles refuses to allow Polynices his turn as ruler of Thebes, thus causing Polynices to raise an army and march on Thebes. Statius is treating traditional material, but he brings a radically new approach. As C. S. Lewis saw in *The Allegory of Love*, in Statius' hands the gods move towards becoming personifications and personifications begin to occupy the space vacated by the gods. From Denis Feeney's sympathetic and persuasive discussion of allegory in the *Thebaid*, I draw just two examples, that of Mars and that of the Furies.

13.13 Statius' depiction of Mars in the *Thebaid* sees the god altered from a divine character who has particular motivations for his interventions in the fighting – the kind of character he is in Homer, where Ares is a Trojan partisan, and in Virgil, where Mars is, among other things, the national god of Rome as the father of Romulus and Remus. Instead, he is represented as 'an embodiment of the madness which is activating the human characters' (Feeney). Feeney argues that Statius draws attention to his innovation by having Venus try to stop him:

> On Thebes shall you bring war, you, illustrious
> father of her first queen – war to decimate
> your own descendants? Do Harmonia's
> own offspring, or heaven's happy wedding feast,
> or these tears of mine, you madman, give you no brief pause?
> > (Statius *Thebaid* 3.269–72, adapted
> > from A. D. Melville)

In Feeney's words, 'she is asking him, in effect, "Have you quite forgotten your mythological personality and allegiances? Are you now nothing more than an allegory?"'.

13.14 As Mars shifts towards the allegorical personification of battle-lust, so the allegorical personifications of earlier epic take over the role of prime movers in Statius' narrative. *Virtus* (Excellence) and *Pietas* (Devotion), for example, appear on the battlefield and intervene in the action. At 10.628–77 *Virtus* visits Menoeceus to tell him to offer himself as a sacrifice on behalf of his people:

> > So she spoke
> and as he wavered placed her hand upon
> his breast to cheer him silently and left
> herself within his heart. And he, as swiftly
> as a lightning-blasted cypress drinks the flame
> from stem to summit, mightily inspired,
> his spirit soaring, seized the love of death.
> > (Statius *Thebaid* 10.672–7)

At 11.457–96 Pietas attempts to prevent the internecine battle between
the brothers:

> From the sky she leapt and under the dark clouds
> her trail was white, despite her sorrow.
> She had no sooner landed than a sudden peace
> softened the armies and they knew their crime.
> Tears poured down cheeks and breasts and horror stole
> in silence deep into the brothers' hearts.
>> (Statius *Thebaid* 11.472–6)

13.15   At the same time, Statius takes the Furies, Tisiphone and
Megaera, and gives to these highly allegorical figures the central role
in the terrible duel between the two brothers in Book 11. Statius is
explicit about this displacement:

> So on the field the guilt of kindred stood,
> huge conflict of one womb, helmeted faces paired.
> Then standards quaked, the trumpets silenced, horns
> dumbfounded. Three times the avid lord of Hell
> thundered from his dark shores and three times shook the
>> world's
> foundations. Even the gods of battle fled.
> Nowhere was glorious Valour, far away
> Mars rushed his frightened horses, the War-goddess
> put out her torches and Pallas, Gorgon-fierce,
> withdrew, and in their places came the Stygian sisters.
>> (Statius *Thebaid* 11.407–15)

Even more graphic is the rout of Pietas by Tisiphone:

> She made some impact on their doubts until
> wild Tisiphone observed her disguise
> and swifter than heaven's flame was at her side,
> rebuking: 'Why should you obstruct war's feats,
> you sluggard deity, obsessed with peace?
> Begone, for shame! This is my field, my day.

You come to guilty Thebes' defence too late.
Where were you then, when Bacchus summoned war,
and orgies maddened the mothers whom he armed?'
                                    . . . At this
the goddess quailed abashed and, as she shrank
recoiling, in her face the Fury thrust
her torch and hissing snakes. Over her eyes
she drew her robe and fled to heaven above
to protest to almighty Jupiter.
                        (Statius *Thebaid* 11.482–8 and 492–6)

As Feeney says:

> Tisiphone and her sister Megaera are far more than avengers
> of blood-guilt, as they were originally in Greek thought, and in
> the early versions of the Theban myth. Under the pressure of
> Vergil's, Ovid's, and Seneca's creations, Statius' Furies represent
> every evil of which human beings are capable. As narrative
> embodiments of attributes of human nature which are regarded
> as timeless, they demand to be read allegorically. . . . [Statius is
> engaged in] an experiment in universalizing the moral experi-
> ences described in the action. . . . For modern readers, with
> our knowledge of the subsequent development of allegory, the
> confrontation of Pietas and Tisiphone is a numinous moment.
> One has the sense of being present at the birth of an entire
> tradition of composition, and the tingle in one's spine is increased
> by the realization that Statius is utterly – arrogantly – in com-
> mand of this manner of composition.

13.16 Feeney is right: Statius' allegorical mode of composition was
taken up and developed by later writers, especially writers with a
Christian message. I conclude this chapter by glancing at just one such
example, the *Soul-Battle*, a Christian poem consisting of 915 epic
hexameters on the struggle between the Vices and the Virtues in the
human soul, written by the lawyer and civil servant Prudentius in
the fourth century CE. The poem features epic-style duels between
allegorical personifications, including Faith versus Idolatry, Chastity

versus Lust, Patience versus Anger and Humility versus Arrogance. Prudentius seems to revel in gruesome detail. For example, when Faith strangles Idolatry, her eyes pop out:

> Look! Pagan Idolatry, challenged by Faith
> to a test of strength, dares strike the first blow.
> But rising to her full height, Faith strikes to the ground her
>   enemy's
> head and hair adorned with heathen fillets and crushes in the
>   dirt
> that face fed on the blood of sacrificial beasts and with her foot
> she tramples the eyes bulging in death, and the scarce breath
> is strangled by the broken passage of the blocked windpipe,
> and drawn-out gasps make an exhausting and difficult death.
> The victorious troops leap for joy, amassed from a thousand
> martyrs by their queen Faith for inspiration against their foe.
>   (Prudentius *Soul-Battle* 28–37)

13.17   The Christian message is conveyed by the speeches put into the mouths of the victorious Virtues, for example, when Chastity revels in her defeat of Lust:

> 'A hit!,' shouts the victorious queen. 'This will be
> your final end, you will lie prostrate for ever,
> no more will you scatter those fatal flames
> against the servants and maidservants of God – the inmost veins
> of their pure souls blaze with the torch of Christ . . .
>   (Prudentius *Soul-Battle* 53–7)

– and so on for another forty lines.

13.18   Prudentius concludes the poem by apparently acknowledging the allegory he has created:

> Dreadful wars are blazing, they blaze
> within our bones, human nature in its internal conflict boils
> with rebellion. The body's guts, crafted

from clay, oppress the mind, while the mind, created
from pure breath, seethes in its dark prison of the heart
and in its tight chains it rejects the body's filth.
With their opposing spirits light and darkness fight
and our twofold substance inspires the opposing forces
until Christ our God comes to help by placing all
the jewels of the Virtues in a purified setting
and by establishing his golden-halled temple where sin has
     reigned
and creating from the sight of its morality
adornments for the soul which so delight Wisdom
who will reign for ever, rich on her beautiful throne.

                    (Prudentius *Soul-Battle* 902–15)

What we are seeing here is the adaptation of the Virtues from Roman polytheism to Christian monotheism, an adaptation for which the pagan epic of Statius perhaps prepared the ground. The significant difference is that, whereas in pagan literature the personified Virtues were forces of the cosmos, in Christian literature they are confined to the soul. As Marcus Wilson says in an essay on 'The Virtues at Rome', 'pagan theology became Christian psychology' and 'the individual becomes a militarized zone, split between the Virtues, on the one side, and Vices, Passions or Sin on the other. In the world of *Soul-Battle* there is no individual at all, except as a battle in progress.'

13.19   And this allegorical message struck home. The vividness of Prudentius' narrative pictures inspired iconographic and literary representations of individual Virtues and Vices through the Middle Ages and the Renaissance. This is evident in the many illustrated manuscripts of Prudentius, an example of which is shown in Figure 8, including the passage cited at 13.16 above, which in turn inspired representations of the cycle of virtues and vices such as that on the central porch of the façade of Notre Dame Cathedral in Paris, dating from the early thirteenth century, shown in Figure 9. So in the 1530s Andrea Alciato published his influential *Book of Emblems* which combined pictures and epigrams conveying allegorical interpretations of the pictures. So, too, Spenser in *The Faerie Queene* presents the

FIGURE 8 Prudentius *Psychomachia* (Cotton MSS Cleopatra C VIII, folio 7b)

By permission of the British Library

FIGURE 9   Cycle of virtues and vices on Notre Dame Cathedral, central porch

Courtesy of Giraudon/Art Resource NY

adventures of the knights of Queen Elizabeth I in allegorical form, with, for example, Sir Guyon, the Knight of Temperance, visiting the Cave of Mammon and destroying Acrasia (an allegory for Intemperance) and her Bower of Bliss (Book 2). This kind of allegorical representation has also left a profound legacy to later European society, shaping the way in which we view the Virtues as personal qualities and as national emblems. Justice and Temperance and Fortitude and Prudence are with us still, in mottoes and in crests and in logos.

Further reading and study

The fullest discussion of allegory in Latin literature is probably Denis Feeney *The Gods in Epic* (Oxford, 1991) pages 5–56. For discussion of the storm episode in *Aeneid* 1 see Philip Hardie *Virgil's Aeneid: Cosmos and Imperium* (Oxford, 1986) pages 90–7 and Feeney's synopsis of the same material at pages 132–3. On allegory of the *Eclogues* see R. J. Starr 'Vergil's seventh *Eclogue* and its readers: biographical allegory as an interpretative strategy in antiquity and late antiquity' *Classical Philology* 90 (1995) 129–38. The quotation from Robert Coleman comes from his commentary on the *Eclogues* (Cambridge, 1977) page 173, and that from Charles Martindale is from his essay 'Green politics' in *The Cambridge Companion to Virgil* (edited by Charles Martindale, Cambridge 1997) 107–24 at page 117.

For C. S. Lewis' views of Statius' *Thebaid* see *The Allegory of Love* (Oxford, 1936) especially pages 49–50. My discussion is inspired by Feeney pages 364–91 (quotations from pages 367, 368, 377, 380–1 and 389).

For a modern perspective on the Virtues along with insightful discussion of the Virtues throughout western culture, see the artist Megan Jenkinson's pictures in *Under the Aegis: The Virtues* (Auckland, 1997) and the essays that accompany them. Of these, especially relevant is Marcus Wilson 'The Virtues at Rome' pages 125–35 (quotation from page 135); and Denis Drysdall '*Emblema Quid?* What is an emblem?' discusses Alciato's *Book of Emblems*.

One crucial issue raised by allegory is the question of whether it resides in authorial intent or at the point of reception. Another relates to the impermeability (or otherwise) of the surface of an allegorical work: do we think that the surface level should be self-consistent, or is it acceptable to include a few hints at an allegorical reading? This becomes especially important if the submerged message is at all controversial. Further study topics that arise include the moral and religious dimensions of Apuleius' *Metamorphoses*: do the adventures of Lucius while he is in the form of a donkey relate to his religious conversion to Isis with which the novel closes? And what kinds of allegorical readings have been suggested for the story of Cupid and Psyche at the centre of the novel?

Another related issue is the allegorical use of drama. A famous example from Roman times is the danger incurred by the orator-turned-poet Maternus by giving a reading from his play *Cato*, which is clearly depicted by Tacitus as a politically threatening subject in court circles. Maternus' courageous response to warnings by his friends is to promise an excerpt from his *Thyestes* at his next reading – an even more politically sensitive theme (*Dialogue of Orators* 2–3). Similarly, we know that Greek tragedies such as Sophocles' *Antigone* were staged under the rule of the Colonels in Greece during the 1970s with the apparent intention of conveying an anti-autocratic message through a medium which could not be objected to by the authorities. It would be an exciting project to search out classical works that could be endowed with a contemporary political message for our own times through allegorical readings.

Chapter 14

Overcoming an inferiority complex: the relationship with Greek literature

14.1 The debt of Latin literature to Greek literature is inescapable. Throughout the chapters of this book, time and again, I have mentioned that Roman authors use Greek texts as models and patterns and treat them as a source of authority and of challenge (see especially Chapters 3 and 11). The Roman attitude towards Greek models is a blend of imitation (*imitatio*) and competition (*aemulatio*). Whichever attitude dominated, for Roman authors, Greek literature was (almost) always there, from the first beginnings of Latin literature in the third century BCE through the fourth century CE when we find the poet Claudian going back to Greek literature for mythological themes. It was a relationship as inevitable as that between a child and its parents. And like that relationship, it was often felt in terms of Rome's inferiority to Greece. A key quotation from Horace's discussion of Latin poetry makes that sentiment clear:

> Captured Greece took captive her rough conqueror
> and brought the arts to rustic Latium. Then the primitive
> metre of Saturn ran dry and cleanliness drove out
> the fetid smell, though all the same for many years
> there remained, and still remain today, signs of the farmyard.
>
> (Horace *Epistles* 2.1.156–60)

And this attitude persisted even after Latin literature clearly had some 'classics' of its own to set alongside the classics of Greek literature. So much is clear from the way in which Quintilian describes his ideal school curriculum in his *Training of the Orator* (10.1.37–131). He assumes the superiority or at least the priority of the study of Greek literature when he discusses the ideal Greek authors for the school student first (10.1.46–84) and only afterwards moves on to discuss the ideal Latin authors (10.1.85–131). What is more, his discussion of Latin authors is conducted entirely in relation to their Greek predecessors, as we see in his remarks on, for example, elegy and tragedy:

> In elegy too we challenge the supremacy of the Greeks. Of our elegiac poets Tibullus seems to me the most terse and elegant. But there are people who prefer Propertius. Ovid is more playful than either, while Gallus is more severe. ... The *Thyestes* of Varius is a match for any Greek tragedy and Ovid's *Medea* suggests to me his potential for excellence if he had been prepared to control his talent rather than indulge it.
>
> (Quintilian *Training of the Orator*
> 10.1.93 and 98)

The only exception to this is the case of Roman satire, with no exact Greek precedent (though plenty of Greek inspiration), where Quintilian proudly declares at the start of his discussion (10.1.93): 'Satire is entirely ours'. In this penultimate chapter of the book, I shall start by adopting Quintilian's – and the Roman – backwards perspective with a focus upon two particular manifestations of the relationship with Greek literature: the reworking of Greek tragedy by Roman poets and the arrival at Rome of the poetic principles of the poets of the Ptolemaic court at Alexandria in Egypt. In both cases I shall argue that the Latin poets took their Greek originals as an inspiration that did not shackle them but opened up new creative possibilities that would speak to a Roman literary audience. I shall conclude the chapter with a discussion of the different models we use to categorize ancient texts and with the suggestion that Latin literature has developed from its origins in Greek literature to prove a remarkably flexible vehicle for the culture's concerns. Then the final chapter will seal the book with the coming of age of Latin poetry in the form of triumphal assertions of immortality expressed by three Augustan poets.

14.2 One of the most remarkable features of Greek tragedy – the name we often give to what should more correctly be called Attic tragedy, since it was specifically produced in and for the Athenian dramatic festivals in Attica of the fifth century BCE – is the number of strong female characters. This is remarkable because it does not reflect women's role in Athenian society, a society in which 'democracy' meant that playing a role in public life was confined to only the men of a relatively small number of clans. (It is estimated that less than one in ten of the population of Attica enjoyed full political rights.) In short, there was no place for the visible and outspoken female in democratic Athens. But Athenian tragedy has a plethora of them – Antigone, Cassandra, Clytemnestra, Electra, Hecuba, Helen and, above all, Medea. Of these, the story of Medea seems to have exerted a special fascination on Roman dramatists and poets. Dramatists early in the history of Latin literature including Ennius, Pacuvius and Accius tried their hands at recasting the famous play of Euripides, for example:

> truly I would rather risk my life three times in battle
> than give birth just once.
>
> (Ennius *Medea* 269–70)

This fascination continued during the early empire too, with Ovid handling the story at least three times in different genres – in his *Letters of Heroines* 12, his epic poem *Metamorphoses* (7.1–424) and in a tragedy, *Medea*, which sadly does not survive – and with Seneca the philosopher and tutor to the young Nero also writing a tragedy, as discussed above in Chapter 10.

14.3 I shall return to the persistent influence of the Medea of Greek literature in a moment. But first, let me draw attention to another important feature of Greek tragedy. The stories which provide the material for Athenian tragedy are mostly set in a distant past of kings and heroes. And yet it is clear that the tragedians shaped the treatment of their material to link with contemporary concerns in the fifth-century democratic city state of Athens. One telling example is the *Oresteia* by Aeschylus, a trilogy dealing with the return home to Argos of King Agamemnon after the Trojan War, his murder by his wife Clytemnestra and her lover Aegisthus, and the vengeance enacted by Agamemnon's son Orestes. Towards the end of the third play in the trilogy, there seems to be no end in sight to this cycle of revenge killings as the Furies, the primitive goddesses of the vendetta, hound Orestes for the murder of his mother. Orestes goes to Athens for refuge and there his case is heard in the homicide court, where he is acquitted when Athena gives the casting vote. This play, then, celebrates the Athenian practice of trial by jury as an advance on the primitive practice of the vendetta and demonstrates how the material of Greek myth could be harnessed to current concerns. We find the same phenomenon in Roman adaptations of Greek tragedy.

14.4   This is especially true in the plays which deal with the quality of kingship exercised by a ruler. Many of Seneca's plays confront issues of good and bad kingship. These were undoubtedly live issues among the Roman elite at this period, as we can see from the ways that the emperors themselves attempted to manipulate their own and their predecessors' images and the ways that their advisers attempted to influence their behaviour by appealing to models of good and bad rule. The literature produced around the accession of Nero in 54 CE provides the clearest proof of this concern with the nature of kingship, for example in Seneca's satire against the deceased emperor Claudius in his *Pumpkinification* and in his essay *On Clemency* which he addressed to the new emperor Nero, in which he urged the exercise of self-control. In his plays, which were written under the emperors Claudius and/or Nero (we have no sure way of dating them precisely), Seneca depicts graphic cases of corrupt and immoral kingship, for example the tyrant Lycus in *Mad Hercules*, Agamemnon in *Trojan Women* and especially Atreus in *Thyestes.* And at times he explicitly raises the question of how the ideal king should behave. For instance, early in his *Oedipus* he makes Jocasta reproach Oedipus for not behaving like a proper king with his despondency about the plague which is afflicting Thebes and which he fears he has somehow caused:

> Oedipus, my husband. What use is complaining?
> It only makes bad things worse. To my mind the essence of
>   being a king
> is to take on challenges. The more your throne trembles,
> the faster your power and majesty slip into decline, then all the
>   more
> fearlessly you should take your stand, controlled, unwavering.
> Running away is not behaviour for a man.
>
> > (Seneca *Oedipus* 81–6, adapted from
> > David Anthony Turner's translation)

In other words, Seneca has taken the material of Greek tragedy and adapted it to specific Roman concerns that would have been eloquent to his audience of the Roman elite.

14.5   This concern with the nature of monarchy is perhaps one of the features that made Seneca's plays so popular and influential with English playwrights of the Renaissance. It is clear that Shakespeare and other Elizabethan and Jacobean dramatists were influenced and inspired by Seneca's tragedies, which were translated into English by Jasper Heywood and others from the 1560s onwards. As Polonius says in Act II, Scene ii of *Hamlet*, 'Seneca cannot be too heavy'. Familiarity with Seneca helps to explain the marked shift from sacred to secular themes in drama of the late sixteenth century and the intense focus upon the themes of revenge and absolute power, themes manifested in plays such as *Titus Andronicus* and *Macbeth*, *Richard III* and *King Lear*. My example comes not from Shakespeare but from his younger contemporary, the poet and dramatist John Marston (perhaps 1575–1634). Here Marston adapts a passage from Seneca's *Thyestes* where he has the Chorus reflect upon the nature of ideal kingship (339–403) and introduces it into his play *Antonio and Mellida*:

> Why man, I never was a Prince till now.
> Tis not the bared pate, the bended knees,
> Guilt tipstaves, Tyrrian purple, chaires of state,
> Troopes of pide butterflies, that flutter still
> In greatnesse summer, that confirme a prince:

Tis not the unsavory breath of multitudes,
Showting and clapping, with confused dinne;
That makes a Prince. No, *Lucio*, he's a king,
A true right king, that dares doe aught, save wrong,
Feares nothing mortall, but to be unjust,
Who is not blowne up with the flattering puffes
Of spungy Sycophants: Who stands unmov'd,
Despight the justling of opinion:
Who can enjoy himselfe, maugre the throng
That strive to presse his quiet out of him:
Who sits upon *Joves* footstoole, as I doe,
Adoring, not affecting, majestie.

(Marston *Antonio and Mellida* IV i 46–62)

The playwrights of the Renaissance found in Seneca's tragedies material that would speak to the socio-political concerns of their own times, just as Seneca (and the other Roman tragedians) had seen that material from Athenian tragedy could be adapted to make it alive and contemporary. Seneca was immersed in his predecessors in the genre, but he was never overwhelmed by them.

14.6   Now I want to return to the story of Medea, leaving the direct relationship between Seneca and Greek tragedy to look at the indirect relationship between Greek and Latin literature, again with the intention of showing how the implicit inferiority complex was overcome. I shall demonstrate how the portrayal of Medea in Greek literature influenced Virgil's depiction in his *Aeneid* of Dido, the queen of Carthage and lover of Aeneas for one winter (see Chapter 1.5, 1.7).

14.7   Another important treatment of the Medea story in Greek literature besides Euripides' tragedy was the epic *Journey of the Argonauts* written by Apollonius of Rhodes, one of the coterie of Greek scholar-poets who gathered at the Greek court of Ptolemy II Philadelphus at Alexandria in Egypt during the late third century BCE. (We shall meet some of the other important 'Alexandrian' poets later in this chapter.) Apollonius took the classic narrative of Jason and the Argonauts and made from it an innovative kind of epic, in which the hero was not a superman but an all-too-human character with weaknesses and failings. And when he treated the theme of the liaison between Jason and Medea he created a sensitive portrait of a young woman falling in love against her better judgement. He used a striking simile to convey her emotional turmoil:

> Then night drew darkness over the earth, and on the sea
> sailors from their ships looked towards the Bear
> and the stars of Orion, and now the traveller and doorkeeper
> longed for sleep, and a pall of slumber enfolded
> the mother whose children were dead,
> and through the city there was no barking of dogs or echoing
> voices, but silence held the blackening gloom.
> But Medea was not overtaken by sweet sleep.
> In her desire for Aeson's son, many anxieties kept her awake,
> in her dread of the mighty strength of the bulls, who were likely
> to bring his destruction in an unseemly fate on the field of Ares.
> Pulsing, her heart throbbed within her breast,
> as a sunbeam quivers on a wall, leaping up
> from the water when it is just poured out
> from a bowl or a bucket. Here and there
> with rapid eddying it shimmers and darts.
> Just like that the virgin's heart quivered in her breast.
>
> (Apollonius *Journey of the Argonauts* 3.744–60)

14.8 Apollonius' treatment of Jason and Medea provided a rich source of inspiration for Virgil in his handling of Dido and Aeneas. This case of intertextuality was recognized in antiquity. The fourth-century scholar and teacher Servius wrote in his commentary on the *Aeneid* 'Apollonius wrote *Journey of the Argonauts* and in his third book introduced Medea in love. This entire book [*Aeneid* 4] is taken from there.' Servius is, basically, right. Virgil uses Apollonius to evoke for his audience a depiction of Medea as a vulnerable young woman who is manipulated by the gods for their own ends into falling in love and playing the role of what we can call 'the helpful princess', using a term from studies of folklore (see Chapter 10.8); this is how he frames his story of Dido. (And of course the Medea of Greek tragedy also illuminates Virgil's Dido: when we first meet her, Dido is a strong and assertive woman, like Euripides' Medea, and later she will become vengeful and bitter about the help she freely and optimistically gave to the stranger on her shores, like Euripides' Medea.) But the inter-textuality between Virgil and Apollonius is not straightforward. For example, Virgil adapts Apollonius' description of Medea falling in love to the point where he depicts Dido's state of psychological anguish after Aeneas has told her he is leaving her.

> Night had come, and weary in every land
> people's bodies took the boon of peaceful sleep.
> The woods and wild seas had quieted
> at that hour when the stars are in mid-course,
> when every field is still, when cattle and gleaming
> birds that haunt the limpid lakes or nest in thickets
> in the country places were all asleep under the silent night.
> But not the agonized Phoenician queen:
> she never slackened into sleep and never
> allowed the tranquil night to rest
> upon her eyelids or within her heart.
> Her pain redoubled and savage love
> came on again and on her bed she tossed
> in a great surge of anger.
>
> (Virgil *Aeneid* 4.522–32, adapted
> from Robert Fitzgerald)

What is even more interesting is how Virgil reuses Apollonius' simile of the sunbeams reflecting from the bucket. Whereas the Greek author used this to depict Medea's emotional state, in Virgil the simile appears not in Book 4 but in Book 8 of the *Aeneid*, depicting Aeneas' in-decision.

> And the hero of Laomedon's line,
> who saw the whole scene, tossed in a great surge
> of troubles. This way and that way
> he let his mind run, passing quickly over
> everything he might do, as when from bronze bowls
> of unstilled water, struck by a ray of sun

> or the bright disk of moon, a flickering light
> plays over walls and corners and flies up
> to hit high roofbeams and a coffered ceiling.
>
> (Virgil *Aeneid* 8.18–25)

These examples clearly show Virgil deliberately choosing to rework Apollonius' setting and simile, in this way appropriating the Greek material and setting it to work in his national epic of Rome.

14.9   Virgil was by no means the first Latin poet to take inspiration from the Alexandrian (or 'Hellenistic') poets of the late third century BCE. In fact, Latin authors of the second century BCE from Ennius onwards were clearly familiar with their work. But from the middle of the first century BCE, Alexandrian poets seem to have provided an important inspiration for Latin poets seeking an alternative voice to that of nationalistic literature on a grand scale. Before we consider the impact of these poets on Latin literature, it is essential to understand their appeal. The key name is Callimachus of Cyrene who, along with Philetas of Cos, Theocritus of Syracuse, Aratus of Cilicia and Apollonius of Rhodes, was among a group of scholar-poets who were attracted by the patronage of the ruler Ptolemy II Philadelphus to the recently founded Library and Museum (which literally means 'House of the Muses') at Alexandria. There they were able to combine research into earlier literature with their own experimental literary activities. They seem to have rebelled against the repetitive and unimaginative re-hashes of the classics like Homer and to have argued for a new set of poetic standards in which value was assessed in quality not quantity. Callimachus sets out his poetic manifesto in the prologue to his *Origins*, a learned, episodic poem on the origins of cities, names, festivals and rituals. In accordance with his principles, he produced the *Hecale*, a miniature form of epic (which we call an 'epyllion', though this is not an ancient term) which deviates from the conventional heroic ethos by focusing on a part of the story of Theseus in which he shelters in the hut of an old woman called Hecale who narrates stories to him. Several features of this work seem to be typical of the Alexandrian poets: its story-within-a-story structure, its treatment of standard myth from a novel perspective, its interest in female psychology. The Alexandrian poets privilege miniature genres such as epigram and Theocritus perhaps even invented a new miniature genre, which we call pastoral. The difference between Alexandrian poetry and earlier Greek poetry, which was largely produced for the context of public performance in the classical city state, is enormous. The idea of poetry as something exquisite produced for a sophisticated and select audience (see the end of Callimachus *Hymn* 2 and *Epigram* 28) seems to have struck a chord at Rome during the middle of the first century BCE, where there was a similar context of a highly educated and intellectual elite. Hence Catullus and the other 'neoterics' in the 60s and 50s; Gallus and Virgil (*Eclogues* and *Georgics*) in the 40s and 30s; Tibullus, Propertius and Horace in the 20s; and Ovid for most of his poetic career over the next three decades were all influenced and inspired by Callimachus and the other Alexandrians.

14.10   The maverick experimental poet Catullus (perhaps 84–54 BCE) and his literary 'set' played a major part in formulating a Roman version of Callimachus' poetic principles. In this poem, Catullus praises a work finally produced by another member of his group after long years of work in terms that recall Callimachus' poetic manifesto:

> *Zmyrna*, my friend Cinna's, finally brought forth, nine harvests
> and nine winters after her conception,
> while Hortensius' five hundred thousand in one
> [year] . . . ,
> *Zmyrna* will travel far – to the sunken waves of Satrachus,
> *Zmyrna* will long be read by the white-haired centuries.
> Volusius' *Annals*, though, will die beside the Padua
> and often make loose jackets for mackerel.
> Dear to my heart is my friend's small-scale monument.
> I'll let the crowd enjoy their long-winded Antimachus.
> (Catullus Poem 95, adapted from Guy Lee)

Cinna's *Zmyrna*, which has not survived, took the typical Alexandrian themes of unhappy love and metamorphosis and was clearly short and learned, just like Catullus' compliment to his friend in this difficult but elegant poem, which is best understood in relation to the water imagery at the end of Callimachus' second *Hymn*. The fact that Cicero disparagingly dubs this group 'the new poets' (*poetae novi* and, using Greek, *hoi neoteroi*, which gives rise to the term 'neoteric' sometimes used of them) indicates that their innovation and experimentation was felt to be threatening. Roman culture, after all, generally valued the traditional and familiar over the new, as we can see from the Latin expression for 'revolution': 'new things' (*res novae*).

14.11 Catullus paid Callimachus the explicit tribute of translating into Latin a famous passage from his *Origins* on the lock of hair of Queen Berenice (Poem 66). His most obviously Alexandrian work is Poem 64. This is a miniature epic in hexameters, 408 lines long, often called an 'epyllion' by modern critics. It adopts the story-within-a-story technique of Callimachus' *Hecale* by telling the story of Theseus and Ariadne within the story of the marriage of Peleus with the goddess Thetis. The link between the two narratives is achieved by the device of ecphrasis – that is, the inner narrative is supposedly embroidered on the marvellous bedspread adorning the marriage-bed. Ecphrasis – which is literally a 'speaking-away' from the narrative, usually a description of a work of art – was not an invention of the Alexandrian poets (the first example is the description of the shield of Achilles in *Iliad* 18), but with their interest in artistry in any and every medium it was a feature which flourished in their hands. Catullus also follows the Alexandrian precedent in giving a non-heroic version of these famous stories. For example, towards the end of the poem, when he has the Fates sing a song looking ahead to the son that will be born from this marriage, the climax of Achilles' achievements is presented as the slaughter of the Trojan princess Polyxena as an appeasement to his ghost:

> Last witness will be the prize given him even in death
> when his rounded tomb, heaped up in a lofty mound,
> receives the snow-white limbs of a butchered virgin.
>   Run, spindles, drawing out the weft, run on.
> For soon as Fortune grants the weary Achaeans means
> to undo Neptune's knot around the Dardanian city,
> his high tomb will be drenched in Polyxena's blood.

> She, like a sacrificial victim falling to the two-edged sword,
> shall lay down, sinking to her knees, a headless body.
>   Run, spindles, drawing out the weft, run on.
> Come then and consort in long-desired love.
> Her consort shall accept the goddess in glad treaty
> and at long last the bride shall be given to the eager groom.
>   Run spindles, drawing out the weft, run on.
>   (Catullus 64.363–75, adapted from Guy Lee)

Not for Catullus the conventional praise of Achilles. Instead, he produces a chilling focus on the sacrifice of a virgin as the climax to the wedding song addressed by the Fates to Peleus and Thetis. This alternative focus applies to the inner story too. With Ariadne centre-stage, Catullus portrays Theseus as thoughtless and selfish and not in the least heroic. Ariadne is another 'helpful princess' on the pattern of Medea and, later, Dido, who is abandoned by the man she has assisted. She allows Catullus to combine two central themes favoured by the Alexandrian poets – female psychology and unhappy love.

14.12 By far the most experimental poem in Catullus' collection is Poem 63, which we already glanced at in Chapter 8. This is the only fully surviving example in Latin or Greek of an entire poem in the strange and disturbing galliambic metre, which is marked by many short syllables, conveying an agitation which matches the subject matter. Catullus seems to have taken over this metre from Alexandrian poetry on the theme of the cult of Cybele and produces his own, Romanized, version of the terrors posed by abandonment to religious ecstasy. In this dramatic poem of less than 100 lines, the young devotee Attis castrates himself and immerses himself in the worship of Cybele, then wakes to regret his actions, and attempts to escape without success. In form and content, then, this poem is thoroughly Alexandrian in its inspiration, while reflecting Catullus' particular concerns with the psychology of gender, identity and abjection. It is an excellent example of how Alexandrian poetry could influence and inspire a Roman poet to achieve an unprecedented creative level. There is a debt here, but no sense of inferiority.

14.13   The same is true in the next generation. Too little of Gallus' poetry survives for us to elaborate the point, but Virgil implies in his *Eclogues* (written in the late 40s–early 30s BCE) that Gallus wrote a learned poem inspired by the Alexandrian poet Euphorion on the origins of the Grynean grove sacred to Apollo. Virgil's *Eclogues* provide a clearer case of the adaptation of Alexandrian poetry to the Roman context. In this exquisite book of ten highly crafted short poems, Virgil is clearly inspired by the miniature *Idylls* written by Theocritus in the third century BCE which we identify as the inception of the genre of pastoral. Like Theocritus, he uses the pastoral framework to comment on the writing of poetry, with the 'song' of the herdsmen representing poetry that he praises or criticizes. Just as Theocritus in *Idyll* 7 presents his version of Callimachus' poetic manifesto, so Virgil starts *Eclogue* 6 with a motif taken directly from Callimachus' *Origins*:

> So when I first placed a tablet on my knees, Lycian Apollo said
>   to me:
> '. . . poet, feed the victim to make it as fat as possible but,
>   friend, keep the Muse slender.'
> > (Callimachus *Origins* fragment 1 lines 23–4)

> When I was singing kings and battles, Cynthius [= Apollo]
>   tugged
> my ear in admonition: 'A shepherd, Tityrus,
> should feed his flock fat, but recite a thin-spun song.'
> > (Virgil *Eclogues* 6.3–5, adapted from Guy Lee)

He then puts into the mouth of the satyr Silenus a song which presents what could easily be read as a statement in miniature of Alexandrian poetic principles, complete with a narrative of origins, an unhappy love affair, a story-within-a-story and several metamorphoses.

14.14   But Virgil also extends the boundaries of this genre from Theocritus' (highly stylized) treatment of the loves and hates of rustic herdsmen to incorporate comment on contemporary socio-political matters. In Chapter 13.7–8 we saw how allegory operates in *Eclogue* 5 to convey a political panegyric of Julius Caesar without disrupting the pastoral surface of the praise of the archetypal herdsman, Daphnis. The same phenomenon occurs in the even more experimental *Eclogue* 4, in which Virgil celebrates the prospect of the return of the Golden Age along with the birth of a mysterious child. Virgil explicitly announces the extension of the genre to include political material in the opening lines:

> Sicilian Muses, grant me a slightly grander song.
> Not everyone delights in trees and lowly tamarisks;
> Let woods, if woods we sing, be worthy of a consul.
>
> (Virgil *Eclogue* 4.1–3)

This is a programmatic passage in which Virgil is explaining how the poem is to be read. His reference to 'Sicilian Muses' makes clear his debt to Theocritus, who came from Sicily and who often uses a Sicilian setting for his pastorals, while making the 'woods . . . be worthy of a consul' indicates his political development of the genre. Again, Alexandrian poetry inspires its Roman imitators but by no means confines them.

14.15 Another generation on and we find the elegist Propertius explicitly styling himself the 'Roman Callimachus' in the fourth book of his poems (4.1.64) and following the model of Callimachus' *Origins* by exploring myths and rituals of Roman culture. So, for example, he creates an illusion of a religious ritual inspired by Callimachus' *Hymns* and then turns the occasion to praise of Augustus (here called Caesar):

> The bard is sacrificing: let mouths be favourably hushed for
> sacrifice
>   and the smitten heifer fall before my altar-hearth.
> Let the Roman garland vie with Philetas' ivy-clusters
>   and the urn provide Callimachean water. . . .
> Muse, we shall tell of Palatine Apollo's temple.
>   The theme deserves your blessing, Calliope.
> My song is shaped in Caesar's name. While Caesar
>   is sung, please attend in person, Jupiter.
>
> (Propertius 4.6.1–4 and 11–14,
> adapted from Guy Lee)

This was an idea that Ovid developed at greater length in his *Roman Holidays*. The concept of this work was to devote one book of poetry to each month of the Roman calendar, explaining the myths and customs associated with the festivals and anniversaries as a series of 'Origins' inspired by the poem of Callimachus. In fact, Ovid completed only the first six of the twelve books, but this is more than enough to demonstrate his transformation of Alexandrian intellectual inquiry into civic poetry that is thoroughly Roman, and thoroughly Ovidian too, in its playfulness and wit. In this excerpt he imagines an epiphany (the manifestation of a god) as he is sitting in truly Callimachean pose, trying to write.

> Yet what god am I to call you, two-shaped Janus?
>> Greece has no divinity like you.
> And tell the reason why you are the only god
>> to see what is behind and what ahead.
> While I contemplated this, my writing-tablets in my hand,
>> the house seemed brighter than before.
> Suddenly holy Janus in marvellous two-headed form
>> thrust his binary face before my eyes.
> I panicked and I felt my hair spike with fear,
>> my heart iced over with a sudden chill.
> Clutching a staff in his right hand, a key in his left,
>> he delivered this from his facing face:
> 'Lose your fear, industrious poet of the days,
>> learn what you seek and mark my words.
> The ancients (since I'm a primitive thing) called me
>> Chaos. Watch me sing events of long ago.
> This lucid air and the other three elements,
>> fire, water and earth, were a single heap.
> Once discord of its components had split the mass,
>> which departed for new homes,
> flame headed for the heights, the next place took the air,
>> earth and the ocean settled in mid-ground.
> Then I, who had been a ball and a shapeless hulk,
>> got the looks and limbs proper to a god.

Now, as a small token of my once chaotic shape,
        my front and back appear identical.'
                        (Ovid *Roman Holidays* 1.89–114, adapted
                            from A. J. Boyle and R. D. Woodard)

It seems that each of the Roman poets who takes inspiration from the Alexandrians, above all from Callimachus, reinvents himself as a new 'Roman Callimachus'. These poets are not expressing their inferiority to Greek literature but proudly asserting their Romanness, a topic to which I shall return in Chapter 15.

14.16 But first, I want to offer a brief discussion of some of the models we use to relate texts to one another, above all, the model that we call 'genre'. Because genre is so central to our attempts as moderns to grasp Graeco-Roman literature, it becomes crucial to interrogate our preconceptions of what is entailed in genre. For the ancients, the genres formed a kind of hierarchy. In undisputed top position was epic. The unwritten 'rules' that governed epic required it to be grand poetry on a large scale in the hexameter metre on themes of patriotic interest, incorporating the heroes and gods of myth and/or the military exploits of leaders of the more recent past. Within that framework, certain set pieces (we might call them *topoi*, borrowing a Greek word) could be expected, such as a council of the gods, arming for battle, heroic feats performed by an individual on the battlefield, a duel, the sack of a city, felling trees for funeral pyres, lamentations for the dead, and so on. Homer's *Iliad* provided the ultimate model and, in Latin, poems like Ennius' *Annals*, Virgil's *Aeneid* and Silius' *Punic War* fulfilled these expectations marvellously. The tradition still survives today, by the way, in a work like Derek Walcott's *Omeros* (1990), a huge poem set in the Caribbean which deals with themes of displacement, imperialism and colonialism as well as the mundane lives and loves of his characters. In prose, historiography came nearest to the role of epic in poetry, with its elevated tone, huge scale and opportunity to introduce patriotic themes in a way that was both educational and entertaining. Of course in both genres there were authors who challenged those unwritten 'rules' – Ovid's *Metamorphoses* and

Lucan's *Civil War* in their different ways both flout the epic pattern exemplified by Virgil, while in historiography Tacitus makes the genre something importantly different from Livy's monument to Rome. In the field of drama, both comedy and tragedy had their distinct 'rules', although Plautus has fun by labelling his *Amphitryo* a 'tragi-comedy'. Poetry besides epic that was written in hexameters has attracted several different generic labels. Modern critics talk of 'didactic' as a category that includes Lucretius' wonderful poem *On the Nature of the Universe* and Virgil's *Georgics*, while 'pastoral' describes the miniatures we call *Eclogues* produced by Virgil and later poets. Whether Lucretius and Virgil would have thought of their poems as anything other than variations on epic is not certain. A clearer case is that of satire, also written in hexameters, where we have Quintilian's guarantee that this was seen as a separate category, as was the prose form of satire that we label 'Menippean satire'. So too with elegy, written in the elegiac couplet, and lyric poetry, such as the *Odes* of Horace. I could go on, but this is enough to suggest the ways in which 'genre' can be used as a hermeneutic tool – as a way of organizing ancient texts into relationships with one another which will aid interpretation. It also illustrates that any attempt at classification immediately runs into problems with the works that don't quite fit – the ones that, deliberately or otherwise, straddle the boundaries.

14.17   At this point, it is relevant to emphasize that, although modern critics talk freely about genre when they discuss ancient literature, the term 'genre' is actually a latecomer. According to the *Oxford English Dictionary*, the first attested use of the word in our sense in English is as recent as 1770. On the other hand, it is clear that the ancients were interested in classifying their literary artefacts. The Hellenistic scholars, for example, devoted huge amounts of time and energy to developing Aristotle's systems of classification. In Latin literature, the idea of genre seems to be represented in the lines by the Republican tragedian Accius: 'Learn, Baebius, how varied are the types of poems and how much they differ from one another' (fr. 8), in the imperial historian Velleius's ruminations on the flourishing and fading of genres at certain moments (*Histories* 1.16–18) and in Quintilian's discussion of which types of literature the budding orator should read (*Training* *of the Orator* 10.1.46–131) where he uses categories which we can recognize as genres. That said, there is no theoretical discussion in Latin literature of 'genre' or even of the preferred concept of imitation (*imitatio*). That leaves it to *us* to interrogate the concept.

14.18 One essential question here is how the idea of 'genre' is formed. Is our concept of 'genre' descriptive or prescriptive? Is it based upon deduction or induction? In other words, does it start by looking at particular texts and deriving from them an idea or ideal of 'epic' or 'lyric'? Or does it operate the other way around and start from an idealized form or formula against which it measures each particular instantiation of the genre?

14.19 These are not easy questions to answer, whether we are scholars immersed in ancient literature or newcomers to the field. Proof of the difficulty around the concept of genre is the frequency with which critics invoke metaphors to explain their interpretation and exploitation of genre in literary criticism. One important metaphor is that of genealogy, according to which the critic can construct a family tree which explains the pedigree of the text under study. According to this image, you can trace the genealogy of epic backwards from, say, Silius to Virgil to Ennius to Naevius to Homer. The problem here is that there will always be poems that do not fit. Another is the related metaphor from biology and genetics, in which the focus is upon the production of texts, which are seen either as pure or as hybrids, produced by parents of two different genres. Such cross-fertilization can, of course, be rich and productive, but the image also opens up the possibility of value judgements about the 'purity' or 'impurity' of specific works of literature. Another image sees genre as a recipe which offers formulae for the cooking or concoction of literary works through combinations of standard ingredients. This metaphor connects with the modern fantasy of computer-generated literature. But just as computer-generated Bach or Mozart performs the technicalities without the touch of genius, so it is clear that this metaphor cannot account for every element in a work of creative literature. In other words, while these metaphors help us think about 'genre' in their different ways, none of them produces a really close fit.

14.20   One of the most persistent images used by critics for the operation of genre is that of mapping. According to this image, the critic is involved in mapping the works of literature on to a two-dimensional descriptive grid. If you get the coordinates right you can locate any text on to this matrix. This has its uses as well as its limitations. One of the most provocative 'maps' of genres known to me is contained in Northrop Frye's *Anatomy of Criticism* (Princeton, 1957). He uses the seasons to organize literature (his discussion ranges wide through European literature) into a system consisting of two opposed pairs, rather like a two-dimensional disc divided into four quadrants: Mythos of Spring – Comedy; Mythos of Summer – Romance; Mythos of Autumn – Tragedy; Mythos of Winter – Irony and Satire. This map of literature captures the potential for the development of genres as they situate themselves at and across the boundaries between the 'seasons'. So, for example, spring shades into summer in the case of romantic comedy and summer into spring in the comic romance, while the interface between comedy and satire is located at the shift from winter into spring. I still find Frye's approach to genre exciting and rewarding.

14.21   The concept of genre, then, seems always to bring us to the subject of boundaries, sooner or later. Whichever model or metaphor we use, genre always involves a balance between consistency and innovation, framework and deviation. That means that the richest texts for generic studies are not the supposed archetypes (though these we also need) but those which explore and breach the boundaries. And when we look at the development of Latin literature through time, from its origins in the classics of Greek literature, I believe we can see an amazing fluidity and adaptability which ultimately sees epic written in non-epic metres. Milestones on this path include Lucretius' *On the Nature of the Universe*, Ovid's *Metamorphoses* and Prudentius' *Soul-Battle*. The story of Latin literature is one of assimilation of new materials and creative responses to new challenges. A literature that starts with the genre of epic, modelled on Greek patterns, has within four hundred years discovered that prose can be the vehicle for the same concerns of morality, identity and allegiance in a work such as Apuleius' *Metamorphoses*. After another two centuries or so, Latin then generates a very modern-looking form of prose in Augustine's *Confessions*. These two works together, Apuleius' *Metamorphoses* and Augustine's *Confessions*, contain in them the seeds of the literary form which gradually rose to prominence during the sixteenth and seventeenth centuries and which since the eighteenth century has been the dominant and pre-eminent literary form in our culture. Sir Walter Scott's 1824 definition of the novel as 'a fictitious narrative . . . accommodated to the ordinary train of human events' reveals how the novel has displaced epic as the vehicle of central cultural ideas and ideals.

14.22 One problem with this focus upon genre, though, is that it tends to treat texts as objects and to invite us to neglect the role of authors and of audiences. With my emphasis upon authors and their contexts in the preceding chapters, there can be little danger of 'the death of the author' here. But I have said much less about the role of audiences – not just the first audience of any performance or reading, but also the audiences of reperformances and rereadings. In different ways, these audiences (the first audience and subsequent audiences, including us) become detectives in search of clues. Ideally, the text constructs its own audience, in the sense that it creates a literary competence in its readership, as Wordsworth said in his Prefatory Essay to the 1815 edition of his works:

> If there be one conclusion more forcibly pressed upon us than any other by the review which has been given of the fortunes and fate of poetical Works, it is this, – that every author, as far as he is great and at the same time original, has had the task of creating the taste by which he is to be enjoyed: so has it been, so will it continue to be.

But sometimes the text is just too alien, or the cultural context which produced it is too remote, for this to work without some extra help, such as I aim to provide in this book. And sometimes it happens that the author has pushed the genre unrecognizably beyond its boundaries, beyond the competence or tolerance of his audience. In such cases, we have experiments that fail. I believe it is important to allow room in our account of Latin literature for such failures of communication, provided we have made every effort to understand all the possible texts and contexts that could illuminate the subject of study.

Further reading and study

Many books on Latin literature and on individual authors and texts will provide insights into the relationship between Greek and Latin literature. Starting points are offered by 'The blending of Greek and Roman', in *Tradition and Originality in Roman Poetry* by Gordon Williams (Oxford, 1968) chapter 5, pages 250–357, by several of the essays in *Creative Imitation and Latin Literature* (edited by David West and Tony Woodman, Cambridge, 1979) and by Thomas Habinek's essays 'Latin literature and the problem of Rome' and 'Why was Latin literature invented?' in his *The Politics of Latin Literature* (Princeton, 1998) pages 15–68. On the influence of the Alexandrian Greek poets on Latin literature see W. Clausen 'Callimachus and Latin poetry' *Greek, Roman and Byzantine Studies* 5 (1964) 181–96 and R. O. A. M. Lyne 'The neoteric poets' *Classical Quarterly* 28 (1978) 168–87. Alan Cameron offers a new (and controversial) assessment of the role of Callimachus in literary history in *Callimachus and his Critics* (Princeton, 1995). Alessandro Barchiesi in *The Poet and the Prince: Ovid and Augustan Discourse* (Berkeley, 1997) demonstrates how a Callimachean voice can operate under the early Principate, while Carole Newlands in *Playing with Time: A Study of Ovid's 'Fasti'* (Ithaca, 1995) offers a study of Ovid's inventiveness. On wider aspects of the Romans' relationship with Greek culture see A. Momigliano *Alien Wisdom: The Limits of Hellenization* (Cambridge, 1975) and the work of Erich Gruen, including *The Hellenistic World and the Coming of Rome* (Berkeley, 1984), *Studies in Greek Culture and Roman Policy* (Leiden, 1990) and *Culture and National Identity in Republican Rome* (Ithaca, 1992).

On the descriptive grid of mapping genres see G. B. Conte and G. W. Most, 'Genre' in the *Oxford Classical Dictionary*, 3rd edition. For the image of the genres as seasons see Northrop Frye *Anatomy of Criticism* (Princeton, 1957) pages 158–239. The quotation from Wordsworth comes from *The Complete Poetical Works of William Wordsworth* (vol. 1, Boston and New York, 1911) page 100.

The topic of the relationship between Greek and Latin literature offers countless ideas for further study. These include the rehandling of the themes of Homeric epic and Athenian tragedy in Latin epic, tragedy, lyric and elegy, for example, in Ennius, Catullus, Virgil, Horace, Propertius, Ovid, Seneca and Statius. Topics here include the stories of Agamemnon and Odysseus, Oedipus and the Seven Against Thebes, Hercules and Medea. Particularly intriguing is the portrayal of Ulysses (= Odysseus) as a wily Greek scoundrel in Roman texts (such as Virgil *Aeneid* 2 and Seneca's *Trojan Women*), which influenced later European literature (for example, Dante's *Inferno*): see W. B. Stanford *The Ulysses Theme* (Oxford, 1963). Another, similar, angle would consist of tracing the development of the Aeneas legend in Rome, by asking what cultural uses this myth of a Trojan prince and enemy of the Greeks served Rome and by exploring how Carthage is brought into the legend. The fact that Virgil fashions his telling of the Aeneas story as a Roman complement to Greek epic rather than a retelling of Homeric material is significant. The essays on Dido by Horsfall and Hexter – N. Horsfall 'Dido in the light of history', in *Oxford Readings in Vergil's Aeneid* (edited by S. J. Harrison, Oxford, 1990) pages 127–44; and Ralph Hexter 'Sidonian Dido' in *Innovations of Antiquity* (edited by Ralph Hexter and Daniel Harrison, New York and London, 1992) pages 332–84 – contain helpful ideas for this enquiry. And one can continue the trajectory to trace Virgil's influence on later epics of empire, on which see David Quint *Epic and Empire: Politics and Generic Form from Virgil to Milton* (Princeton, 1993).

The influence of the Alexandrian poets on poetry of the late Republic and early Principate still yields new insights, for example, Callimachus' influence on Statius was the subject of a recent US PhD dissertation. But this topic does not just invite a backwards look to what preceded Latin literature. The fact that Roman poets adopted and adapted the themes of Greek tragedy has had immense significance for the development of later European literature. It may come as a sobering and surprising realization that Shakespeare had no first-hand acquaintance with Greek tragedy and that his knowledge of Greek tragedy was mediated through Latin authors. Most important of these were Ovid, thanks to his 'repackaging' of Greek mythology in his

Letters of Heroines and *Metamorphoses*, and Seneca, whose tragedies were translated into English by various authors including Jasper Heywood and published in 1581, with highly significant consequences, as T. S. Eliot realized. On Seneca's influence on later tragedy see Gordon Braden *Renaissance Tragedy and the Senecan Tradition: Anger's Privilege* (New Haven, 1985) and R. S. Miola *Shakespeare and Classical Tragedy: The Influence of Seneca* (Oxford, 1992). So a further topic is the investigation of how Latin poetry mediated Greek stories for English poets of the Renaissance and later. Finally, study of the implications of the different models of genre is a fruitful way into Latin literature, especially in terms of the actual or implied relationships between author, text and audience(s).

Chapter 15

Building Rome and building Roman literature

15.1   By the time of Augustus, it seems that the Romans had overcome their cultural inferiority complex to the Greeks and were capable of celebrating their achievement in literature that was not just Latin but Roman, by which I mean rooted in the fabric of the city of Rome itself. In this brief final chapter I shall focus upon three poetic texts, by Virgil, Horace and Ovid, that commemorate Romanness – *Romanitas* – in a new voice of self-confidence. I shall also suggest that it is no coincidence that two of these three texts use architectural imagery to emphasize the solidity of their poetic achievements. These are designed to be lasting monuments to Romanness. The third text, as we shall see, prefers the image of imperial territory as an intimation of immortality. And perhaps that is better. Anyone who has visited Rome, or seen pictures of Rome, knows that the buildings constructed two thousand years ago are in various states of dilapidation, even if they have endured remarkably well (and probably better than anything we can build). On the other hand, there is a sense in which we are still inhabiting the Roman Empire. *Romanitas* rules. That is why I shall give the last word to Ovid. And en route, I shall allow myself a brief consideration of the role of this book in the study of Latin literature.

15.2   If there is a definitive moment which pinpoints when Latin literature comes of age, I suggest (and this is bound to be controversial) that it is in 29 BCE, the year of Octavian's return from the East to celebrate his triple triumph over his conquered enemies. Virgil marks the moment with a bold statement of poetic and political self-confidence that comes, significantly, at the very centre of his four-book poem *Georgics*, a poem dedicated to his patron Maecenas (see Chapter 7.17–18) in which he offers a complex and nuanced view of the relationship between human beings and their environment. At the start of Book 3 he announces a future poem in praise of 'Caesar' (Octavian).

> I will be first, if life is granted me,
> to lead in triumph the Muses from
> Greek Helicon to my native land. I will be first
> to bring you, Mantua, Idumaean palms,
> and in green meadows raise a marble temple
> beside the water where great Mincius,
> embroidering his banks with tender rushes,
> in lingering loops meanders.
> In the middle of the shrine, as patron god,
> I will have Caesar placed, and in his honour
> myself as victor in resplendent Tyrian purple
> will drive a hundred chariots by the river.
> For me the whole of Greece, deserting the Alpheus,
> Olympia's river, and the groves of Nemea
> will compete in racing and in boxing.
> And I will offer gifts, my brow with olive
> wreathed. I see myself already
> leading the solemn procession joyfully
> to the shrine and watching bullocks sacrificed,
> or in the theatre viewing the change of scenes
> and Britons rising woven in crimson curtains.
> On the temple doors I will have carved in gold
> and solid ivory the hordes of Ganges
> in battle and our Romulus' victory,
> and here great Nile in flood, surging with war,

and columns rising decked with prows of bronze.
I'll add the Asian cities tamed, Niphates' heights
conquered, the Parthian cunning in his flight
shooting his arrows backward, and two trophies
won from far separated enemies,
a double Triumph from two furthest shores. . . .
Meanwhile however let my Muse pursue
the woods and glades of the Dryads, virgin territory,
no soft assignment on your command, Maecenas.

> (Virgil *Georgics* 3.10–33 and 40–1,
> adapted from L. P. Wilkinson)

This is a remarkable promise of a future epic poem which will celebrate Octavian's military exploits at the furthest ends of the world, a promise that will be fulfilled, if in rather oblique terms, in the *Aeneid*. The passage is important in several respects. First, Virgil explicitly promises an appropriation of Greek literature for Roman purposes and even claims that all of Greece will abandon its celebration of its festivals to participate in his festival. Second, he introduces his poetic exploit in distinctly militaristic terms, as if he were a triumphing general. Third, he uses the monumental image of a temple to depict his poetry, so creating an equivalence with the temples in Rome built and restored by Octavian (*Achievements of the Divine Augustus* 19–21). Fourth, he situates his own architectural achievement not in Rome but in his home city of Mantua, beside the river Mincius, so linking Roman military and political power with the land and people of Italy in a way that matched Octavian's own drive to unify Italy. Fifth, he places Caesar 'as patron god' in the centre of the temple, elevating Octavian to extraordinary superhuman status and responding to that with his own role as the priest in charge of the sacrifices and ceremony. And sixth, he promises an ecphrasis (see Chapter 14.11) of carvings on the temple doors which will glorify the military achievements of Caesar, here called 'our Romulus', a reference to one of the names Octavian contemplated taking before he settled on 'Augustus' in 27 BCE. This elaborate evocation of a physical monument is at once a high compliment to Caesar, an assertion of Virgil's future poetic ambitions, and a statement that political leaders need poets.

15.3   Just a few years later, in 23 BCE, in a poem which shows remarkable similarities to Virgil's monumental and triumphal imagery, Horace concludes his collection of *Odes* 1–3 with a flourish full of ambitions of immortality.

> I have completed a memorial more lasting than bronze
> and higher than the royal grave of the pyramids,
> that neither biting rain nor the north wind in its fury
> can destroy nor the unnumbered
>
> series of years and the flight of ages.
> I shall not completely die and a great part of me
> shall escape the Goddess of Funerals: I shall grow ever renewed
> in the praise of posterity, as long as the Pontifex
>
> shall climb the Capitol with the silent Vestal Virgin.
> I shall be spoken of where violent Aufidus roars
> and where Daunus, poor in water, has always ruled
> over his rustic peoples, as the one, famous from a humble
>   origin,
>
> who was the first to spin Aeolian poetry
> to Italian rhythms: take on a pride
> that has been won by your merits and kindly encircle
> my brow, Melpomene, with Delphic laurel.
>
>   (Horace *Odes* 3.30, adapted from
>   Gordon Williams' translation)

In this extraordinary assertion of the durability of his poetry, which starts with monumental imagery and goes on to link his poetry with the institutions of Rome and with his home territory in southern Italy near the rivers Aufidus and Daunus, Horace here talks directly about his relationship with Greek literature. He claims to have been the first to produce an Italian version of Aeolian poetry, by which he means the Greek lyric poets from Lesbos, Sappho and Alcaeus, and he depicts himself garlanded with a laurel crown from Delphi. The symbolism of this is twofold. Most obviously, in a thoroughly Greek image, he means to indicate that he is the supreme champion of Apollo, the god of Delphi and the god of poetry. But for a Roman audience the laurel crown inevitably suggested a triumphant general as he processed through Rome on his way along the Sacred Way to the Capitol (see Chapter 5.17). This single image, then, deftly represents the appropriation of Greek literature by Roman culture.

15.4   These two texts contain supreme assertions of Roman self-confidence in the realms of poetic as well as political power. Here we see shrugged off the debt of the Romans to their Greek predecessors that had earlier been felt as a burden and as a cultural inferiority complex – a classic case of the anxiety of influence (see Chapter 3.10 on early Latin literature as translations of Greek, 12.16 on belatedness, and Chapter 14.1–15 generally). Without abandoning their Greek heritage, these poets have produced works which merit the label of 'classic' in their own right – and they know it and say it. The monumental imagery and the imagery of the triumphing general found here are quintessentially Roman features and mark the coming of age of Latin literature, as it changes from being literature in Latin to being truly 'Roman' literature.

15.5   This seems the moment to ask what a history of Latin literature could or should look like. It will by now be clear that this book is not a conventional literary history. If it were, it would trundle through the notional periods of Latin literary history, such as The Early and Middle Republics, The Late Republic, The Age of Augustus, The Early Empire and The Late Empire. Or it would present Latin authors as a series of heroes in a broadly diachronic sequence of, say, Livius Andronicus – Naevius – Ennius – Plautus – Terence – Lucilius – Cicero – Lucretius – Catullus – Caesar – Sallust – Virgil – Horace – Tibullus – Propertius – Livy – Ovid – Seneca the Elder – Seneca the Younger – Lucan – Persius – Petronius – Pliny the Elder – Valerius Flaccus – Statius – Silius Italicus – Quintilian – Martial – Pliny the Younger – Tacitus – Juvenal – Suetonius – Apuleius – Ausonius – Claudian – Prudentius – Jerome – Augustine and the Church Fathers. There are plenty of other books that do that. Their aim at comprehensiveness makes them immensely useful as works of reference, if rather too large and heavy to sit down with and read all the way through. The volume of *The Cambridge History of Classical Literature* devoted to Latin literature (edited by E. J. Kenney and W. V. Clausen, Cambridge 1982) consists of 42 essays by 18 scholars in 974 pages. Gian Biagio Conte's *Latin Literature: A History* (Baltimore, 1994) numbers 827 pages in its translation from the Italian original and Michael von Albrecht's two volume work in German, *A History of Roman Literature* (Leiden, 1997), weighs in at a resounding 1,843 pages in its English translation. There is a great danger that, under this heap of words and scholarship, 'the work disappears', to quote the warning expressed by Roland Barthes.

15.6   So instead I chose a novel organizational principle – by topics, topics that I see as providing key insights into Roman literary culture. This is designed not to supplant but to complement the fuller discussions in the encyclopedic literary histories mentioned above. It is also designed to complement the approach shared by some of the most important books on Latin literature to appear in the last four decades – *Tradition and Originality in Roman Poetry* by Gordon Williams (Oxford, 1968), *Generic Composition in Greek and Roman Poetry* by Francis Cairns (Edinburgh, 1972), *The Rhetoric of Imitation: Genre and Poetic Memory in Virgil and Other Latin Poets* by Gian Biagio Conte (English translation, Ithaca and London, 1986) and now *Allusion and Intertext: Dynamics of Appropriation in Roman Poetry* by Stephen Hinds (Cambridge, 1998). All these books assess Latin literature primarily in terms of a dialogue between texts and in terms of the interaction of elements within texts. All of these books have produced interpretations that have profoundly affected the way we read Latin poetry. What I try to do here is go beyond the relationship between text and text and to privilege the relationship between text and context(s).

15.7   To close, I would like to invite reflection for a moment on the activity of writing a book like this – a book that attempts to introduce readers new to Latin literature to what is most important and most valuable. In his provocatively titled book *Is Literary History Possible?* David Perkins says: 'The writing of literary history involves selection, generalization, organization, and a point of view.' It takes only a moment's thought to see that the issues Perkins is raising under the rubrics of selection, generalization and organization are issues that have concerned us in this volume too. It is his fourth heading that I want to draw attention to. He suggests that the writing of literary history involves 'a point of view'. Not everyone would agree with that, or, to be more precise, not everyone would approve of that. It seems to me that the big books designed to be used as reference books – such as the *Cambridge History of Classical Literature*, along with the *Oxford Classical Dictionary* and other massive tomes – aspire to an authority that speaks with an impersonal voice which deters any challenges to the expertise there displayed. I do not believe that this should be the aim of any author of literary history. Rather, I suggest that literary history is more effective when it is expressed with a marked point of view, so that the sense of an individual behind the very particular judgements offered is palpable and contestable. That is why I have so deliberately used a 'personal voice' in this book. I hope that students and teachers alike will be moved to agree and to disagree with the views and judgements expressed here. And if I have done my job well, the best proof and the highest compliment will be that readers new to Latin literature will now be inspired to throw away this introduction and go directly to the texts themselves.

15.8   That is why I choose to finish not with my voice but with the voice of a Roman poet, a Roman poet asserting his immortality. This is Ovid at the close of his epic masterpiece, *Metamorphoses,* usually dated 8 CE. And it marks a crucial moment in the history of Latin literature. Instead of appealing to a precedent in Greek literature, Ovid takes as his model a Latin poet. The opening words of this passage proclaim the intertextual relationship with Horace *Odes* 3.30 (above in Section 15.3): Ovid deliberately reuses the opening word of Horace's poem, *exegi* ('completed') – exactly the same verb in exactly the same form. He proceeds to adapt Horace's catalogue of obstacles to dura-bility, to replay Horace's 'a great part of me' as 'the finer part of me' and to refigure Horace's image of national ceremonies at the temple of Jupiter Optimus Maximus on the Capitol as an image of Rome's domination of the world. And finally, in his very last word, he takes Horace's 'I shall not completely die' and turns it into the triumphant proclamation, 'I'll live to all eternity'. The truth of his assertion lies in the fact that, two thousand years later, we are still studying Ovid.

> Now stands my task completed, such a work
> as not the wrath of Jupiter, nor fire nor sword
> nor the devouring ages can destroy.
> Let, when it will, that day, that has no claim
> but to my mortal body, end the span
> of my uncertain years. Yet I'll be borne,
> the finer part of me, above the stars,
> immortal, and my name shall never die.
> Wherever through the lands beneath her sway
> the might of Rome extends, my words shall be
> upon the lips of men. If truth at all
> is stablished by poetic prophecy,
> in fame I'll live to all eternity.
>
> (Ovid *Metamorphoses* 15.871–9,
> adapted from A. D. Melville)

Further reading and study

On the deeply militaristic nature of Roman culture, including the significance of the triumph ceremony, see Chapter 5. Alongside the monumental imagery in these texts it is essential to study the visual imagery provided by monuments. A classic study of the visual dimension of Augustus' reign is provided by Paul Zanker *The Power of Images in the Age of Augustus* (translated by Alan Shapiro, Ann Arbor, 1988).

The study of Roman literature should take us back to the study of Rome itself. An excellent book about representations of the city of Rome in literature is Catharine Edwards' *Writing Rome: Textual Approaches to the City* (Cambridge, 1996). A fine visual introduction to the monuments and sites of the city of Rome is Amanda Claridge's *Rome: An Oxford Archaeological Guide* (Oxford, 1998). There is of course no substitute for visiting the city in person.

For more conventional literary history see *The Cambridge History of Classical Literature: Latin Literature* (edited by E. J. Kenney and W. V. Clausen, Cambridge, 1982), Gian Biagio Conte *Latin Literature: A History* (translated by J. Solodow, Baltimore, 1994), and Michael von Albrecht *A History of Roman Literature* (English translation, Leiden, 1997). Elaine Fantham *Roman Literary Culture from Cicero to Apuleius* (Baltimore and London, 1996) is important for the way she extends the contexts in which literature is viewed. Landmark studies of Latin literature during the last few decades include Gordon Williams *Tradition and Originality in Roman Poetry* (Oxford, 1968), Francis Cairns *Generic Composition in Greek and Roman Poetry* (Edinburgh, 1972), Gian Biagio Conte *The Rhetoric of Imitation: Genre and Poetic Memory in Virgil and Other Latin Poets* (English translation, Ithaca and London, 1986) and Stephen Hinds *Allusion and Intertext: Dynamics of Appropriation in Roman Poetry* (Cambridge, 1998).

On the actual project of literary history see David Perkins *Is Literary History Possible?* (Baltimore, 1992), quotation in the text from page 19.

Further study could lead to texts which discuss the fabric of the city of Rome, its buildings, monuments and spaces. Examples include the anticipations of the future city provided in Virgil's description of King Evander's settlement on the site of Rome in *Aeneid* 8; Livy's careful recording of extensions to the city walls and boundaries (*pomerium*) and significant building projects, such as temples and aqueducts, in *From the Foundation of Rome*; Propertius' poems about Rome, especially in Book 4 (4.1, 4.9, 4.10 and 4.11; also 3.11); Ovid's memorialization of the foundation of buildings and of myths in his *Roman Holidays*, such as Livia's shrine to Concord (1.637–50 and 6.637–48), the Ara Pacis ('Altar of Peace', 1.709–24), the temple of Mars the Avenger (5.545–98) and the temple of Hercules of the Muses (6.799–812); Juvenal's representation of a Rome that has become un-Roman in *Satire* 3; and the historian Ammianus Marcellinus' potted history of Rome as a rise to splendour through a pact between Virtue and Fortune, followed by his satirical portrayal of Rome's subsequent decline at 14.6.

The idea of Italy and the idea of Rome are also rich fields for study. The unification of Italy is not an issue confined to recent history: a study of Virgil's *Georgics* in its historical context will reveal the intersection of literature and politics in Octavian's agenda.

On the city of Rome, Catharine Edwards' book (above) will offer some provocations here, such as her quotation (on page 27) of Freud's famous use of the city of Rome as an analogy for the human mind with its archaeological layers and locations with multiple associations. In terms of ancient texts, Augustine's *City of God* is especially suggestive, with its deconstruction of the Roman claim to cultural hegemony and replacement of Roman citizenship with citizenship of heaven.

Another idea which is currently exciting attention, is the study of the modern city of Rome with emphasis on the ways in which architecture and topography articulate cultural messages, as seen in *Roman Presences: Reception of Rome in European Culture, 1789–1945* (edited by Catharine Edwards, Cambridge, 1999). The appearance of the letters SPQR on drain covers and the changes wrought by Mussolini in his quest for a new ancient Romanness are fascinating topics. Finally, you might investigate the continuing existence within Rome of the Vatican City, a separate state where Latin is still spoken. Since 'Vatican' refers to the 'song of the prophet/poet', we can ponder the foresight of the poet Ovid when he prophesied that his poems would still be read so long as Rome exercised power in the world.

Extract from
Darkness Visible
by W. R. Johnson*

There are, then, at present two quite distinct schools of Vergilian criticism that seek to explain and to justify the *Aeneid* by constructing for it two radically opposed political allegories. The major achievement of the essentially optimistic European school has been to show that what had been taken as Vergil's chief defects might better be seen as his particular virtues. What had been named a slavish or incompetent dependence of Homer becomes in their hands a brilliant recreation, a thorough and fresh rethinking of Homeric problems and Homeric solutions. For them, the genre of epic is not so much artificially resuscitated by Vergil as it is reinvented. If, for instance, a constant complaint throughout the nineteenth and much of the twentieth century had been that Aeneas is a poor excuse for a hero, the European school counters that it is not a question of Aeneas' failing as a hero but a question of Vergil's rethinking the concept of heroism which was a process that entailed a distillation of post-Socratic ethical speculation and that implied some criticism of the Homeric concept of heroism. . . . This school of Vergilian criticism has ventured on a tremendously difficult task and has performed it with extraordinary success, so it is with real

*W. R. Johnson *Darkness Visible: A Study of Vergil's* Aeneid (Berkeley, 1976), pages 8–9, 11 and 15.

diffidence that I turn from the strengths of this school to its weaknesses. Those weaknesses can best be described by their being contrasted with the strengths of the somewhat pessimistic Harvard school. In this reading of the poem the superior virtues and the high ideals of Aeneas are sometimes grudgingly allowed him, but he is in the wrong poem. His being in the wrong poem furnishes it with a kind of tragic greatness that calls into question not only the heroisms of Homer's poems but also Augustan heroism and indeed any heroism. The presence of the Stoic or the Epicurean sage on the Homeric battlefield creates a *concordia discors* that is clearly wrong for a celebration of *Roma aeterna* and evades any possible kind of good resolution to the conflicts the poem mirrors. The historical and the metaphysical stakes in this race between order and disorder are too high, and the hero, the order, and the disorder are all gathered up into, and at last devoured by, an implacable and unintelligible nihilism. . . .

The major weakness of the Harvard school is, as I see it, that it is obviously rooted in our peculiarly contemporary brand of pessimism. It is hard to imagine how this reading of the poem could exist without the support of our agnostic and atheistic existentialisms. And it is therefore only too possible that such readings of the poem project back upon Vergil a taste for the cult of failure and for the sense of the absurd and the meaningless that ancients, even the ancients that Dodds characterizes so well, would have found all but incomprehensible. Furthermore, it is clearly impossible to ignore Vergil's very real (if qualified) admiration for Augustus, his hope for political salvation, his desire to believe in cosmic order, and, failing a strong faith in human nature, his reverence for human dignity.

Who's afraid of literary theory?
by Simon Goldhill*

> Oh, do not ask 'What is it?'
> Let us go and make our visit.
>
> T. S. Eliot

An oblivion of one's own

The MacCabe affair; structuralism bandied in the *Daily Telegraph*; the heady Seventies; Paris and the hairy Sixties. What *is* literary theory and *why* are they saying such horrid things about it . . . ?

Why not turn to an unlikely source of enlightenment – Oxford? The Thomas Wharton Professor of English offers a clarion call:

> Without some kind of theory, however unreflective and implicit, we would not know what a 'literary work' was in the first place, or how to read it. Hostility to theory usually means an opposition to other people's theories and an oblivion of one's own.

There's the rub. 'Theory' isn't something one tacks on to reading. It's what makes reading *possible*. It's there already. Always. The

*Simon Goldhill 'Who's afraid of literary theory?' *JACT Review* 10 (1991) pages 8–11.

question is how explicit to make it and how to make it explicit. How hard to think about it. What literary theorists do is to try to understand the process of reading. What we do to books and books do to us. . . . An anatomy of the life-blood of teaching.

Don't look now . . .

It is this desire to make explicit – placing what we do *es meson* as they say in democratic Athens – that causes most of the fuss and bother. For some classicists, just doing well what they have been taught to do, is enough. And granted our institutional structures, it often has been enough for status, jobs, power. Keeping one's head down. . . . Literary theorists, however, advertise to students the excitement and empowerment of rebellion and revelation: unmasking the hidden agenda, discovering the credo, recognizing the unrecognized. Plus the thrill of the attack on the entrenched position (which, as Stormin' Norman said, needs six attackers for each defender – in theory). Hence the *agon*. Head in the sand versus superiority (up) in the air. . . .

It seems to me – but then it would, wouldn't it? – that only one side of the *agon* is *intellectually* tenable. Because, like Socrates, it seems to me that the unexamined life isn't worth living – especially for a *critic*. Just doing what we do – as a credo – is to fall headlong into the oblivion of one's own.

Finding one's place

Particularly for classicists, who have such a developed sense of intellectual tradition, it is ludicrous myth-making to pretend what we do now is what we've always done. That there is – simply and self-evidently – a *natural* way to read. An unchanging classical tradition. Wilamowitz was once a trendy young Turk, a *Gastarbeiter* in the profession, arguing for a new scientific classics, *Altertumswissenschaft*, against the dilettantes and aesthetes (as well as Nietzsche). We are the heirs of that faddish continental turn to theory. And like Wilamowitz, we are also heirs to a Romantic commitment to emotion, spontaneity, the sublime, unity, truth, the artist. . . . When we forget the history of terms like 'realism', 'description', 'literature', 'character', 'nature', – because they seem the most . . . natural words to use – we forget how their assumed meaning is the product of a series of continuing theoretical and ideological battles. (Social 'realism'; psychological 'realism'; political 'realism'; dirty 'realism'. . . .) Literary theory as the investigation of the history of criticism – especially for what it can tell us of why we are what we are – is particularly relevant and necessary for classicists, then. For classics consists in the history of such re-evaluations, re-appropriations, renaissances of the past. We do not read a Greek play like Sophocles *or* like Virgil, *or* like St Augustine, *or* Dante, *or* Nietzsche, *or* . . . and to ask why, is both to engage in literary theory and to try to find one's own place within an intellectual tradition. Not to take one's place for granted. To resist the oblivion of one's own.

Business as usual

But so many theories! Semiotics, structuralism, post-structuralism, deconstruction, feminism, psychoanalysis, narratology . . . isn't the proliferation in itself a sign of instability, faddishness and fashion? To profess allegiance to a theory – isn't that to be as entrenched as the positions you said theory set out to attack?

I'd rather see the proliferation of work on literary theory as a testimony to its remarkable verve and ability to generate excitement and new insight. When the questions stop, so too does the theory. Different branches of theoretical investigation look at different aspects of literature. Some compete; some overlap. For example, it would be hard to find a feminist who was not interested in psychoanalysis (to gloss a complex engagement as neutrally as possible); and as the name suggests, post-structuralism is specifically a challenge and response to structuralism. The rhetoric that sees heated debate, new questions and developing attitudes merely as a sign of 'faddishness' is a rhetoric sadly committed to the slow, unreflective rolling of the status quo. Don't look now. As a classicist, my priority is to understand as best as possible the ancient world and my involvement with it, and I am ready to read whatever will help me. (I am describing here the norm in most other branches of classics. Imagine a classical philosopher or classical archaeologist pretending contemporary methodology in philosophy or archaeology was irrelevant to his or her work!) Studying literature, studying literature of the past, studying literature of another culture – these are shared problems in the humanities, and what arrogance and foolishness would it be to assume that the right questions and answers can come only from within classics! (The best piece of textual criticism I have read recently is on Shakespeare and is written by a vaguely Marxist art historian.)

But it's not one way traffic. Derrida, Barthes, Foucault – those luminaries of the French theoretical (and intellectual) scene – write on Plato, classical rhetoric, and the history of sexuality in the ancient world (and their questions and responses have influenced a generation of scholars inside and outside classics). It is our duty (and pleasure and opportunity and stimulus) to engage critically with their writings. We can inform the work of theory as much as we can be informed by it.

So, in the face of the profusion of critical theory, not so much 'eclecticism' as *engagement*; not so much 'allegiance' as a continuing work of *enquiry*. Above all, not the smugness of Business As Usual. Which will condemn classics to an oblivion of its own.

The S word

When the editors asked me to write this piece – yes, they did, and twice – they asked particularly for some explication of the power of the S word. Even before the national press put it on their front pages, 'What is Structuralism?' was a question asked much more often than it was answered. (I first asked it in my first year as an undergraduate, just after being nearly killed by a don who was driving me to a cricket match and who was arguing a theoretical point with a graduate so intently that the car left the road.) So, what is it again?

Let me begin the two minute version with two pieces of background. At the beginning of the century, Ferdinand de Saussure, a French linguist, offered a course in which he outlined the importance of understanding the *structure* of a language, if we wish to understand how meaning is formed. He outlined the structural elements that he thought crucial, focusing on the *sign*, which is made up indissolubly by a *signifier* (e.g. the sound 't-r-e-e') and a *signified* (e.g. the notion 'tree'). He asserted that the relationship between signifier and signified is arbitrary, that is, with the exception of certain onomatopoeic words like 'plop', there is no necessary or inevitable connection between the sound 't-r-e-e' and the meaning 'tree'. He saw signs put together in a series or sequence – the *syntagm* (e.g. 'The tree is green' or 'Green is the tree', but not 'Tree green the is') – and selected from the possible set, the *paratagm* (e.g. 'a/the etc. tree/bush etc. is/was etc. green/tall etc). The perception of sound and meaning itself, argued Saussure, were produced by such diacritics: 't-r-e-e' is perceived as not 'b-e-e', 's-e-e', or 'w-e-e' etc.; and it means not 'bush', 'is', 'tall' etc. As words can only be defined by other words, so meaning is produced in this system of differences. This is the beginning of what is known as 'structural linguistics', and despite Chomsky's revolution, this has remained a standard part of linguistics.

My second background. In 1949, Claude Lévi-Strauss published a seminal work of anthropology, *The Elementary Structures of Kinship* and, later, *Structural Anthropology*. Here, developing Saussure's ideas of a system of differences, he used the idea of *polarities* in particular to explore first kinship and, second, myth. To understand the bizarre rules of kinship and the bizarre narratives of myth, Lévi-Strauss looked at how these rules and narratives could be read as formulated within a grid of polarities, and in one of his most famous analyses (of the story of Asdiwal) he took a particularly intractable tale and showed how it utilized a set of polarized terms – up/down, inside/outside, raw/cooked etc. – crucial to the culture in which the story was told, to produce a message about that culture. Myths, argued Lévi-Strauss, are narratives which mediate – and mediate on – a culture's own structuring oppositions. 'Structural anthropology' has remained a standard part of anthropology.

In the 1960s, this burgeoning work in anthropology and linguistics became an important influence for literary studies. Roland Barthes is a good figure to sum up this part of the story. Barthes' early influential work was within the tradition of 'semiotics', the 'science of signs' that Saussure had predicted as the outcome of his thesis on language. He analyzed both the 'fashion system' – and how self-reflexive that 'fashion' should be the object of his work! – and elements of modern myth: e.g. Brigitte Bardot's face, wrestling, the cover of Paris Match. He was interested in how signs functioned in culture –

the *codes* or systems in and by which signs developed meaning – and he drew explicitly on the work of Saussure and Lévi-Strauss. But in *S/Z*, his magnum opus, Barthes turned to analyze a short story of Balzac, *Sarrasine*. He divided the text up minutely to analyze the different codes and different structures of the work, in order to anatomize how the story's meaning was produced. (The story is 30 pages, the analysis 230. . . .) It is a *tour de force*, that combines passages of elegant and deeply serious essay writing on a vast range of topics – from 'character', to 'reality', to 'castration' – with an appearance of careful, even scientific dissection of the language of the story. Indeed, structuralism's grids of oppositions, its demonstrations of how such oppositions structure a culture's narratives, claimed to offer the hope of an objective, even scientific analysis of literature, rather than vague and evaluative 'appreciations' or histories of sources that traditional criticism all too often provided. It is in a work such as *S/Z* that literary structuralism finds its apogee.

So what is meant in general by the S word in literary criticism is the methodological utilization of a model developed from linguistics and anthropology that sees meaning produced in and by a structured system of differences, polarizations and their mediations, within a culture and its texts. Okay?

Now try to define 'christianity' or 'socialism' and you will see what happens when you try to do a two minute version . . . Insufficient, superficial, misleading. . . .

But what about us?

As one might expect for a society that gave us μέν and δέ (not to mention νόμος and φύσις) this idea of a polarized set of oppositions structuring a culture's view of itself (even as a 'culture' as opposed to, say, 'nature') has proved extremely profitable in the study of ancient Greece in particular. And it would be hard to find a classicist worth his or her salt – yes, even Hugh Lloyd-Jones – who would not confess to being influenced by these ideas, especially mediated by Jean-Pierre Vernant and Pierre Vidal-Naquet and the scholars around them in Paris. In as it were 'anthropological' questions – religion, the ordering of space in the city, how myths work, and the like – structuralist methodology has led to important and lasting insights, that are already standard. Even in books written for sixth-formers. Take sacrifice, for instance, that central ritual of Greek religion. It has become understood as an institution that sites man within a community and within a set of interrelations with the divine and animal world – indeed, that helps define these different categories of being. It is a way of defining 'human culture' as 'culture' as opposed to 'nature' and the suprahuman immortals. It is also to be understood in contrast to hunting and agriculture in particular as other institutions for the production and consumption of food. Sacrifice is, in other words, a fundamental *expression of social order* (and thus corrupt sacrifice becomes a crucial image for the collapse of social order particularly in tragedy and epic). Both this very general model and the complex details of its working out (which I can't deal with here) are the product of classics' fruitful interaction with structural anthropology, an interaction that has been crucial in uncovering the *categories* in which ancient society thinks (about) itself and by which ancient society is ordered. It would be simply impossible today to discuss 'sacrifice' (and many other topics) without taking account of these analyses.

In classical literature, too, there are by now standard works deeply indebted to structuralist methodology. James Redfield's book on Homer, for example, *Nature and Culture in the Iliad*, is the best available exploration of the society depicted in the Homeric poems, and it depends heavily on the structuring of polarity of 'nature' and 'culture' to express many aspects of the poem's depiction of social life and war. With this fine study too, structuralist methodology has proved essential in uncovering the culturally specific categories in and by which meaning is formed.

So it would be wrong to think of structuralist influence as marginal or localized. It is by now across the world integral to classics as a discipline. Our students will all be its heirs. . . .

Then and now

The responses to structuralism have been multiform, and if it seems strange to turn back to the 1960s (and beyond) to introduce literary theory, it is a sensible strategy in as much as what has happened since and is happening now can be seen as a reaction to that movement. Post-structuralism and deconstruction, for example, have explicitly challenged the security of the polarized opposition (that central motif of structuralism) and have explored the hierarchies and tensions within such structuring dualities. Narratology has attempted to continue structuralism's (claims to a) scientific approach but has reintroduced a dynamic of narrative progress into structuralism's often static descriptions of systems of meaning. Feminism and Marxism have challenged the apparently apolitical stance of structuralism's understanding of meaning. Foucault's history, too, has developed the idea of 'code' towards a more flexible notion of 'discourse' and reinscribed 'power' as a major term in any discussion of culture and meaning. The struggle to refine the process by which we approach the ancient world goes on. . . .

Those questions and my answers

Are you a structuralist/post-structuralist/deconstructionist?
I am a classicist.

Why all that jargon?
Each branch of study has a technical vocabulary. Do you think your critical vocabulary was God-given? The worst jargon of all is the jargon of 'natural', 'simple', 'common-sense', jargon. . . .

Why does theory seem so deliberately obscure?
In part because of your unfamiliarity with the technical vocabulary. Partly because some difficult arguments are hard to read (try Kant, Hegel, Plato). And someone said 'if anyone fully understood what was written in a daily newspaper, he would go mad'. Newspapers are clear for the punters, aren't they?

A final story

There's a party/pub game that goes like this: each person chooses five adjectives or nouns that he or she thinks offer the most essential definition of him or herself. (You know, 'male, heterosexual, married, depressed, teacher', that sort of thing.) A funny thing is that I've never met a black person who *didn't* say 'black' and I've never met a white person who *did* say 'white'. Theory's a bit like that. People don't recognize their own until they're made to. . . .

So the next time you hear someone – even yourself – denying an interest in theory or denying its importance, just think of what theory *is* being espoused. . . .

Finally, finally

As the epigraph suggested. And a map of the preceding . . .

An O of one's own

On MacCabe, see D. Simpson 'New Brooms at Fawlty Towers' in *Intellectuals: Aesthetics, Politics, Academics*, ed. B. Robbins (Minneapolis, 1990).
The quote: from T. Eagleton *Literary Theory* (Oxford, 1983).

Don't L now

See P. de Man *The Resistance to Theory* (Minneapolis, 1986) 3–26.

Finding one's P

On major shifts in 'world-pictures', see M. Foucault *The Order of Things* (London, 1970).
For classicists' attempts to do a job on 'character', see P. Easterling and S. Goldhill in *Characterization and Individuality in Greek Literature* ed. C. Pelling (Oxford, 1990).

S as usual

On many theories: see J. Culler *The Pursuit of Signs* (London, 1981); Eagleton (above); F. Lentricchia *After the New Criticism* (London, 1980).
On psychoanalysis and feminism, see J. Mitchell *Psychoanalysis and Feminism* (New York, 1974); J. Gallop *Feminism and Psychoanalysis* (London, 1982).

On textual critcism, see J. Barrell 'Editing out', in his *Poetry, Language and Politics* (Manchester, 1988).

On French luminaries: J. Derrida 'Plato's Pharmacy' in *Dissemination* tr. B. Johnson (Chicago, 1981); R. Barthes 'L'ancienne rhétorique, aide-mémoire', *Communications 16* (1970) 172–237; M. Foucault *A History of Sexuality* vol. 2 and vol. 3 (*The Care of the Self* and *The Uses of Pleasure* [New York, 1985 & 1986]). And for classics engaging, see J. Winkler *The Constraints of Desire* (New York, 1990).

5. The S word

Intros: J. Culler *Structuralist Poetics* (Ithaca, 1975); R. Scholes *Structuralism in Literature* (New Haven, 1974). More advanced: F. Jameson *The Prison House of Language* (Princeton, 1972); R. Macksey and E. Donato eds *The Languages of Criticism and the Science of Man* (Baltimore, 1970).

Backgrounds: F. de Saussure *Course in General Linguistics* (New York, 1959); C. Lévi-Strauss *Elementary Structures of Kinship* (Boston, 1969); *Structural Anthropology* (New York, 1963). On Lévi-Strauss, see e.g. E. Leach *Lévi-Strauss* (London, 1970).

R. Barthes *Mythologies* (London, 1972); *Elements of Semiology* (London, 1967); *The Fashion System* (London, 1984); *S/Z* (London, 1975).

6. But what about U?

Good general intro: R. Gordon ed. *Myth, Religion and Society* (Cambridge, 1981); J.-P. Vernant *Myth and Thought among the Greeks* (London, 1983); J.-P. Vernant and P. Vidal-Naquet *Myth and Tragedy in Ancient Greece* (Brighton, 1981).

Sacrifice: e.g. M. Detienne and J.-P. Vernant *La cuisine du sacrifice* (Paris 1979), and articles in Gordon (above).

Schools intro to Greek religion: J. Gould 'On making sense of Greek religion', in P. Easterling and J. Muir eds *Greek Religion and Society* (Cambridge, 1985).

7. Then and N

Post-Structuralism etc: J. Culler *On Deconstruction* (London, 1983); R. Young *Untying the Text* (Boston, 1981); C. Norris *Deconstruction* (London, 1982); J. Harrari ed. *Textual Strategies* (Ithaca, 1979).

Narratology: G. Genette *Narrative Discourse* (Oxford, 1980); *Figures of Literary Discourse* (Oxford, 1982).

Feminism: E. Showalter ed. *The New Feminist Criticism* (New York, 1985); N. Miller ed. *The Poetics of Gender* (New York, 1986); E. Abel ed. *Writing and Sexual Difference* (Brighton, 1982).

tword

Pretty well all the above are paperbacks in English ... and they all have more reading too. ... If you want to read one starting article, try P. Vidal-Naquet 'Land and Sacrifice in the Odyssey', in Gordon ed. (see section 6); lots of the above material is used for Greek literature in e.g. J. Redfield *Nature and Culture in the Iliad* (Chicago, 1975) and in S. Goldhill (well, I had to finally) *Reading Greek Tragedy* (Cambridge, 1986).

Authors and texts

Latin and Greek authors and texts used or mentioned in this book, giving the conventional Latin title where appropriate. * means that excerpts are presented in this book.

Accius: Lucius Accius, 170–86 BCE (Funaioli's numbering)
*Achievements of the Divine Augustus = Res Gestae Divi Augusti
Aeschylus (Greek): perhaps 525–455 BCE
    Oresteia
    Seven Against Thebes
Alcaeus (Greek): born perhaps 625 BCE
Ammianus Marcellinus: perhaps 330–95 CE
    History = Res Gestae
Apollonius of Rhodes (Greek): third century BCE
    Journey of the Argonauts = Argonautica
Apuleius: perhaps 125–70 CE
    Apology = Apologia
    Metamorphoses (also called *The Golden Ass*)
Aratus (Greek): third century BCE
Aristotle (Greek): 384–322 BCE
Augustan History = Historia Augusta, biographies of emperors 117–284 CE
Augustine: Aurelius Augustinus, 354–430 CE
    City of God = De Civitate Dei
    Confessions
    Letters

Boethius: Anicius Manlius Severinus Boethius, perhaps 480–524 CE
    Consolation of Philosophy
Caesar: Gaius Iulius Caesar, 100–44 BCE
    Civil War = Bellum civile
    Gallic War = Bellum gallicum
Callimachus (Greek): third century BCE
    Epigrams (Pfeiffer's numbering)
    Hecale
    Hymns
    Origins = Aetia
Calpurnius Siculus: probably Neronian
    Eclogues
Cato: Marcus Porcius Cato, 234–149 BCE
    Origins = Origines
Catullus: Gaius Valerius Catullus, perhaps 84–54 BCE
    Poems
Cicero: Marcus Tullius Cicero 106–43 BCE
    For Archias = Pro Archia
    For Caelius = Pro Caelio
    For Marcellus = Pro Marcello
    Letters to Atticus = Epistulae ad Atticum
    Letters to his Friends = Epistulae ad familiares
    On Friendship/Laelius = De amicitia/Laelius
    On the Command of Gnaeus Pompeius/In Support of the Manilian
        Law = De imperio Cn. Pompeii/Pro lege Manilia
    On the Republic = De Republica
    Philippics = Orationes Philippicae
Cinna: Gaius Helvius Cinna, friend of Catullus
    Zmyrna
Claudian: Claudius Claudianus, perhaps 370–404 CE
Dio, Cassius (Greek): perhaps 150–235 CE
    Roman History
Dionysius of Halicarnassus (Greek): Augustan
    Roman Antiquities
Donatus: Aelius Donatus, fourth century CE
    Commentaries on Virgil and Terence
Egeria: ?late fourth century CE
    Egeria's Travels = Itinerarium Egeriae
Ennius: Quintus Ennius, 239–169 BCE
    Ambracia
    Annals = Annales (Warmington's numbering)

Epigrams (Warmington's numbering)
Medea (Warmington's numbering)
Scipio
Euphorion (Greek): third century BCE
Euripides (Greek): born probably in 480s BCE
Medea
Gallus: Gaius Cornelius Gallus, perhaps 69–26 BCE
Elegies
Gellius: Aulus Gellius, born *c*.125/128 CE
Attic Nights = *Noctes Atticae*
Hecateus (Greek): late sixth century BCE
Hesiod (Greek): around 700 BCE
Theogony
Homer (Greek): poems usually dated to eighth century BCE
Iliad
Odyssey
*Horace: Quintus Horatius Flaccus, 65–8 BCE
Art of Poetry = *Ars Poetica*
Epistles
Epodes
Hymn for the Age = *Carmen Saeculare*
Odes (sometimes called *Carmina*)
Satires (sometimes called *Sermones*)
Juvenal: Decimus Iunius Iuvenalis, perhaps 60s–130s CE
Satires
Laberius: Decimus Laberius, perhaps 106–43 BCE
Mimes
Livius Andronicus: Lucius Livius Andronicus, wrote from 240 BCE
Odyssey = *Odyssia*
Livy: Titus Livius, 59 BCE–17 CE
From the Foundation of Rome = *Ab Vrbe condita*
Lucan: Marcus Annaeus Lucanus, 39–65 CE
Civil War = *Bellum Civile* (sometimes called *Pharsalia*)
Lucilius: Gaius Lucilius, perhaps 180–102 BCE
Satires (Warmington's numbering)
Lucretius: Titus Lucretius, perhaps 94–55 BCE
On the Nature of the Universe = *De rerum natura*
Macrobius: Ambrosius Theodosius Macrobius, late fourth or early fifth century CE
Saturnalia

Marcus Aurelius (Greek): emperor 161–80 CE
  Meditations
Martial: Marcus Valerius Martialis, perhaps 40–98 CE
  Epigrams
Martyrdom of Perpetua and Felicitas = Passio Perpetuae et Felicitatis, third
  century CE
Menander (Greek): fourth century BCE
Naevius: Gnaeus Naevius, wrote perhaps 235–205 BCE
Nepos: Cornelius Nepos, perhaps 110–24 BCE
  On Famous Men = De viris illustribus
Ovid: Publius Ovidius Naso, 43 BCE–17 CE
  Art of Loving = Ars amatoria
  Letters from the Black Sea = Epistulae ex Ponto
  Letters of Heroines = Heroides
  *Loves = Amores
  Medea
  *Metamorphoses
  *Roman Holidays = Fasti
  *Sorrows = Tristia
Pacuvius: Marcus Pacuvius, perhaps 220–130 BCE
Panegyric of Messalla = Panegyricus Messallae, perhaps 31 or 20s BCE
Persius: Aules Persius Flaccus, 34–62 CE
  *Satires
Petronius: Petronius Arbiter, died 66 CE
  *Satyrica
Philetas (Greek): also spelled Philitas, third century BCE
Philodemus (Greek): perhaps 110–35 BCE
  On the Good King According to Homer
Plato (Greek): perhaps 429–347 BCE
  Phaedrus
  Republic
  Symposium
Plautus: Titus Maccius Plautus, wrote perhaps 205–184 BCE
  Amphitryo
  *Pseudolus
  *Three-Dollar Day = Trinummus
Pliny the Elder: Gaius Plinius Secundus, 23–79 CE
  Natural History = Naturalis historia
Pliny the Younger: Gaius Plinius Caecilius Secundus, perhaps 61–112 CE
  *Letters
  *Panegyric = Panegyricus

Plutarch (Greek): born before 50 and died after 120 CE
    Parallel Lives
Polybius (Greek): perhaps 200–118 BCE
    Histories
Praise of Piso = Laus Pisonis: perhaps Neronian
**Praise of Turia = Laudatio Turiae = ILS* 8393: late first century BCE
Proba: fourth century CE
Propertius: Sextus Propertius, perhaps 48–16 BCE
    *Elegies
Prudentius: Aurelius Clemens Prudentius, 348–410 CE
    **Soul-Battle = Psychomachia*
Quintilian: Marcus Fabius Quintilianus, born perhaps 35 CE
    **Training of the Orator = Institutio oratoria*
Rhetorical Treatise to Herennius = Rhetorica ad Herennium, written perhaps
    82 BCE
Sallust: Gaius Sallustius Crispus, perhaps 86–35 BCE
    War with Catiline/The Catilinarian Conspiracy = Bellum Catilinae/De
        Catilinae coniuratione
    War with Jugurtha = Bellum Iugurthinum
Sappho (Greek): seventh–sixth century BCE
Seneca the Elder: Lucius Annaeus Seneca, perhaps 50 BCE–40 CE
    **Persuasions = Suasoriae*
Seneca the Younger: Lucius Annaeus Seneca, perhaps 4 BCE–65 CE
    **Consolation to Helvia*
    Mad Hercules = Hercules Furens
    *Medea
    Moral Letters
    *Oedipus
    On Anger = De ira
    On Clemency = De clementia
    **On Providence = De providentia*
    Pumpkinification = Apocolocyntosis
    Thyestes
    Trojan Women = Troades
Servius: Marius Servius Honoratus, fourth century CE
    Commentary on Virgil
Silius Italicus: Tiberius Catius Asconius Silius Italicus, 26–102 CE
    **Punic War = Punica*
Sophocles (Greek): active 468–406 BCE
    Antigone

Statius: Publius Papinius Statius, born around 50 CE
    Lumber = Silvae
    Thebaid
Suetonius: Gaius Suetonius Tranquillus, born around 70 CE
    Caesars
Sulpicia: late first century BCE
    Elegies
Sulpicia: reign of Domitian, 81–96 CE
Tacitus: Cornelius Tacitus, perhaps 56–120s CE
    Agricola
    Annals = Annales
    Dialogue of Orators = Dialogus
    Histories
Terence: Publius Terentius Afer, died after 160 BCE
    The Brothers = Adelphoe
Theocritus (Greek): third century BCE
    Idylls
Thucydides (Greek): perhaps 460–400 BCE
    History of the Peloponnesian War
Tibullus: Albius Tibullus, died 19 BCE
    Elegies
Valerius Flaccus: Gaius Valerius Flaccus Setinus Balbus, died before 95 CE
    Argonautica
Valerius Maximus: reign of Tiberius
    Memorable Acts and Sayings = Facta et dicta memorabilia
Varius Rufus: friend of Virgil, reign of Augustus
    Thyestes
Varro: Marcus Terentius Varro, 116–27 BCE
    Likenesses = Imagines
Velleius: Velleius Paterculus, reign of Tiberius
    Histories
Virgil (also spelt Vergil): Publius Vergilius Maro, 70–19 BCE
    Eclogues (sometimes called *Bucolica*)
    Georgics
    Aeneid
Xenophon (Greek): fifth–fourth centuries BCE

Time-line

Foundation of city of Rome 753 BCE (traditional date)

The Seven Kings of Rome, 753–509 BCE, including:

Romulus	735–717
Numa	717–674
Servius Tullius	580–533
Tarquinius Superbus	533–509

The Republic, 509–31 BCE, including:

first war with Carthage	264–241
second war with Carthage	218–201
sack of Carthage and Corinth	146
tribunate of Tiberius Gracchus	133
wars with Mithradates	88–64
dictatorship of Sulla	82–79
conspiracy of Catiline and Cicero's consulship	63
Julius Caesar's conquest of Gaul	58–50
civil war between Julius Caesar and Pompey	49–48
assassination of Julius Caesar	44
triumvirate of Antony, Octavian and Lepidus	43 onwards
battle of Actium	31

The Roman Empire, 31 BCE–476 CE, including:

Augustus	31 BCE–14 CE
Tiberius	14–37
Caligula	37–41

Claudius	41–54
Nero	54–68
the year of four emperors	68–9
Vespasian	69–79
Titus	79–81
Domitian	81–96
Nerva	96–8
Trajan	98–117
Hadrian	117–38
Antoninus Pius	138–61
Marcus Aurelius	161–80
Diocletian	284–305
Constantine	306–37
Romulus Augustulus	475–6

Translations used/adapted

Apuleius *Cupid and Psyche*: E. J. Kenney (Cambridge, 1990)

Augustine *Confessions*: Henry Chadwick (Oxford World's Classics, 1992)

Catullus: Guy Lee (Oxford World's Classics, 1990)

Cicero *De Republica, Laelius, On Friendship* and *The Dream of Scipio*: Jonathan Powell (Aris & Phillips, Warminster, 1990)

Cicero *In Defence of Marcus Caelius Rufus, In Support of Marcus Claudius Marcellus* and *On the Command of Cnaeus Pompeius*: Michael Grant *Selected Political Speeches* (Penguin Classics, 1989)

Cicero *Letters to his Friends*: D. R. Shackleton Bailey (Penguin Classics, 1978)

Cicero *Second Philippic*: Amy Richlin in her book *The Garden of Priapus: Sexuality and Aggression in Roman Humor* (New York and Oxford, 1997 (revised edition)) pages 14–15

Cicero *Selected Letters*: D. R. Shackleton Bailey (Penguin Classics, 1983)

Horace *Odes and Carmen Saeculare*: Guy Lee (Francis Cairns, Leeds, 1998)

Horace *Odes* 3: Gordon Williams (Oxford, 1969)

Horace *Satires*: Niall Rudd (Penguin Classics, 1979)

Laudatio Turiae: E. Wistrand (Lund, 1976)

Lucan *Civil War*: S. H. Braund (Oxford World's Classics, 1992)

Lucretius: R. Melville (Oxford World's Classics, 1997)

Lucretius *De Rerum Natura*: R. E. Latham (Penguin Classics, 1951)

Ovid *Amores*: A. D. Melville (Oxford World's Classics, 1990)

Ovid *Fasti*: A. J. Boyle and R. Woodard (Penguin Classics, 2000)

Ovid *Metamorphoses*: A. D. Melville (Oxford World's Classics, 1986)

Ovid *Tristia*: Peter Green (Penguin Classics, 1994)

Petronius *Satyrica*: J. P. Sullivan (Penguin Classics, 1969)

Plautus *Pseudolus*: E. F. Watling *The Pot of Gold and other plays* (Penguin Classics, 1965)

Propertius: Guy Lee (Oxford World's Classics, 1994)

Seneca *Letters*: Robin Campbell (Penguin Classics, 1969)

Seneca *Medea*: Fred Ahl (Ithaca, 1986)

Seneca *Oedipus*: David Anthony Turner, in *Classical Tragedy, Greek and Roman* (edited by Robert Corrigan, New York, 1990)

Statius *Silvae* IV: Kathleen Coleman (Oxford, 1988)

Statius *Thebaid*: A. D. Melville (Oxford World's Classics, 1992)

Tacitus *Annals*: A. J. Church and W. J. Brodribb (reprint, The Franklin Library, Pennsylvania, 1982)

Terence *The Brothers*: Betty Radice (Penguin Classics, 1965)

Tibullus *Elegies*: Guy Lee (2nd edition, Francis Cairns, Liverpool, 1982)

Virgil *Aeneid*: Robert Fitzgerald (Penguin Classics, 1985)

Virgil *Eclogues*: Guy Lee (Penguin Classics, 1984)

Virgil *Georgics*: L. P. Wilkinson (Penguin Classics, 1982)

Note: apart from this list, all translations are my own.

Index of names and topics

Index of passages quoted

7864 30